Also by Kate Evans

Negotiating the Self

For the May Queen

Complementary Colors

Like All We Love

Call It Wonder

an odyssey of love, sex, spirit, and travel

Kate Evans

Coyote Creek Books | San José | California

ISBN: 978-0-9961824-2-3

Printed in the United States of America

Published by Coyote Creek Books
www.coyotecreekbooks.com

Portions of this work were previously published as "The Healing
Machine" in *elephant journal* (October 16, 2014). Reprinted with
permission.

Portions of this work were previously published as "Infinity" in
Three, edited by Spike Wong, Jan McCutcheon, and Kelly Harrison.
(PushPen Press, Santa Cruz and San Jose CA, 2013).

Excerpt from *Arrowsmith* by Sinclair Lewis. Copyright 1925 by
Houghton Mifflin Harcourt Publishing Company and renewed 1953
by Michael Lewis. Reprinted with permission of Houghton Mifflin
Harcourt Publishing Company. All rights reserved.

"Give Yourself to Love" by Kate Wolf, © 1982 Another Sundown
Publishing Company. Used with gracious permission of Max Wolf.

"Restoration" by Stacey Knapp. Used with gracious permission of the
author.

"Something New" by Nat Keefe/Hot Buttered Rum. © 2011 Hot
Buttered Rum. Used with the gracious permission of the band.

The words of Gabriele Rico, as quoted in Suzanne Rico's blog (www.
suzannerico.com). Used with the gracious permission of Suzanne
Rico.

For Dave

Don't call it uncertainty—call it wonder.
Don't call it insecurity—call it freedom.

OSHO

This is a true story, as true as memory can be. To write this book I relied primarily on my memories, but also on the blog I've kept since 2008 and the journals that I kept since 1970 (and that have since met their demise). In addition, I consulted with several people who appear in these pages. I have changed some names and identifying details. I take full responsibility for the strengths and defects of my remembrances—and the ways I chose to tell them—for all narratives are constructed. If they weren't, they'd be as long as life.

1

The Trip of a Lifetime

You road I enter upon and look around, I believe you are not
all that is here,
I believe that much unseen is also here.
—*Walt Whitman*

I awake to a charley horse in my thigh.

I've had a few charley horses in my life, the bizarre uncontrollable bulging of a muscle, especially when I was a teenaged synchronized swimmer spending dehydrating aerobic hours in the water, flexing and contracting my legs. Sometimes the cramp happened at home, sometimes in the pool. I'd be on my back, hands cupped and sculling hard, my leg straight up in "ballet leg" position, my toe pointed hard as a gymnast's—and as though it had a mind of its own, my calf muscle would fist up, curling and turning tightly beneath my skin like a fetus beneath a belly. Sometimes it happened in the middle of the night, jolting me awake.

That's what I think is happening this early morning, a charley horse. I am fifty years old.

My first thought is to jump up from bed. Yet suddenly I know that would be impossible. As I am pulled from sleep into waking, it dawns on me I am not experiencing your ordinary charley horse. Something is different. Significantly different. The muscle spasm grips not only my leg but, I soon realize, my whole body. Every muscle, every inch of skin—every internal organ, it seems—is seizing, transmuting from supple to solid. My toes cross. My fingers curl. An electrical force stampedes through me. A roaring—like the mysterious force of the world unleashed—fills my head. I try to yell out. An uncanny bellow emerges, a noise not belonging to me.

It's as though I am simultaneously struck by lightning and run over by a truck.

Oh my God, I'm having a stroke or a seizure.

There is no way to cease this hurricane barreling through my body. This force will run its own course, and it's going to take me with it, no matter what I do. I'm certain I'm dying.

A memory surfaces. It's the memory of a dream I'd been having moments ago, of Gabriele, my mentor, my friend, my other mother. She's been dead for five months. Cancer carried her away. In the dream, she was aglow with health and light and love. Incredibly, right before I awakened into this bodily nightmare, as I was poised on the pinpoint between life and death, she said to me:

The veil between the worlds is thinner than you think. When you really look, you can see the perfect beauty of it all. Moving from one state to the next is like lifting a gauze curtain. There's no reason, ever, to be afraid of dying.

The dream felt so real—more like a visitation than a dream. Spoken to me moments before from another realm, her words resonate through the rock of my body, despite the deafening roar that shrouds me.

I have been living my authentic life, says a voice. This voice is somehow internal and external, somehow mine and not mine. *I've been saying yes to life. I have no regrets. We all must go sometime. It's okay. Release to this experience. Release, release. No matter what, you are all right.*

As though this mine/not mine voice waves a magic wand, fear melts away. I know I am on the brink of an adventure, the greatest adventure of all. It's as though I am poised at the top of life's roller coaster, suspended between ascent and descent. That liminal space, that profound pause, that border that's both here and there, that silence between breaths, between heartbeats. And I am buckled in, safe.

Deliberately, purposefully, I let go of all resistance. I release to the plunge. I open my arms and my heart to the wonder, to the grand adventure, to the trip of a lifetime.

Here I go! It's okay. It's all okay.

And I disperse into nothingness.

Eight months earlier, in winter 2012, my husband Dave is driving us from our seaside town of Santa Cruz, California, up into the Sierra Nevada mountains for a few days of skiing. Chitty Chitty

Bang Bang—our blue Subaru—bumps along the freeway in her knobby snow tires. It's one of those crystalline winter days. The East Bay's emerald hills stand out like pop-up book mountains against an indigo sky.

My phone rings. It's our property manager telling me that the Love Nest, our Santa Cruz townhouse that we've rented for almost two years, is going up for sale.

We moved to small-town Santa Cruz from a sixth-floor apartment complex in downtown San Jose. That apartment was conveniently located across the street from the campus where I teach, and two miles from Dave's job at a start-up. We liked the urban life, walking to restaurants, the grocery store, the yearly blues festival, and campus events.

Yet in addition to being light filled, the apartment was bug filled. One too many bouts with cockroaches and bedbugs had left us with painful welts on our bodies and psyches. This assault was a profound challenge to my belief that we create our own reality. I mean, really? Part of me *wanted* these damn bugs to keep invading? Part of me *wanted* to be jolted from sleep because minuscule vampires were sucking my blood? Part of me *wanted* to throw away our mattress and wash every piece of clothing and bedding while our home-sweet-home was injected with clouds of poison whose yellow residue had to be laboriously scraped from the inside of the windows?

For weeks I sat awake on the corner of our sectional couch, scratching the red ridges on my legs and belly where the bugs had had a feast. During those long, sleepless nights I'd said in my head, over and over, *Something good is going to come from this. Something good is going to come from this.*

I wondered if Job endured God's wrath with such a mantra.

I figured that whether or not I created my reality, I had a choice about how to respond to it. Why not focus on a happy outcome?

Indeed, something good came from the pestilence: it launched us out of the city apartment and into the Love Nest, three blocks from the beach. I've never lived in such a cool pad. It was built from redwood in 1962, the year of my birth. Its centerpiece is a globular fireplace suspended from a beam on the high ceiling. A spiral staircase leads up to an office loft and a light-filled bedroom. Rumor has it that the six-unit complex—with its unique wavy roofline—appeared in *Sunset* magazine back in the day. From the deck we can see a sparkly creek lined by bird-filled trees and hear sea lions barking from the wharf. In nice weather, faraway screams drift through the windows when the Boardwalk roller coaster drops from its heights.

Dave and I love the water. He's been a scuba diver for many years. When I first saw him dive into a pool and swim with the ease of a dolphin, I fell in love with him all over again. In our California towns a hundred miles apart, we both grew up swimming all summer, boating, fishing, water skiing, snorkeling. As a teenaged synchronized swimmer on a team called the Mermaids, I fashioned myself a half-sea, half-land creature. And now, after meeting and marrying midlife, Dave is my merman. It must have been meant to be since his family crest features a mermaid.

Because the ocean is cold in Santa Cruz, we don't do much swimming. But we love to walk or jog on the beach, our feet invigorated by icy surf. We ride our bikes on paths that hug the shore.

Sometimes we do yoga on the sand. We wander out to watch the sunset, breathing in the salt air. We watch the pelicans and gulls, the otters and dolphins. Sometimes we are graced by a whale spout. Once we had a bonfire on the beach with friends. Like teenagers, we were busted by a ranger who made us dump out our wine and beer. We laughed about that for weeks. Every once in a while, I'd remember that an infestation of bedbugs led us here.

So when we get the call that the Love Nest is being put on the market, my heart knocks and my palms sweat. I feel myself gripping harder and harder. *Oh no, our beautiful home.*

We could try to buy the place. But we aren't sure we want to be homeowners, especially in beachside California, some of the most expensive real estate on the planet. We have enough in savings for a down payment. But our income situation isn't conducive to a mortgage. Dave no longer works for the start-up. And I have recently decided to take an early retirement, at age fifty, from the university. After spending my whole life as either a teacher or a student, I have only a few months left in academia.

There are a few things in our favor. Both of us will continue to receive excellent medical coverage upon my retirement. And when I'm ready, I can make as much money as I want—teaching or doing other things—and it won't jeopardize my small pension. Dave has some stocks that have the potential to perform well, but that's like playing the lottery. And he's open to any other business opportunities that might pop up. In the meantime we've planned to rely on our savings and figure it out as we go along.

Upon retirement, I want to write, to read whatever I want, to travel in months other than summer, to broaden my notions of what life can be. Maybe at some point I'll develop writing retreats. In Dave's case, in addition to being the domestic god of the house, he's been doing some part-time telecommuting work. He enjoys cooking and photography. We are flexible and free—or unstable and irresponsible, depending on your point-of-view. This mixed disposition—part responsible citizen, part bohemian—drew us to each other in the first place. As did the fact that we love to travel and have no kids.

Deciding to leave my secure employment is a risk. I am doing it completely on intuition. I have a feeling that by opening up the space and time, unforeseen possibilities will float our way. I want to see what will happen in the fertile void.

And now, as though the universe is answering my call to change, in the vein of *Be careful what you ask for*, our house is being ripped out from under us. As I sit in the car with Dave driving, my mind goes into overdrive. A mass of mixed feelings sweeps through me. I feel dizzy. A little sad. A tinge scared. I forget for a moment the Bedbug Rule: that every single time something "bad" happened in my life, it has led to something good—some new growth, some unforeseen adventure. Something I couldn't have imagined before. Some huge expansion of what life can be.

When I hang up the phone, I turn to face Dave. He sits calmly, hands on the wheel. Although he's heard everything, I reiterate the details. Green hill after green hill rolls past. When I finish the run-down, we sit quietly for a moment.

Then I say, or he says—one of us says, "So, what do you want to do?"

I feel a surge of excitement, a flutter of apprehension. We are on the precipice, the top of the roller coaster, the pause between ascent and descent. *Something good is going to come from this.*

As we cross the Martinez Bridge and speed toward the Sacramento Valley, we begin to talk. And talk. And talk. We play with possible scenarios, from making an offer on the Love Nest, to joining a friend who's starting a communal living situation, to moving to a different town or state, to traveling. As we explore the options, I pay close attention to my feelings. It has taken me years to realize that my feelings are my *guide*. If something feels good, my intuitive needle is pointing true north. When I follow my excitement, I'm being true to myself. If I feel anxious or sad or angry, it's time to ease up and not force myself to make a move. As we talk, when an idea delights me I linger, folding and unfolding the notion like an elaborate origami.

As much as clinging to the Love Nest is my initial inclination, when we float the idea of becoming homeowners, it feels a little like someone's hands are clutching my throat. *But that's the responsible thing to do!* says a voice like my father's. *Home ownership is the American Dream!* says a voice like a public service announcer's. *But who cares if it's the American Dream if it's not my dream?* says my inner compass.

What about renting another place in Santa Cruz? No. Replacing the unique and beautiful Love Nest is impossible. And to try feels like moving backward rather than forward.

Soon it becomes clear that when we talk about doing something *completely different*, something *new*, I'm excited. When we talk about what we love—not what we feel we "should" do—my heart sings.

We love to travel. We love to spend extended time in places, experiencing various versions of life. We love to dive deeply into time with friends. We love to meet new people. We love nature and wild animal encounters. We love dancing to live music and hiking and yoga and skiing, feeling our bodies move in the world. We love trying new things. One of Dave's favorite sayings is, "And now for something completely different."

We enjoy taking advantage of my summer and winter breaks, as well as our frequent flyer miles and Dave's propensity for finding good deals and creating itineraries. In three years together, we've traveled a lot. We've been on an Alaskan cruise, followed by a Western-states car trip, including several weeks in Paradise Valley, Montana, at the place of a friend. We saw bison, bears, elk, moose, and deer in Yellowstone and Grand Teton National Parks. At dawn, we floated down the Snake River and experienced the iconic sunrise photographed by Ansel Adams. We spent several weeks in Mexico City with our friends Martin and Cathy. With two other couples, we took a rowdy music cruise in the Caribbean. Afterward we drove from Ft. Lauderdale to New Orleans. We road-tripped down to Southern California to visit groups of friends and my sister and her family. More recently, we got married in Hawaii. We swam with dolphins, snorkeled with turtles, and flew on a zip-line across a canopy of trees.

For my fiftieth birthday the previous November, Dave took me to Yosemite for a night in the magnificent Ahwahnee Hotel. The desk clerk upgraded us to the Library Suite, complete with massive fireplace, four-poster bed, and a view of Yosemite Falls splashing down thousands of feet of granite. I felt my parents' presence. They met in Yosemite in 1956. Now, more than fifty-five years later, they were both gone. Dave knew being in Yosemite would be meaningful to me as I stepped into midlife.

Each journey takes us to a deeper level. Each trip extends our sense of what it means to move through, and be in, the world. Travel has become something more than a hobby. Travel, for us, isn't separate from real life. We take literally the notion that life is a journey. Each trip, each adventure, *is* life.

It's the perfect storm. In a few months, at the end of May, neither one of us will be locked into a job. And if we don't replace the Love Nest with another house—if we aren't paying rent or a mortgage—we'll have more money to finance traveling. We can go places we've dreamed about. We can spend time with friends all over the world who've invited us to visit.

Suddenly it's clear. I pull a notepad and pen from my purse. A spark has lit the fire within. Like two beings connected at the brain and heart, we create a list of things we'd like to do as a home-free couple.

We've barely reached the foothills of the Sierra Nevada mountains when we've charted out a year plan. We'll talk to the landlord to see if we can stay two more months. Then I'll be done with the semester, and we'll be divested of our stuff: we'll sell it, give it away, or put it in storage. The first of June, I'll be officially retired, and we'll be off.

In less than an hour, we've transitioned from home-dwelling creatures to nomadic ones. We've created the plan of our dreams. I know there are lots of details to square away, but we'll take care of them as they come. No need to worry about tackling them now.

Perhaps the decision to hop on the open road is impulsive, but it makes sense.

"You know what?" says Dave. His reflection wavers in the windshield. "We've been training for this our whole lives."

I tuck the piece of paper into my purse. I feel a little dizzy. Unanchored. It's time to sit back and watch the road unfold. I sense inside of me a kind of openness that simultaneously feels like flying and free fall.

I reach over to the dashboard, push a button to turn on a CD. The song "Something New" by Hot Buttered Rum fills the car, a personal message to us:

We could fall away from here
but I have faith that the footholds will appear…
There's not a force in this world, any place any time,
like the human soul on fire.

2

Teacher

Believing what you think, you're carried into
the endless dramas of the self.
—Byron Katie

It was 6:30 a.m. My car crept down the freeway toward my high school English teaching job. It was a cold, dark morning. On the radio, an NPR correspondent reported bad news in a soothing voice. It was 1987; I was twenty-five years old.

I stuffed miniature candy bar after miniature candy bar into my mouth from a bag splayed open on the passenger seat. The waistband of my skirt dug into my side. I'd stopped at 7-Eleven to buy several bags of candy. For months now I'd been buying sweets for my students. I didn't understand why I couldn't stop eating them.

I kept the candy in my desk drawer, handing it out when students did well on quizzes, or weren't tardy, or won a vocabulary game. Lately I showed a lot of movies in class. Sitting in the back of the classroom while *The Great Gatsby* or *Romeo and Juliet* flickered on the screen, I'd reach into the drawer and eat candy for an hour in the dark.

I was never hungry. I was always hungry.

I hated getting up in the black, cold early morning while Ray—my husband of two years—pulled a pillow over his head. I dreaded having to pick an outfit to wear that never felt quite right on my skin. My daily shower was drudgery. My hair was dry and static prone from washing it every day, but going to work with unwashed hair felt even worse.

I thought about Timmy, a dark-haired, dark-eyed junior who, at seventeen, looked like a man in his twenties. I hoped he'd be absent from class. He was often absent, thank God. A couple of weeks ago, we'd been reading aloud *Death of a Salesman* when he started ad-libbing Biff's lines, putting pornographic words in the character's mouth. When I told him to leave class, he loomed over me, an eerie smile on his face. I asked the principal to suspend him, transfer him, do *something* with him. Timmy returned in two days. I was glad when he took the toilet pass to the bathroom because he'd be gone for up to twenty minutes. He'd return smelling like pot. I didn't want to be his parole officer. I didn't want to spend one more day in his presence. I wondered why he didn't drop out of school. I would if I were him. I envied his rebellion.

I thought guiltily about the mountain of student papers—at least two hundred by now—heaped on my coffee table back home. I had promised myself I'd grade them over the weekend. As Ray and I drove to the store, I read half an essay then gave up, tossing it onto the back seat. The stack sat ignored on the coffee table while we watched football. Even though I lugged them with me, I didn't touch the dreaded papers when we ate dinner at my parents' house. I also didn't touch much of my food. I detected my mom wordlessly scrutinizing my body. I heard her thoughts: *you're gaining weight.*

One hand on the steering wheel, I shoved a Kit Kat in my mouth. I didn't even like Kit Kats. The chocolate tasted like wax. Brake lights glared red in front of me. Rush hour. In the rearview mirror, my face looked cadaver gray.

A tsunami of negativity threatened to pull me into an undertow. My mind seemed incapable of an encouraging thought.

God, I hated my job. How had things gotten so bad? My teacher education classes had been fun. I enjoyed creating lesson plans and indulged myself in imagining a classroom of students whose lives would be touched by literature and writing. But the reality was a chaotic mass of thirty-five restless bodies, of seven-period days, of classrooms that reeked of sweat, of desks crammed into every inch of the room, of tripping over sprawled legs and backpacks, of gossip and sassiness and eye-rolls, of jarring bells ringing every forty-five minutes, of homework—if completed—scrawled out thoughtlessly in cluttered handwriting.

My colleague Leanne and I had started going to happy hour on Fridays. Like me, she was an overwhelmed and disillusioned young teacher. We shot off campus at 3:30, the minute we were allowed to leave. Eventually we began drinking on Thursdays too. Lately, we squeezed in a Wednesday now and then. We drank until we could laugh—and laugh hard—at what we'd felt guilty about an hour before: the inept way we'd disciplined a kid, the lesson plan gone down the toilet, the endless stream of grading haunting us. Ever creative with her disciplinary tactics, Leanne once sent a girl to my classroom with a note for me, folded and stapled around the edges. When the girl left, I pulled the note open. In Leanne's loopy script it read, "This girl is driving me crazy. I had to get her out of the room for a few minutes." We roared every time we retold that story.

After happy hour, even though I was full of beer and greasy appetizers, I'd stop at a deli to buy a turkey-and-cheese sub. It tasted so good—salty and sweet and chewy and crunchy. Even my tipsiness could not abate my self-loathing as I shoved down that whole sandwich on my drive home. I dispensed of the paper evidence out the window, adding littering and drunk driving to my litany of sins.

Ray was probably puzzled as he watched me pick at dinner, even though I was clearly gaining weight. The first year of our marriage, I'd dropped twenty pounds on Weight Watchers. He loved my new, slim body. As the weight slowly crept back on, his dissatisfaction was clear. I was mortified.

We'd been married such a short time, and I didn't like having sex with him anymore. I used to love sex. I had plenty in high school and college. So much, in fact, I'd felt out of control, which probably factored into why I got married: to put boundaries around myself, to make myself into a wife.

Ray and I had become like his parents. His mom, always on a diet and nibbling at her meals, snuck bites as she cooked. His father teased her about her weight. The fact that my father-in-law was pudgy enraged me. What a double standard! Women's bodies were up for scrutiny in ways men's weren't. But I never said a word.

Once, as I ate a peanut butter and jelly sandwich, Ray said, "Isn't that fattening?" Defiant on the outside and ashamed on the inside, I numbly ate the rest without tasting it. One Christmas he bought me clothes two sizes too small. An odd, unspoken conspiracy of shame about my body plagued our relationship.

When we first started going out, Ray was still in school, finishing his engineering degree and working part time at a grocery store. He wanted us to save every penny so we could buy a house. Being a homeowner meant everything to him. When we were engaged, I won two thousand dollars on a slot machine. He insisted we use it to buy a couch for our dream home. I didn't want to use it for that, but I wasn't sure what I wanted to use it for. Possibly travel somewhere? But he said a house should be our priority. I didn't insist. I didn't know myself well enough.

I was only in my twenties, but I felt old. What had I been thinking, getting engaged at twenty and married at twenty-two? Why had I been in a rush to grow up? To be a wife and have a career? What had been the alternatives? I couldn't recall, although I had a vague memory of having wanted to be a writer who traveled the world. What a harebrained fantasy.

A student asked me if I was pregnant. It was my worst nightmare; people were watching me and judging my body. People thought I was fat. People I had to stand up in front of every day. I lied and told her I had been pregnant, but I'd miscarried. I hoped she'd spread this lie to the other students. The shame was excruciating. If someone would have asked Lisa that question, she would have roared with laughter, perhaps chiding the student, "Oh, you think I'm *fat*?" Lisa was a friend of my mother's, a large woman who wore floral, flowing clothes and chunky jewelry. She was always smiling and didn't seem to give a damn what anyone thought of her size. She lived in herself happily, like her body was a fun house or a rococo painting. Why couldn't I be peaceful in my body, no matter its shape or size? The times I came closest to that feeling was when I was drunk.

Recently I'd gone to the doctor. I'd had a pain in my side for months that made it hard to take a deep breath. For weeks before the appointment, I'd fantasized about telling the doctor I was deeply depressed, or that I thought I was going crazy. I imagined breaking down and crying hysterically. Then he'd do something—wouldn't he?—to save me. Wouldn't he send me to a psych ward or insist I take a leave of absence from my job? It was hard to imagine. It seemed melodramatic, like a scene from a Victorian novel.

At the appointment, I averted my eyes when the nurse weighed me, and I talked to the doctor only about the side pain. After the exam, he left the room for a few minutes. Sitting alone under fluorescent lights on crinkly antiseptic paper that covered the exam table, I cried. I bawled. I sobbed. I hoped the doctor or nurse would come in and catch me in the act.

I stopped crying the minute he walked back in.

"Are you okay?" he asked.

"Yes," I said, praying he'd see the *no* in my eyes. A judge in my head said I was being silly, histrionic. I thought the doctor—

in his authoritative white coat and dependable stethoscope—might somehow hear the judge and overrule him.

The doctor tore a prescription for painkillers off the pad and handed it to me, then walked out the door.

Traffic was picking up. That meant I'd be on campus in about ten minutes. I ate a mini Snickers, the nuts and caramel sticking to my molars. A chill slid through my body. Silently, tears began to fall, smearing my mascara, blurring the road. I didn't want to be in this body anymore. I didn't want to be in this life anymore. I felt worse than atrocious. I felt numb, blunt, unable to touch anything real.

I merged my car into the slow lane. So what if I were a few minutes late to work? We were supposed to be on campus at 7 a.m., but classes didn't start until 7:30. No one wanted to be there that early—not the students, not the teachers, not the administrators. The only ones who didn't seem to mind were the cafeteria ladies, their hair caged in hairnets. Sometimes I yearned to be one of them: no papers to grade, no hormonally charged students to force archaic literature upon. All the cafeteria ladies were fat and didn't seem to care.

One flick of the wheel. My mind suddenly became hyper focused.

One flick of the wheel and I'll fly off into a ditch, maybe hit a tree. Maybe I'll be lucky and die immediately. Or perhaps I'll break up my body badly enough that I can go on disability. I'll be paid to do nothing. At the minimum, I won't have to teach today.

I watched my hands. The crevices of my wedding ring were encrusted with residual hand lotion. My fingernails were ragged, chewed down. These hands could play "Für Elise" on the piano.

They typed ninety words a minute. As a synchronized swimmer, my cupped hands pushed water with such force that I could hold my straight-as-an-arrow body upside down and thigh high in the water. These hands had held innumerable pens and pencils, writing poems and stories since I was a kid. I wondered if these hands would dare to yank the wheel to the right. To send me over the edge. To make the decision for me.

Something inside me sputtered. In the midst of desolation, a kernel of life thrust forth, a seed, a morsel of awareness. I could make my hands do it. I could kill myself if I wanted to. Or maim my body. But I knew—even in the depths of misery—that I didn't want to.

No, I didn't want to harm myself. I didn't want to die. Yes, I wanted things to change. But no one else was going to save me. Even as inept as I felt, I knew that I alone had the power to save me. I just didn't have a clue how to do it.

Later that semester, I taught Thornton Wilder's *Our Town*. Before we started the play, I asked the students to write about a typical day. What did they do between the time they got up and came to school? What was their first class of the day like? What did they do after school, in the afternoon? Where and with whom did they have dinner? What did they do before bed?

Over the next few days, we read the play aloud. Toward the end, Heather—the one student who always volunteered—read Emily's famous "good-bye speech." Emily—who has died in childbirth—returns to the land of the living. It's her twelfth birthday. She's amazed at the beauty of everyday life: her youthful mother cooking breakfast, the clock ticking, the smell of coffee. But her mother is rushing Emily to get ready for school, not pausing meaningfully as the ghostly Emily craves. Emily realizes as a dead person she cannot bear the beautiful land of the living. The living don't inhabit life with the deep knowledge that everything is evanescent, that one day life as they know it will vanish. So she says good-bye to the world to return to her grave. She leaves, knowing that human beings squander their lives.

The girls had tears in their eyes. The boys looked down at their books. In silence, I handed back to the class the papers they'd written about a typical day.

"Imagine," I said, "that you have a chance to relive this day you wrote about. Imagine you get to go back and experience it again. What would you do differently? What would you think? How would you feel?"

As they bent their heads to their papers, my throat tightened. It wasn't enough, but it was something: I had used literature to touch their lives, even if for a mere moment. I wasn't so far gone that *Our Town* didn't stir me anymore.

I believed in a sublime vision of life. I had been an exuberant child. As my mom cooked in the kitchen, I'd come in and spin around in circles. She teased me about being a Tasmanian devil. I learned to read at age four and kept a journal almost every day, starting in third grade. I loved riding my bike. I loved the feeling of the warm sun on my cool skin when I pulled my slick body out of the pool. I loved family trips and playing with friends, but I also loved holing up in my room with my imagination for company. I had a tape recorder, and I'd walk through the house, or through the trees, taping enticing sounds. *Harriet the Spy* was my favorite book. Harriet was a passionate girl; she rode her bike around, spied on people, and wrote stories in her notebook. She helped me see that writers perceive life richly.

I remembered when most everything felt like an adventure.

Although she was buried down deep, that exuberant child still lived in me. I wanted to see beauty with my eyes and heart, to feel passion again. I wanted to be like audacious Harriet. I didn't want to be like dead Emily, mourning life's beauty as a ghost.

*

Having made the decision to be homeless, or more aptly "home-free," Dave and I have two months to disperse our things. We don't have much stuff. The Love Nest has one bedroom, a loft office, a living room, and a kitchen. Oh, and a garage and storage room. And we have some stuff stored in our friend Jerry's garage in San Jose. It's surprising how much "a little" stuff can actually be.

I know it's time to get rid of things I've been clinging to. I start with the early 1960s colonial-style table that came to me after my father died, when my mom—Alzheimer's creeping up—moved into assisted living.

This was the table where Mom served dinners with at least two different-colored vegetables. This was the table—when we went out to dinner for Mom's birthday—that our cockapoo jumped on, licking the frosting off Mom's birthday cake. This was the table where my two sisters, my parents, and I sat in our usual places. Sometimes after dinner we'd get up and move the next chair over. We role-played the other person, talking the way they talked, exaggerating their mannerisms. Whoever was my father bossed people around, whoever was me talked a lot, whoever was my older sister sulked, whoever was my younger sister fell asleep with her head on the table, and whoever was my mom rolled her eyes at everything.

With a nomadic life in the works, it's time to let it go. On Craigslist in the free section, I post a listing. I want to give it away. I want to rip off the Band-Aid quickly.

Minutes after I post the ad, my inbox fills with messages. After reading the first few emails, I come across one from a guy who runs a sober living home for men. I message him that he can have it. And I thank him, saying I know people whose lives have been saved by the kind of work he does.

He writes me back and says he does this work because he's been "blessed in abundance." He adds, "I used to live in a converted chicken coop and wanted to die. I have been overly compensated in life and have been clean/sober for over twenty-three years." He says without the love of spirit and desire to give back, he would be "dead or incarcerated certainly."

There was a time in my life I would have sneered at this thinly veiled God-talk. But now, only the goodness touches me through cyberspace. I don't care about the specifics—what version of God he believes in, or if he thinks the Twelve Steps are the "only way" to sobriety. I just appreciate the vibe of his words.

The next afternoon, a truck with huge wheels pulls up. A bulky, tattooed man emerges, arms spread wide.

"Hi Kate!" he says. We hug. "This is Teddy," he adds.

I look down and see a—nine-year-old, twelve-year-old?—child. It's difficult to place his age because of his telltale Down syndrome features: hunched body, softly sloping eyes, round face. Teddy grins at me.

"Would you like a hug, too?" I ask.

He nods. He reaches up to me. So supple. Almost as though he has no bones in his body.

They drive away with the table and chairs piled in the back of the truck. I imagine a group of men sitting around the table, working to re-spark their inherent goodness; a group of men getting their lives back on track; a group of men communing around the table as my family did. I have no idea how Teddy fits in, but I love that he does.

*

In 1989, when my husband of five years, Ray, left—him devastated, me relieved—he took only his clothes, his history books, and his vintage bomber jackets. I was surprised he didn't want the Mikasa china, the Oneida silverware, the Waterford crystal. After all, he'd chosen the designs and had initiated the wedding gift registration at Macy's. I understood from following his lead that this is what people-who-are-marrying do, what people-who-are-marrying care about. Five years after the wedding, most of those fine domestic gifts were still nestled in boxes, awaiting the never-to-arrive day we'd buy a house. He didn't even take the Fiesta bowls or Art

Nouveau statuettes or Art Deco prints—things he'd combed antique stores for, things I thought of as his.

I was about to move into my own apartment, a studio in a sketchy neighborhood. It was in my price range and had my number one requirement, a pool. My new digs were so small there'd be no room for the stuff of my marriage. Besides, I didn't want to drag around the dregs of my old life. I was starting over. All I needed was a big bookcase, a foldout couch-bed, my word processor, and a popcorn maker.

I called Goodwill. Two guys in a big truck came and took everything, including my marriage bed. They eyed all that china and silverware. It probably wouldn't make it to the donation bin. I'd considered trying to sell it all, but that seemed like a hassle. I wanted to free myself from this stuff in the easiest way possible. It was satisfying to be so reckless. I believed in my idol Walt Whitman's words, that humans are the only animals "demented with the mania of owning things."

I considered throwing my wedding ring into the ocean while sounding my barbaric yawp. Instead I sold it for one-tenth its purchase price.

I was happy. In a jittery sort of way. I'd been feeling more excited about life, sensing more surges of possibility, ever since Ray and I moved to the Bay Area for his new job. I quit teaching high school and started a master's program in English. Graduate school was a dream of reading, writing, exploring my mind and heart. I feasted on Whitman and Plath, on Swift and Shakespeare. I wrote myself into thrillingly essayistic revelations about Prospero and Antonia and Joe

Christmas.

Shortly before we split up, Ray told me that all this literature was making me "too idealistic." He read the newspaper and watched World War II documentaries. I went to author readings: Maxine Hong Kingston, Margaret Atwood, Isabelle Allende, Robert Bly, Gary Soto, Billy Collins. Sometimes I sat next to Harry, another graduate student. I was enthralled with Harry, who'd lived more life than most thirty-two-year-olds. He'd procured a discharge from the Army because he was an MP who discovered his pacifism and refused to carry a gun. He spent a couple of years in the seminary, where like a number of the other initiates, he indulged his bisexuality. He'd been in the Peace Corps in Africa. A man in his thirties, he spoke with authority in class. I swooned when he read e.e. cummings aloud. Sometimes during class, when the professor was talking, he'd lean over and annotate a page of my book, which thrilled me more than a kiss. We shared the poetry we were writing. He returned my poems with rapturous comments written in elegant script.

I invited Ray to come along to the readings. He declined. I didn't encourage him, didn't say it might save our marriage. I wasn't sure I wanted it saved.

"I have to give you credit," I said. "If you were hanging out with another woman the way I do with Harry, I wouldn't like it."

"Well," he said, looking up from his newspaper, "you're the jealous type."

"I am?" I said, a little surprised at this assessment, but deep down knowing it fit.

He smiled.

"So it really doesn't worry you," I asked, testing him, "that I'm spending so much time with another man?"

"You're not fucking him, are you?"

"No." I was telling the truth, but my heart raced.

He looked me right in the eye, like I was a stranger. "Then what do I have to worry about?"

He had a lot to worry about. I was having an intellectual affair, an erotic experience of the mind. I felt aroused all the time: when I sensed Harry's arm an inch from mine at a reading, when I engaged in class discussion, when I was writing an essay or a poem. Sometimes I even forgot to eat. I'd never felt so alive.

Surprisingly, I wasn't using alcohol to fuel these feelings. Harry was a vegan and didn't drink, so when we were together I abstained. Once at a restaurant after a reading, he ordered pizza without cheese and a glass of water. Who did that? His quirks increased his mysterious allure.

That semester the most glamorous professor I'd ever seen swept into the classroom: Dr. Gabriele Rico. Golden hair, long limbs, a chic sheath dress, frosty pink lipstick. She pushed the podium aside and slipped off her pumps, standing before us in sexy stocking feet. It was fascinating because she was no barefoot hippie; she was a stylish woman.

Dr. Rico shared with us her passion for poetry. She introduced me to Sharon Olds, Lorna Dee Cervantes, Galway Kinnell, Mary Oliver, Louise Glück. Sliding her glasses from the top of her head to the bridge of her nose, she read poetry aloud in her downy voice as though poems were sultry, sacred vessels. She taught us how to listen to—to *feel*, to *believe in*—the magic of language. She taught us how metaphor and rhythm create a transcendent experience. Poets, she said, use words to express what is beyond words. That's the paradox. And paradox gets to the heart of truth. While polarities—true/false, life/death—are opposites they are also related, thus, inseparable. One is not possible without the other. She quoted E.M. Forster: "Only connect."

She referenced physicists and philosophers. She talked about Chaos Theory, that patterns emerged from chaos. She discussed the brain's hemispheres. She said the left brain analyzes. It thinks logically, linearly, in steps. The right brain thinks in patterns, images, emotions. It creates. It's receptive. The left brain is the critic that can take things apart. It's helpful when editing our writing, she said, but if we allow the left brain to dominate too soon, it can usurp our intuitive, passionate right brain.

She encouraged us to allow, not force. Put the critic aside until we needed it. Let the right brain's generative powers flow through us. Let the right brain tap into our unconscious, where profound knowing is generated. She told us to not fear the blank white page. Not to fear chaos or the unknown, which are essential features of the creative process. She told us to trust that something would appear.

She projected slides of paintings—Chagall's floating lovers, Brueghel's plunging Icarus, Michelangelo's God and Adam nearly touching fingers—and read an accompanying poem. We wrote our impressions quickly, so as to surpass our inner critics, shocking ourselves with our insights. She'd read aloud a poem and have us cluster freely on a page. We grabbed words and phrases, spinning a web with circles and arrows, revealing intuitive patterns. She gave us three minutes, telling us to go fast—without overthinking—so we'd bypass logic. Three minutes became a deep and timeless experience. We wrote like we never worried, like we never heard of writer's block, like we were children unconstrained by a lifetime of rules.

She invited us to read aloud. Epiphanies popped up, one after the other. Gabriele called these sudden insights "A-has!" Invariably, as we read to each other we'd spontaneously gasp and applaud and sometimes, cry. We didn't *understand* the poetry. We *felt* it. We *inhabited* it. We *became* it.

Twenty-five years later, Gabriele would appear in my dreams during my seizure, telling me that the veil between the worlds is thin. That life and death aren't opposites, that they are polarities connected by a spectrum. Mysteriously intertwined. What, she implied, is "real"? Is a dream as real as life? And if death is part of living, are we ever really separated from life?

When she was fading away from cancer, she told her mourning daughters and husband that sadness was appropriate—but that they should also feel joy. She was experiencing deep amazement. Her dying journey was revealing profound levels of understanding. Dying, she said, is a grand adventure.

3

Boy Crazy

If the body were not the soul, what is the soul?
—Walt Whitman

While Ray and I were divorcing, Harry—my graduate school poet compatriot—swept me off my feet. He wrote me poems. He held me close, swaying me in an impromptu slow-dance in the living room. He told me if I got pregnant, he'd want to keep the baby. He didn't believe in abortion, and he wanted me to be the mother of his children. He took me on a road trip to his mother's house and, one night, we made love against a tree in the moonlit backyard.

I fantasized about our bohemian life. We'd write, we'd grow vegetables, we'd bake bread. The baby would take a nap in the laundry basket nestled in a pile of clean towels. Instead of being married to an engineer in a house filled with wedding china and heirlooms, I'd be married to a poet in a house of books and bare feet.

Soon, though, Harry was struggling with the master's program.

He needed to take a break from school, so he decided to go to Portland for a while, where his father lived. He wasn't sure how long he'd be there. We talked often on the phone, and he wrote me romantic letters. Eventually, he invited me to visit.

That's when he broke the news:

He was in love with someone else. A man. He considered himself bisexual, but lately he felt that his deepest emotional sympathies lay with guys.

His revelation hit me like a runaway truck, crushing my bohemian farmhouse fantasy. What had happened to my life? Was I really going to be alone? I was almost twenty-eight. Where had my twenties gone? I cried and cried and cried; it felt like I was falling down a dark, deep hole. Harry held me as I sobbed. But he didn't change his mind.

He brought me to the airport. I clung to him in the waiting area. When my flight was called to board, I detected a look of relief pass through his eyes. How could it be that he loved me one minute—wanted me to be the mother of his children—and the next crushed me and threw me away like a used paper cup?

For weeks my stomach was clenched. I couldn't eat. I found perverse satisfaction in the fact that my clothes grew looser by the day. I was disappearing, an act of defiance against life. I dragged myself to class and to my part-time job at a department store.

One day my friend Gina hauled me out of my apartment, where I'd been curled in a blanket on the couch, and took me downtown.

"You have to get out and do something and quit feeling sorry for yourself," she said.

Quit feeling sorry for myself? That stung. How could she even begin to understand my pain? She was beautiful. She'd traveled the world. She spoke several languages. She didn't seem to care if she was in a relationship or not. She didn't bat an eye at having a threesome with two guys on a beach in Greece. To her, life was a scrumptious delight. I'd never feel that way again. But I went with her downtown because going or staying was the same thing.

It was a cold day. The air hurt my lungs. As we walked along the sidewalk, my eyes glazed over at clothes and furniture and food for sale. What was the point?

At a busy intersection, we were crossing the street when something unseen stabbed my heart. I stopped in the crosswalk, frozen. People scurried by. My body solidified to stone. Who was I? The woman who wrote poems and whose soul sung to literature? The woman who wanted to have bohemian babies with a poet? The responsible high school teacher married to an engineer? The free-spirited college girl who'd reveled in sex and partying?

The little red crosswalk man blinked and blinked. My feet were leaden. I could not move forward. I could not move backward.

"Kathleen!" Gina shouted at me from across the street.

I didn't budge. I couldn't. I stood alone in the middle of the crosswalk. The light was about to turn. Gina—in a black coat with a fur collar and knee-high black boots, her raven hair a dark halo—ran to me.

"What are you doing? Come on!"

"I can't move," I said. "I really can't move."

"What are you talking about, silly?" She hooked her arm through mine and yanked me across the street, just as the light changed and cars swooped past. Her eyes sparkled. Her perfumed skin smelled like gingerbread.

Like a good witch, like an angel, she broke the spell. I'd crossed the street. I'd moved forward. Something cracked, like the breaking of a wishbone. I felt Harry lose his grip on me. My fear of being alone was dissipating. My body felt like it was floating. A sensation of looseness, of openness, replaced fear.

Maybe I didn't know who I was. That meant I was like a blank page, ready for the pen. Perhaps I could take Gabriele Rico's advice about writing and apply it to life: *trust that something will come. It always does.*

Could change really be like that, as simple as crossing a street? As uncomplicated as turning a page? Could I really be whoever I wanted to be? That would mean knowing what I wanted. What did I want? To write. What else? I wasn't sure.

But crossing that street had helped me clarify something I *didn't* want: I didn't want to be someone's wife. I didn't want to have someone's babies. At least not now.

I was fourteen, at summer camp. John, the blond-haired blue-eyed water-skiing star, had chosen me. He took me behind the girls' cabins, to the little bridge that spanned the dark, gurgling creek. He put his face to mine, a shadow in the moonlight. He kissed me. I'd been kissed once before, at my eighth-grade graduation dance. But this was different; he thrust his thick tongue into my mouth. A foreign, rubbery thing—weird and dazzling and shocking. I worried he'd cut his tongue on my braces, but he didn't seem concerned. I struggled to breathe through my nose. He pulled me closer, an uncanny hardness pressing against my leg. My body bloomed with an electrical charge, a buzzing of cells. Like Alice down the rabbit hole, I fell into the sensation, marveling that my body had such capacities.

The glare of a flashlight beam interrupted us. "You have five minutes to get back to your cabins," said a male counselor's voice, a god in the dark.

I was fifteen, in the back seat of my boyfriend's car. For the first time, I let him unzip my jeans. I wondered if his brother and brother's girlfriend, who were making out in the front seat, heard the zip. His fingers moved into my pants, pushed aside my underwear, and a finger slipped in. I gasped. How did he know how to do that? Tingling danced up and down my spine, my arms, my throat. I was stunned at my body's response. I clung to him until he moaned, a wet spot appearing on his jeans—a mind-boggling mystery.

I was sixteen, in bed with my boyfriend. Actually, my exboyfriend. We'd broken up a few months before. We'd dated for half the year, and he wanted to go all the way, but I'd always stopped short. Now we were at a party at someone's house, someone whose parents were out of town. Laughter and conversation and music floated in. Red plastic cups of keg beer bolstered my confidence. I was drunk, I wanted to have sex, and I trusted him. I wanted him to be my first.

The room was dark. I couldn't tell for sure, but I assumed he'd taken out his tooth and set it on the dresser. That fake front tooth, attached to what he called a "flipper" wedged in the roof of his mouth, impeded kissing. (The first time I'd seen him remove it was on a ride at the fair. He'd said, "Don't think I'm weird," and then took it out, shoving it in his jeans' pocket. I'd thought it was funny, and a little creepy, and very much like a boy, to have a removable tooth.)

We took off our clothes and got under the covers. We kissed, he climbed on top. I was ready, and when I took him in, my whole body detonated, a drunkenly numb explosion. It was better than I'd imagined. Why had I waited so long? I was keen on this, the high of obliteration.

What I mean to say is: from the beginning I liked sex. I liked touching, and kissing, and mounting and being mounted. I loved the soar and the rise of it, the shuddering exalt, the way time and thought were annihilated. For the same reasons, I liked drinking. The two usually went hand in hand.

As a kid when it was my turn to do the dinner dishes, I inhaled the remnants of musty wine in the bottom of my mother's wine glass. I tipped it to my lips. A sexual warmth swelled in my veins.

In my small-town high school, news spread on Fridays about whose parents were out of town for the weekend. That would be the party zone. Having sex, drunk, at one of those parties in a parents' bedroom was *de rigueur*.

Guys may have used me, but I used them back. Yet when I heard someone had called me a slut, I was humiliated. When my mom found my birth control pills in my room when I was sixteen, her disgrace shamed me.

"But Mom," I said, "you always said if I was going to have sex, be sure to use birth control."

"I didn't think you'd start so young," she responded grimly.

So young? I'd felt sexual my whole life. As a kid on the playground, erotic feelings arose when I hoisted myself onto playground equipment, mounting it between my legs. I had no brothers. I wondered if my mom would feel sixteen was too young for a guy, too. I didn't ask. Double standards enraged me: a guy who had a lot of sex was a stud; a girl was a whore.

To elude a double standard and dive into freedom wasn't easy. Something niggled at me. I rarely had sex sober, as though I needed bolstering to do what I (thought I) really wanted. In high school, drinking and sex went hand in hand. In college, drugs were added to the mix.

Wasn't sex about enjoying the body? If so, why did I need to be mentally altered to partake?

In college, I became a sensate bottomless pit, stuffing into my orifices food, mind-altering substances, and men's body parts. I'd get fat from indiscriminate eating and partying, and then skinny from starving myself. Big, small, big again—like Alice, like Gulliver. Through hedonism and abnegation, it seemed I was seeking to simultaneously ignore myself and infiltrate myself, to numb and pierce myself.

When I came home for summer break after my junior year, my mom took one look at me and said, "Let's put you on a diet." I'd always resented how my svelte mother was so critical of my body—but this time, I was relieved. I'd felt so out of control, and she was going to help rein me in.

I ate lots of salads and stopped drinking booze. Daily, I did aerobics in the family room. I walked the neighborhood, breathing in our small-town air. My extreme mood swings—exacerbated by drugs and alcohol—diminished. As the pounds melted away, my parents praised me. I was happy, yet something stuck in my craw: it seemed all we talked about, and all I thought about, was my body. And my self-discipline. As though my value increased with the decreasing of my size and the increasing of my restraint. I was obsessed and resentful, yet it pleased me to be thought of as pretty and in control.

I was a few pounds from my goal weight when, one afternoon, my friend Natasha called.

"It's so hot," she said, "and I'm bored. Let's make margaritas."

Her blender was on the fritz. We were going to use her boyfriend's blender—but he wasn't home so we needed to get the apartment key from his roommate, Ray, at the grocery store where he worked.

I remember first seeing Ray: tall, dark hair, close-set eyes, wearing a white button-down shirt and red-and-blue striped tie beneath a grocery store smock. A box cutter in his hand. He seemed so composed, so much more mature than all the guys in the dorms.

When he showed up after work at the apartment that evening, Natasha and I had a full-blown party going. Margaritas, beer, music, people hanging out in every room. Ray went to the fridge and pulled out a beer like a man who knew what he wanted. He loosened his tie and rolled up the sleeves of his white shirt, like a businessman after a long day. Clean shaven, boxy jawed. So totally male. Even the way he crossed his legs with determination fed my newly blooming fetish for Mr. Responsible.

He sat next to me, and we started talking about music (we both loved the Doors) and politics (liberal) and our interests (him: flying small airplanes and working on cars, me: reading and swimming) and our goals (he wanted to be an engineer, I wanted to write). I broke my diet getting drunk that night. Drinking margaritas felt so much more adult and civilized than the beer and tequila shots and drug mania of the dorms. He didn't say lewd things; he didn't dare me to a join in a drinking game; he didn't try to entice me into a back bedroom. Like Mickey Rooney or Greg Brady, he asked for my phone number.

On our first date, he took me to a jazz club in his silver Corvette. I wore a sundress, and the whole night I felt like I was playing a role from a 1940s movie. A few days later, we had sex for the first time. Afterward, I put on his button-down shirt like a nightie (very Marilyn Monroe) and made him a sandwich (very Donna Reed). There was something safe and retro about him. I no longer had to consider if I'd drop acid or smoke a joint or have random sex with a stranger. He had his eye on the future: he wanted a job with the airlines, and a house, and nice furniture, and one child. I donned our relationship like a life jacket.

Three months later we were engaged. Two years later we married.

Soon, the life jacket morphed into a straitjacket. Dread spread through me, a constant companion as I listlessly cooked dinner, or ironed Ray's button-down shirts, or rolled over in bed hoping he'd not want sex, or scrawled on student papers with a red pen, or—in his absence—sprawled on the couch eating forbidden food (potato chips, ice cream). Driving to my high school teaching job, I'd contemplated driving my car off the road but enrolled in graduate school instead.

I intuited my freedom magically lay somewhere in Walt Whitman, Henry David Thoreau, Virginia Woolf. Or in Harry, the bisexual poet. It felt delicious to be sexually alive again, to discover my libido hadn't abandoned me. But after I recovered from his breaking up with me—after I'd crossed the road to the other side—I realized that I gave him too much credit. Our sex life hadn't been good merely because of him. I was a sexual being. Such feelings weren't reliant upon another person.

Now that I was single, I had a chance to do something I'd always wanted to do: embrace my sexuality, on my terms. I wasn't in high school or in college anymore, places where people would judge me or pigeonhole me. At twenty-eight, I was an adult woman. And what I wanted was the same thing men had: sexual freedom. I wanted to have sex without recrimination, without guilt. Consciously, deliberately, I decided it was time to sow my wild oats. I wanted to break down double standards. I wanted to have sex like a guy.

As much as self-liberation was involved, so was repeating old patterns. Specifically the sex-plus-drinking prototype. On weekends, I started going to clubs with two friends from the department store where I worked: Caprice, a Grace Kelly-elegant blond from couture, and Carla, a short, dark-haired lovely from lingerie.

The three of us reveled in sweaty dancing, gyrating our bodies with strangers. One night I met a guy who took me from bar to bar. He knew the bartenders at each place who whipped up special cocktails for us. He asked me if I'd go to a hotel room with him.

"Do you have condoms?" I asked. It felt liberating to be so brash.

"No," he said.

"I'll only go to a hotel with you if you stop to get some on the way."

I probably should have been more concerned about his drunk driving. But he did as I demanded and stopped off for condoms. I stayed in the car. By the time we got to the hotel room, he couldn't get hard enough to slip on the condom. Minutes later, he was splayed on the bed, snoring.

I avowed each Monday that I wouldn't party the next weekend and instead would focus on my homework, reading *Beowulf* in the original or writing a paper about religious allegory in *As I Lay Dying*. But by Friday I'd agree to meet Carla and Caprice, and the weekend, yet again, became a blur of drinking and dancing and men.

One morning I awoke suspended in uncertainty. Where was I? A dark-haired man, his back to me, lay snoring in the bed. Flashes from the night before blipped through my mind: sex standing up in the kitchen, against the table, his brawny arms pinning me down. I'd been perched on the pinpoint of pleasure and pain, dulled by the morphine quality of too many cocktails. There had been a fierce vibe about the sex, on the edge of dangerous, something menacing. He didn't hurt me, but clearly he had the potential.

His snore was deep, his mouth quivering. Quietly, I rolled

out of bed. A needle pierced my brain. Nausea rode up my spine. In the light I could see that the apartment was stylishly appointed; long windows looked out over the city. As noiselessly as possible, I pulled on my bra and wrinkled blouse and short skirt. Holding my shoes, I crept across the floor toward the front door. Where were my underwear? Where was my purse?

"Hey, where are you going?" His voice came at me from behind. I turned. He was sitting up in bed, his mountainous chest bare.

"I said, where are you going?" He didn't say this in a sweet, *I don't want you to leave* way. His voice flew at me with an edge, a threat, like the tone of a kidnapper discerning his captive's attempt at escape.

"I have to go," I said, eyeing my purse near the coatrack.

"No, you don't." He pulled back the covers and swung his feet to the floor.

I grabbed my purse and bolted for the door, yanking it open and running out, down the stairs, into the cold, clear morning, my heart a fist. When I finally turned and saw no one, I slowed to a brisk walk, past cafes and stores, past people living normal lives.

I hailed a cab. In the warmth and safety of the taxi, I caught my breath. Had I been in danger? I wondered if my mind had freaked out over nothing. Maybe nothing bad had been about to happen. Maybe I imagined it all. Yet my body, prickling in fear, sent me a different message: *keep this up, and you're asking for trouble.*

The cabby eyed me in the rearview mirror then looked away. I pressed my knees together, hoping he hadn't glimpsed my underwear-less state.

One night when the bars closed down, I went to Carla's apartment to spend the night. When she took her cigarette from her mouth and set it in an ashtray before removing her blouse, I saw what looked like a big bandage on her arm.

"What's that?" I asked.

"This? Oh, it's the patch," she said. "I've been trying to quit smoking for a long time. I've discovered smoking while you're on the patch gives you a killer high, especially if you're drinking."

Talking and drinking tea, we sat on the couch in pajamas. Carla confided in me that Caprice's boyfriend ran a phone sex line, where Caprice worked in addition to the department store. I was both intrigued and repulsed. It was incongruent to me that Caprice—such an elegant woman, who fitted rich women with chic wardrobes—talked dirty to guys for money.

"You think *that's* wild?" said Carla. "Get this: Caprice's boyfriend likes having sex while holding a gun to her head. She doesn't like it, but she does it to please him."

I had no idea what to say. I didn't know Caprice very well. We just got drunk together occasionally and danced at clubs. At work she'd haughtily say "hello" to me on the floor and briskly move on. But somehow I felt implicated in the degradation of her life.

The next morning, Carla and I walked to a corner cafe. The city was bright and cold. I felt disassociated from my body in a not completely unpleasant way. It was like a scene from a film: eating breakfast in a hip cafe with a glamorous friend. A woman at the table next to us looked vaguely familiar. Had I seen her in a made-for-TV movie?

I realized no one knew where I was. None of my graduate school friends, not my parents or my sisters. I had no husband or boyfriend to account to. The memory of Carla's stories about Caprice chilled me and somehow seemed connected to my morning, a few weeks back, where the guy with the mountainous chest didn't want me to leave his apartment. My emotions were fuzzy and all over the place, zinging from happy and free to confused and anxious, and back again.

What was wrong with me? I'd have epiphanies about life, but then their energy would slowly leak away. Could I ever reach clarity about how to best live?

"Here, feel this," said Wes as we lay together in bed. He guided my hand to the spot behind his ear and then drew it down the side of his neck. Beneath my fingers, below his skin, ran something long and firm and snake-like. A foreign object was lodged in his body.

"What is that?" I asked.

I hadn't seen Wes since I was nineteen. It was now ten years later. My partying days with Carla and Caprice were coming to an end. He was in his early thirties and never married. When we saw each other again—meeting at a hotel where he'd come for a conference—sparks flew like they had when we'd met at a concert in 1980.

When I first saw him, I intuited something was different. A dead ringer for the actor John Stamos, he still had his gorgeous dark hair and olive skin and dazzling smile. But something was unusual, as though his face had been dissembled and reassembled askew. As though he was the Doppelganger of the guy I'd known.

"Well," he said, turning toward me in bed, propping his head on his hand. "I fell off a ladder three years ago when I was painting the side of my house. I hit my head and had to have brain surgery."

I shuddered at the thought of a surgeon breaking open his skull.

"What you feel in my neck," he went on, "is part of a shunt. If my brain swells, the liquid drains through a tube that runs down my neck and into my stomach."

Back in the day, Wes' roommate was his good friend James. In a bizarre twist of fate, James now worked for the company that made the very shunt encased in Wes' body.

Wes described the spectacle of his surgery and the brutal aftermath. He made it clear he'd come close to dying.

So that was the difference I'd sensed in him. A softness born from tasting his mortality. I thought about how he used to clean every inch of his car's dashboard with a Q-tip. How he'd done so much coke he had to have his deviated septum operated on. How he'd loved laughing and sex and hot girls. How he'd lied to me about who-knows-how-many women. How he took me to San Francisco for a wine-and-cheese picnic on a blanket in Golden Gate Park. He'd seemed so sophisticated, someone who lived big and knew how to navigate the world. I'd still lived with my parents. I'd been envious of his freedom, his maturity, his maleness.

This new version of him had softened, yet he retained an exuberance toward life. It was nice to be with him on different terms. I was no longer anxiously waiting for him to call, no longer craving a monogamy he wasn't capable of. We lived hours away from each other. I knew I didn't want much more than this day at the hotel, and neither did he. We were friends, a sweet surprise I'd never imagined possible. Our reunion was infused with a tenderness of two comrades who'd been youngsters together, and who'd since come of age.

While we had sex, and while we talked for hours in bed afterward, I felt a deep appreciation for something intangible. For the way everything changes and yet, in some mysterious way, is timeless.

Over the next few months, Wes and I talked on the phone now and then. One day, his mother picked up when I called.

"Wes is in the hospital," she said. "He had some brain swelling and the shunt malfunctioned. He had to have another surgery."

I called the hospital. Wes sounded good. He briefly relayed what had happened and then joked about the sexiness of one of his nurses.

"I'd like to come visit you," I said.

"Not now. In a while. I don't want you to see me without my hair." He laughed.

A few days later, I called again. His mom answered.

"Oh, my dear," she said, her voice tight. "Wes died."

"Oh my God, I'm so sorry," I said, not sure if that was the right thing to say. She gave me details about the funeral. I hung up, stunned.

Other than my sweet-but-aloof maternal grandmother, I'd never known someone who'd died. Nana had wasted away with lung cancer. Grandparents were expected to die. But young and vibrant Wes? I sat like a stone, my hand still on the phone's receiver. It didn't seem true.

On my way to Wes' funeral, my steering wheel went wonky.

I pulled over to the side of the freeway, a flat tire whomp-whomp-whomping. This was in the days before cell phones, and I had no idea how to fix a flat tire. The January morning was hazy and frigid. As cars whipped past, gusts of cold burned my face.

A truck pulled off the road and stopped in front of my car. When the door opened, a man in jeans, a flannel shirt, and a cowboy hat emerged. This tall man, this sturdy handsome cowboy, approached. I put his age at forty. Suddenly I was self-conscious of my short black skirt, shiny heels, and blond hair. Was I a roadside neon sign shouting "victim"?

A clear signal shot through me. I had choice: I could be filled with fear, or I could trust that everything would be okay. I thought about Wes. Something about the gravity of his death helped me. I sent him a mind-message, even though I had never before done anything like it before: *hey, take care of me, okay?* The minute I sent him that plea, calm saturated me like warm water.

"Can I help you here?" asked the cowboy.

"Thank you, that would be great," I answered.

"Do you have a jack and a spare tire?"

"I'm not sure." I opened the trunk to a mountain of stuff. I'd been home for Christmas, and my car was filled with presents. Patiently, he helped me remove them and set them next to the car. In the cold, my fingers were numb.

He found the spare tire but not a jack. He went back to his truck and pulled out a jack and a wrench. And then he knelt before the flat.

There was a composed confidence to his movements. I could

imagine a horse responding to him with a subtle shift in the saddle or on the reins.

When he finished, he stood, wiping his hands on his jeans.

"I don't know how to thank you enough," I said, reaching into my purse to pull out a twenty. He held up his hands.

"No," he said. "I won't take money for this."

I was shocked. Really? If I believed in angels—much less ones who looked like cowboys—I'd say he dropped from the sky.

An inspired thought came to me, born from all the Christmas stuff in my car. "Hey, do you drink coffee?"

He nodded.

"I got this coffee machine for Christmas, but I already have one. I won't use it. Would you take it? Please?"

With the same deadpan look in his eyes he'd had the whole time, he reached out and accepted it, thanking me.

When I arrived at the church, which was packed, I slipped in a back pew. I sat in a kind of trance amidst the Catholic trappings so familiar to me from childhood: stained-glass windows, velvet kneeling bench, robed priest at the altar. As a kid, it seemed the purpose of church was to test my patience. It was one of the few times in life I became excruciatingly bored. I was relieved when we'd happen upon a folk mass. A bearded priest playing the guitar and leading the congregation in "Blowing in the Wind" was as good as church got. There were, though, aspects of church I found soothing: the light blue of Mother Mary's gown, the sugary waft of incense.

That was the paradox of church, simultaneously comforting and alienating. A funeral reached the pinnacle of this contradiction.

A solace and a lament. At Nana's funeral, my mom had bent down and kissed her mother's waxy, dead cheek. I was shocked because my mom wasn't the kissing type. Mom hadn't shed a tear that I'd seen, yet she'd stiffly bent down and pressed her lips against her mother's cadaver. At the time I'd felt my mom was playing a role, performing her part from a script. I pitied her because that's how death was, right? It befuddled us all.

I glimpsed Wes' nose peeking from the casket. I had no desire to walk to the front, when the time came, and view his body. So odd, so strange, to think of his body up there—when not long ago, his body lay next to mine, his hand guiding my fingers down his neck so I could feel the tube that had saved him and then betrayed him. In the hotel, his body was animated with something that made him *him*. But that body up there, laid out for show? That was no longer Wes. It was some kind of weird, empty vessel.

The minute that thought passed through me, I heard Wes' voice. I could tell he was there, actually *there* in the church, but not in that body. I couldn't see him but I sensed his presence up in the corner of the church. That presence hovered in a specific spot, up high and to the right of the coffin. I felt his smile, heard his unique tone of voice conveying to me without words: *yep, I'm not in that body anymore. All is well.*

Once when I was about twelve or thirteen, I was very upset—I don't remember why—and as I sprawled on my bed, sobbing, I felt a presence sit beside me, stroking my head to comfort me. The presence, whom I'd thought of at the time as Mother Mary, was deeply soothing. There was wisdom in her touch that told me everything would be all right. Later, in my early twenties, when I was distressed and driving my car alone, the song "Bridge Over Troubled Water" came on the radio. I'd never before paid much attention to that song. But at that moment it seemed a force greater than myself sang it directly to me, assuring me I was safe and loved.

And now here was Wes, talking to me mind to mind, or soul to soul. His presence was as true as the fact that not too long ago, we'd lain together in a hotel bed. Actually, this moment felt truer. The past was like a dream. The present moment was a sensory reality. Wes' talking to me from the corner of the church *was* happening. It was happening *now*. I wasn't seeing him or hearing him with my usual senses. I experienced him in an extrasensory way, the same way I'd felt the comforting woman sit next to me on my bed, the same way I'd perceived that "Bridge Over Troubled Water" was being played for me.

Wes was dead but not. He spoke but without words. I couldn't see him but I could feel him. These paradoxes were real. Wes' disembodied presence was real. Whatever "real" meant.

*

From the time I was a teenager, my mom gave me a hard time about guys. "You are boy crazy. You love being in love," she chided. She saw my lust as weakness. She was harshly judgmental of anyone whose decisions were fueled by emotion or libido. People who had extramarital affairs were especially atrocious; they didn't care whom they hurt. After my divorce, Mom didn't want to meet Harry. "It's too soon," she said. One day she found a book of e.e. cummings poems that Harry had inscribed to me, dated before my separation from Ray. Angrily, she accused me of having destroyed my marriage.

"It's just so selfish," she said, "to do whatever you feel like, on whim, without thinking about others."

Decades later, after my father died, my sisters and I took Mom on a cruise of her beloved Hawaiian islands. Her first job out of nursing school in the early 1950s had been on the Big Island. As a kid, I pored over her Hawaii scrapbook, turning the thick pages, gazing at the black-and-white pictures affixed by the corners with gold triangular appliqués. The smooth-skinned version of my mom was proof she'd existed when I didn't yet. She reclined on the beach in a one-piece bathing suit; dressed in a pineapple-print muumuu, she read the newspaper in the nurse's dorms. The muumuu was long and form fitting; she still had it and would wear it now and then, proud that her middle-aged figure was as slim as her young one. Sometimes she entertained my sisters and me with a hula dance, her hands flowing like streamers. She called sandals *zorris* and urination *shee-shee*, terms she learned in Hawaii. Mom wasn't very coordinated or good at sports, but she could kick butt at ping-pong, which she'd perfected in Hawaii. And she had a ukulele, which she'd sometimes strum. Over the years, my parents took trips to the islands, returning tanned and relaxed. Hawaii was her own personal paradise.

So with my father gone, and dementia sliding over Mom's brain like a glacier, and the geriatric neurologist encouraging her to live her life to the fullest *now* because soon she'd be too incapacitated—we went on a Hawaiian cruise. Just us four women.

Carrying her cane and wearing tennis shoes, Mom did a great job walking around, given that she'd recently had several falls and was recovering from a broken arm and a gluteal hematoma—a massive, deep bruise that covered her tiny butt cheek in black, purple, and orange. We explored Maui, Kauai, and the Kona side of the Big Island. Bad weather had rerouted the ship away from the Hilo side, so we didn't get a chance to visit together the place she'd lived more than fifty years before. (I was a tad relieved. I worried about taking her to see the old nurses' dorms that I knew to be deteriorated, covered in moss and mildew, all the windows broken out.) Still, we explored beaches, reveling in the green and blue of it all—and then at sunset, the spectacular orange, purple, and fuchsia.

One night at dinner, Mom was feeling good from several Lava Flows, blended drinks that went down like milkshakes. Because of the medications she was on, she wasn't supposed to drink alcohol. But my sisters and I shared the belief that she should be as free as possible to do what made her happy. As she drank and loosened up, we talked about her life in Hawaii. I asked her why she'd decided to quit her island job and come back to California.

"Man complications," she said, with a rare sideways grin that I knew to be self-deprecating. And "man complications"? I'd never heard her say anything like that before.

"Really?" I said, smiling, leaning in toward her like a girlfriend eager for some good gossip.

Her words came in fits and starts, but eventually she admitted she'd been "dating," as she put it, a married man, a doctor. I couldn't figure out if she was saying she told his wife—or if his wife found out on her own—but apparently Mom and the wife met to talk about the situation.

I thought of all the years Mom had said derogatory things about people who had extramarital affairs or even flirted with people who weren't their spouses. I thought about how she criticized me for being too taken with guys rather than focusing on my own strengths, my own life. Now here was Mom telling me she had left her beloved Hawaii and given up her job because of a man. A married man.

"I wish I hadn't been so boy crazy," she said.

4

Freedom

I stopped waiting for the world to give me what I wanted;
I started giving it to myself.
—Byron Katie

In two months, Dave and I will leave the Love Nest. After my family table is hauled off by the former addict and the huggable kid with Downs syndrome, our snow tires are taken by a toothless man. As he shoves the tires in his truck bed, he says that finding them for free on Craigslist was a miracle. His daughter, who lives in Reno, has a Subaru they'll fit. He tells me the whole family lives up there: his five adult children and twenty-six grandchildren. He loves driving to Reno to visit, to help them out, to bring them things.

"You sound like a wonderful father and grandfather," I say.

"Well, that's not always been the case," he says, rubbing his chin stubble. "Was some years in there when we all didn't talk." His eyes move far away. "When I retired I felt that I didn't have much of a purpose. But now I'm realizing helping out the clan is my purpose."

A week later, we are invited for dinner at the home of our friends Mary and Wayne. As couples, we are on different trajectories. Dave and I are giving up a house, and they just bought one, a ranch-style with four bedrooms and a pool. In their late sixties, they want to create a life where friends and family can visit and where they can throw parties.

On our way out the door, Dave says, "Hey, let's bring Mary and Wayne our fireplace tools." They have three fireplaces, after all. That leads him to grab the wood stand and other fireplace paraphernalia. I wonder what else they might like. I have a set of china I've never used. My mom won it in a raffle and gave it to me years ago. It's pretty, white with Chinese-style red and gold trim. I've never removed it from the boxes. I like knowing pieces of us will be incorporated into others' lives.

Dave's tent, backpack, and rubber wellies go to Rob, who runs a small farm. (Later he tells us he uses the boots every day—and each time he slips them on, he thinks about us.) Several pieces of our furniture fill the empty spots in the home of our bachelor friend Jerry. Plants are gifted to Roxy, our friend with a green thumb.

The biggest challenge is my books. I have so many that I've been lugging around for years, some signed by the writers, many dog-eared and Post-it noted. And what about my high school yearbooks? They are the heaviest, most unused books on my shelves. They've been with me for more than thirty years.

I post a message on Facebook. A woman I haven't seen since high school responds she'd love the yearbooks; a bitter boyfriend burned hers up in a bonfire. I mail them to her. I mail other books to people I think might appreciate them: a couple of novels to my sister, an art book to an artist friend, and a poetic memoir about motherhood to a poet-mother.

One day I am invited to a gathering of five women writers. We teach at the same university. I go through my books to decide what to give to whom: the signed Gloria Steinem to the most flourishing feminist, the stack of memoirs to my nonfiction professor friend, the piles of poetry books to my poet laureate pal, the self-help stack to my friend who wants to change her mind and her life.

I also set aside a heap of books I think my students might enjoy. The next week I play Santa, showing off the covers, telling the class about the books, and throwing them into hands that shoot up in the air. Students laugh and shout as books fly like confetti.

*

At age twenty-eight as a Master's student, I taught freshman composition through the teaching assistant program, headed by Gabriele. Just as she'd ignited in me a passion for poetry and writing, Gabriele turned me onto teaching—quite a feat given how beaten-down I'd become after three years of teaching high school.

She introduced us to innovative writing pedagogy from the likes of Peter Elbow, Don Murray, and Mina Shaughnessy. She helped me see that it's crucial to guide students through the process of writing. Merely assigning an essay taught little. Instead, students should talk about ideas, cluster possibilities, free-write on key topics and subtopics, and reflect on the process along the way. She encouraged us to design our courses to allow students to explore and *play* with their ideas and language. She showed us how to bring other art forms—poetry, visual art, music—into the writing classroom to spark ideas and to influence flow and form. These practices revolutionized my teaching. Suddenly, teaching felt like an authentic, generative act. The class became about sharing our minds and our hearts. And it was actually, for the most part, fun.

However, as in teaching high school, I felt plagued by stacks of papers to grade. Miserably, I'd stare at the mountain on my weekends. It felt like I never had a moment of true freedom where I didn't have to think about work. And it was frustrating to spend so much of my living time marking up students' papers, only to have students glance at the grade then shove the papers in their backpacks.

With Gabriele's guidance, I began to experiment with a variety of ways to lighten the load—and make the paper-grading experience more valuable for my students. I had students share drafts in small groups. I was thrilled when I'd walk around the class hearing them discuss the hook, the flow of the language, the use of examples and images, the grammatical problems. They were learning to *see* and *talk* like writers.

On the day the papers were due, I asked the students to write down the strengths and weaknesses of their papers. Most of them were quite astute about what they'd done well and where they needed improvement. And because they often put on the page what I would have written after reading the paper, it was a huge time saver.

Even so, editing was the most frustrating and time-consuming part of grading. The more hours I edited, the more irritated I became with basic errors. What would start as a desire to help became a slash-and-burn. I'd think, *Don't they even care?* So I stopped editing. Instead, I underlined errors and had the students find and fix the problems. Remarkably, once the students knew where to look, they could correct most of their errors.

One day at Gabriele's house, I watched as she sat on the floor of her living room, student papers spread out around her. As she read, she laughed, *oohed* and *ahhed*. She not only cared about what students had to say; she was totally engaged. Her comments focused less on catching students doing something wrong and more on celebrating what they were doing right. When a line was particularly noteworthy, she'd pen "Woof!" in the margin. She helped me see that grading papers didn't have to be drudgery. It could be fun and enlightening. It was an opportunity to connect with each student. She showed me how to infuse this dreaded task with joy, with love.

I became good friends with several of the other TAs, women who also felt empowered by Gabriele's teaching. Even though we were different ages, we were all undergoing personal transformations. Like me, Emma was going through a divorce. Her situation was more grave, though, because she had two young daughters who were turning against her under the influence of their father. I was in my twenties and Emma was in her thirties. Then there was Mary, who'd been married at seventeen, and was now in her forties. Her thirty-year-old marriage was in turmoil. And then there was Faith, who was in her fifties. The mother of seven children, she'd been letting go of her Mormon religion for several years. We were all seeking, all reaching toward a new freedom.

Upon her divorce, Emma moved from her suburban home to a cozy cabin in the mountains. The four of us—Emma, Mary, Faith, and I—gathered there one afternoon to drink wine and talk. In her living room, I nestled into a chair and into the conversation. Hearing my friends talk about their lives infused me with a honeyed pleasure. I loved the way they examined their pasts. I loved the way they dreamed about the future, spinning glittery webs of possibility. Although I was the youngest, they didn't patronize me. Forty years separated us, but we were peers.

Emma and Mary pulled Tarot cards from a pack, creating elaborate designs on the rug. Mary was especially gifted at riffing on the significance of the cards. Any "negative" card had a positive spin. A death meant an opening up into something new. A blockage was a rich space of learning. Darkness was a place to discover light.

Emma pulled out a joint and asked us if we'd like to smoke it. Mary and I were in. Having been a Mormon her whole life, Faith demurred. But with a little encouragement, she agreed to try it.

I watched Faith take a hit of weed and sip wine. What a contrast to all those years of praying to a Mormon God, studying the teachings of Joseph Smith, and raising seven children. In my small hometown, there were a lot of Mormons. They seemed nice but secretive. I was curious about their beliefs and about what went on behind the doors of the Mormon temple. I asked Faith what had changed for her. Why did she start moving away from the church?

She talked about how her religious beliefs began to fade years ago. It was a glacial process that carved away at tradition. She'd always loved to read, and the more she read, the more she found herself critiquing her faith. She didn't like the gender hierarchies, in particular. She told us that when a couple gets married in the temple, the woman is given a "secret name." The only other person who learns the woman's secret name is her new husband.

"What's the purpose of a secret name?" I asked.

"Well," said Faith. "The only way a wife can get to the highest level of heaven is if her husband calls her over, using her secret name."

"But what if the wife dies first?"

"She waits in the lower level until he dies and can call her over."

"Wait a minute," I said, my revulsion for double standards kicking in. "That sounds like a strategy to coerce wives to keep their husbands happy. I mean, if you piss him off in this life, he might consign you to that lower level in the afterlife."

"Exactly!" said Faith, laughing. "It's things like that, when I really began to think about them, that turned me away from the church."

In our Master's program, Faith was an outspoken feminist. She revered Adrienne Rich and Audre Lorde and, like them, critiqued phallocentric literary traditions.

"So what's your secret name?" I asked in an offhand manner.

Was I seeing it right? Did Faith blanch? Her posture stiffened.

"I can't tell you," she said.

"Wait a minute," I said. "You don't even believe in this stuff anymore! Why can't you tell us?"

"I don't know," she said, her tone softening. "I just can't." Before our eyes, she transformed from a blasé pot-smoking, wine-swilling ex-Mormon to a reverent Mormon wife.

"Come on," urged Mary. "Tell us! It will free you!"

"Yeah!" said Emma.

"And if it's true you need someone to call you over," I said, "I'll do it! I'll call you over!"

Everyone laughed, even Faith. But she wouldn't relent. She wouldn't tell us her secret name.

Now that I was teaching, I no longer worked at the department store. Carla and Caprice and clubbing melted away from my life. I nestled into my studio apartment and became friends with my neighbor, Michael. We met at the pool. His skin was so white it had a light blue tinge. With his dark hair and prominent eyes, he looked like the goth version of the young Paul McCartney. He was quirky and brilliant, a post-doc in neuroscience. I admired the fact that he knew so much about both science and literature. His literary preferences tended toward the dark and esoteric: *Jude the Obscure*, the Biblical Job, Leonardo da Vinci's journals that were written in upside down and backward script.

One night I awoke to a pounding on my apartment door. I glanced at my clock: 1 a.m. Without getting up from my couch bed in the middle of my studio's living room, I yelled through the door. "Hello?"

"Is Marie there?" said a male voice.

"There's no one here by that name," I responded. I heard footsteps walking away down the hall and fell back to sleep.

I re-awoke suddenly. At first I was confused. It was dark and cold. Was that a breeze I felt over my skin? The clock said 2 a.m. Vision seeped in as my eyes adjusted to the light. I realized my sliding glass door was wide open. I couldn't see my front door, but I could tell it was open, too. A cross-current of cold ran over my body.

Oh my God, I thought. *Someone broke into my apartment. Is that person still here, hiding in the kitchen or bathroom?*

My body was frozen in place under the covers. I forced myself to reach over, pick up my phone, and dial 9-1-1.

"What's your emergency?" said a female voice in my ear.

"Someone broke into my apartment," I whispered. "I'm here alone. I don't know if they're still here."

She recited my address, which appeared on her display, and asked me to confirm it.

"The police are on their way," she said. "Stay put, and stay on the phone with me."

"Okay," I whispered, shaking beneath the covers. "I'm scared."

"Hang in there, everything will be fine." As scared as I was, I was grateful that this woman existed in the world and was on the other end of the line. It felt like she could save me even if the guy jumped out and attacked me.

"Oh shit," I whispered. "I hear something." Footsteps. Jingling noises.

"Don't worry, that's the police. They've arrived."

I jumped out of bed and threw on my robe in time to see three tall and handsome cops, like a scene from a romance novel, enter my place. One, gun drawn, kicked opened the bathroom door to nothing.

During their report-taking, I looked around to see if anything was missing. I didn't have much of value. I'd given most everything away a year ago to the guys in the Goodwill truck. I noticed that my purse was slumped on the floor beneath a barstool. My wallet was gone. It'd had six bucks in it.

The cops asked me if I knew any of my neighbors. I called Michael, who came down the hall to my place, face puffed with sleep. The police asked him if he'd seen or heard anything.

"Actually," he said, "I also was awakened a while ago by someone knocking on my door asking for 'Marie.'"

One of the cops said that it was probably the thief casing our places. He chose my apartment because a solo female voice had responded.

Thank God all he'd wanted from me was money.

"An addict," said another of the cops. "There have been a lot of break-ins in the past few weeks. Someone trying to get money for his next fix."

When the police left, Michael said I could come over and sleep on his couch. I did so that night, and the next, and the next. For months I lived more at his place than mine. One night, while we were watching TV, he reached over and started rubbing my feet. When he slipped a finger between my toes, it was reminiscent of my high school boyfriend slipping his finger into me all those years ago. A tingle shot up my spine. I looked over at Michael, but his eyes were glued to the screen.

A few weeks later, we ended up in bed. We'd been friends for months, and the sexual tension had built over time—so when we were finally making out, it felt surreal.

I looked at him—this quirky, genius scientist who'd been my pal for months—and said, "What are we doing?"

"Do we really have to talk about it?" he said, silencing me with kisses.

As Gabriele's devotees, the four of us—Emma, Mary, Faith, and I—attended a conference for teachers of writing. What a thrill to sit in rooms with others who were on fire about writing and teaching, and to hear our idols—Gabriele Rico and Peter Elbow—talk about a pedagogy of the heart. Faith and I shared a room at the conference hotel. The first night, as we changed for dinner, Faith said to me:

"Look at this!" She held up a sexy black bra and matching underwear.

"Nice," I said.

"No more temple garments for me," she said.

"No more what?" I asked.

"You know, Mormon underwear."

"Mormon what?"

She described the white cotton undergarments that Mormon men and women wear their whole lives.

"What's it feel like to not wear it anymore?"

"Wonderful," she said. "I'm still getting used to it."

"What does your husband think?" I asked.

"He doesn't know." She smiled, and turned to walk into the bathroom. I supposed that meant that after seven children, their sex life was over.

The next day, the four of us took a long walk through a forest that spread out from the seaside. We were all keyed up. The conference had deeply inspired us as teachers and writers. I skipped along the path, my long blond hair metronoming on my back. Emma said I looked like Alice in Wonderland. I felt so free. The future was rich and full of possibility.

Michael and I had been together only two months yet he was so temperamental. Sometimes he didn't want to talk all day. A pattern was emerging: we'd have a few wonderful days together, and then he'd disappear. If I called him, he'd not answer—or, if he did, his voice would be glum. He said he was subject to black moods. During those times he couldn't communicate. He couldn't give anything to anyone.

There, on the path with my friends, dappled sunlight and salt air on our faces, still high from the speeches and workshops that I was sure could revolutionize my teaching—my life—the drag of Michael's bad moods lifted from my mind like a helium balloon. I didn't want to be Michael's girlfriend anymore. I wanted to be free. I wanted to be happy. Sure, he was a genius. Sure, when he was in a good mood he was a wonderful boyfriend. But I didn't know from one minute to the next which Michael would face me. It was emotional whiplash. I wanted to be with someone who was, well, happier.

When he came to pick me up from the conference, I jumped in the car feeling so full of life, so sure I was going to break up with him. But the minute I sat down, that feeling vanished. He smiled, kissed me, told me he was happy to see me.

5

End of an Era

Everybody knows in their bones that something is eternal,
and that something has to do with human beings.
—*Stage Manager, Thornton Wilder's* Our Town

It's spring 2013, my last semester of teaching before retiring, and Gabriele is dying. For months she has battled cancer and has finally yielded, surrounded by her daughters and husband, Rich.

I am the age she was when we met.

Rich calls to say Gabriele would like a visit from Dave and me. I'm relieved I get to see her, but also a little nervous. Even though she had cancer twice before—once in her thirties and once in her forties—she's a force of nature. In her fifties and sixties she learned how to wind surf, rock climb and snorkel, and she became a yogini. In her mid-seventies, she glowed. She played like a kid with her grandchildren; her three daughters and their families were the joy of Gabriele's life. But she never subsumed her identity into "Nana." She and Rich traveled the world, and she never stopped writing. Until the last few months of her life, she was still working on several book projects.

I'm so used to the vibrant version of Gabriele that I worry seeing her so ill will be shocking and painful—for both of us.

Dave and I go to the house that I first stepped into almost twenty-five years before. Back then, I worked at her house on textbooks and other writing projects. It's the house where over the years I attended parties on the deck overlooking the canyon. It's an architectural marvel, a California wood-and-glass maze. I once heard someone call it the Cupertino Mystery House, a play on the nearby labyrinthine Winchester Mystery House.

The house's magnificent entry beckons us. Fat koi swim in the glittering pond near the steps. Gabriele's youngest daughter, Simone, emerges from the front door, and we meet in an embrace. She sobs into my shoulder. Seven months earlier my own mother died, and five years before that, my father. I hug her as a woman who has also suffered the illness and loss of her parents.

Rich and Suzanne, Gabriele's middle daughter, greet Dave and me with teary hugs. Gabriele lies upstairs in her bedroom, but her presence is everywhere. The house feels like an extension of her body. Images of Gabriele are on exhibit in many of the rooms. Rich, a photographer, has taken countless pictures of her over their sixteen years of marriage. My favorite is a black-and-white nude of Gabriele in crow pose, crouched with her knees balanced on her elbows, her lithe sixty-something yoga body so sturdy, her blond hair curtaining her face. There is a funny series of black and white photos called

"Godiva Gabriele." Nude, yet adorned by a wig of knee-length blond hair, she's standing next to a tram wearing ski boots in one shot, Rollerblading on a city street in another, and draped over a horse statue in a public park in yet another.

Gabriele loved the female form in art. When I was first getting to know her, I was ambivalent about nudity. I once told her I believed the objectification of women was damaging. I said the historical male gaze placed men in a superior role. In her gauzy voice, Gabriele talked about the beauty of the human form, male or female, but added that there was something exalted about women. She didn't believe that was sexism. She thought it was a timeless truth.

She'd smiled as I persisted in my argument. She didn't belittle my opinion, but she could see my developing ideas were fragile because I was desperate to sway the opinions of others. She was gentle enough, wise enough, to allow me my many transformations. Years after my dogged opinions expressed in that conversation, I posed nude for Rich's camera with Gabriele in the room. It felt like a revolutionary act after so many years of debasing my body. Gabriele accepted all of my changes with grace. She was like a mother to me in many ways—but because she wasn't my mother, we never battled as I radically jumped from one thing to the next.

When Suzanne and Simone guide Gabriele downstairs to the living room couch, my residual anxiety about seeing the dying Gabriele lifts. If possible, she looks more beautiful than ever, as though light glows through her skin. In her bodily fragility, it seems like earthly concerns have lifted, as though her spirit is pure.

Although Gabriele is as imperfect as the next human being, she is enlightened when it comes to mortality. Gabriele said she was experiencing a divine transformation that was leading her to new understandings about the mysteries of life. On her blog, Suzanne wrote these words that Gabriele said:

"I've been interested in the act of dying for years, and I think most people want to run away from it. But I've decided I want to look at it head on: what's involved, what makes it harder, what makes it easier, what it *is*. I've determined I need to be a participant in this because I think dying is somehow equally as significant and important as birthing…. So I've been looking at birth and death not as opposites but as the ends of a single continuum. And I'm trying to determine what that means for me and what it might mean for other people who need to learn. I think we humans are still at a stage at which we really don't know what to think about death, and fear really interferes with how we're able to see it….I've been thinking about what life is for, anyway. In the end, we die. I just have this gut feeling that we are meant to learn things from it that we don't know yet—and that *everything* every human being learns is never lost, but becomes part of the essence of what it means to be human—to be alive in a universe that's a big unknown. I think *that* is the immaterial quality of life which never dies, though the body dies, and is recycled and made part of the earth again."

With a broad smile, Gabriele sits beside me on the couch and hugs me. Suzanne adjusts the pump that runs with a line into her mother's body, feeding her pain medication. In the midst of the hug she calls me her "sixth daughter."

"Wait a minute," I jest. "I thought I was the fourth!"

She laughs her signature laugh, which rumbles up like music from her belly.

Suzanne says, "There are at least a hundred daughters."

We chat a bit in an unremarkable, comforting way. Soon her daughters and Rich leave the room.

Gabriele reaches out her arms, and I lean into her. Dave sits quietly on the end of the couch and snaps a few photos. She holds me and rubs my arms and my head, comforting me, silently telling me everything is as it should be.

Several hundred people attend Gabriele's memorial. It's held on campus—the campus where I met her, where I worked with her for years, where I am teaching my last semester before retiring.

In my creative writing class, I tell my students about her. I read aloud poems and have students cluster then write their own versions, a technique Gabriele developed called Re-creation. The students love the way their minds are set free, the way they can do more with words than they've ever imagined.

Sometimes you have a magical class where everything gels, where students shine and laugh and share freely and fiercely. This is one such group. They respond energetically to almost everything we try.

This is exactly how I felt in Gabriele's class as a graduate student. And it is with this group of students I experience my last day of teaching—perhaps ever. Somehow it feels more like graduation than retirement. We end with a class poetry reading. The students read with passion. We laugh, we are moved to tears, we applaud, just as the students did all those years ago in Gabriele's classes.

Then it's over. I stand in front of the class, a bit numb. I thank them for being an unforgettable group, and for creating an amazing experience on the last day of my San Jose State teaching life.

Silence falls. My eyes are damp. The students sit looking at me. No one glances at a cell phone or zips open a backpack. We are a still life, frozen in time.

Suddenly, one young man who has been on fire all semester—who has been the class cheerleader—jumps up from his seat and yells, "Group hug!"

All twenty-five twenty-somethings stand and rush toward me, arms outstretched, and surround me. It's the end of an era. The hug of a lifetime.

6

Flight

It's time to start living the life you've imagined.
—*Henry James*

It's Dave's and my last day in the Love Nest. To allay the knot in my stomach, I hum a Bob Marley refrain in my head: *every little thing's gonna be alright.*

After the movers take what's left of our stuff to storage, we walk down the street for breakfast at our favorite cafe. While eating, I think about our Tempur-Pedic mattress and purple couch and solid oak desk lodged in a dark storage container for who-knows-how-long. I think about how in a few hours we'll be on the first plane trip of many in the coming months. I think about how we are inhabiting the fertile void, a place of openness and unknowing. Viscerally, I settle into that exciting, unnerving space. I see myself free-floating like an astronaut in the cosmos, lightly attached by an umbilical to the mother ship.

After breakfast we take a final walk by the ocean. A little weepy, I say good-bye to the beach, our beach, my beach.

Two days before my mother died—only weeks after Dave and I got married—I stretched out next to her on her bed, our bodies touching, my face next to hers. Hawaiian music serenaded us on my iPod. She wasn't able to move much, and she hadn't spoken in over a year as dementia whittled away her words. I talked to her about what I loved about her. I told her how grateful I was to have her as a mother. I reminded her of the gift she'd given to me when she'd said, "Don't ever worry about how I will react to your writing. Write whatever you want." When I was a child, she took me to the library each week. At night she sat on my bed so we could read together, me one page, her the next. I thanked her for bringing books into my life. I thanked her for our family trips, told her that her love for travel was contagious. So was her strength as a woman. Every argument we'd ever had, every tension between us, had long fallen away.

When I stopped talking, I held her, rubbing her arms and head. She had never been relaxed with physical touch. It felt extraordinary to have her resting in my arms—and to think about how she had held me when I'd first come into this world.

Two days later, she died. The next morning, I'd awakened feeling numb. No matter how many years she'd been ill, no matter that I was a fifty-year-old woman, no matter how many times I'd prayed for the end to her suffering, it was a shock to lose my mother. I allowed my heart to break. I took a walk down the street toward the beach. My beach.

As I approached, I saw and heard a commotion in the sky and

the water. The closer I got, I saw what was causing the turmoil. Flying and plunging and bobbing were thousands upon thousands of birds: white and brown pelicans, gulls, terns, cormorants. Dozens of harbor seals dove and surfaced, their slick bodies gleaming.

They spoke to me, somehow, of my mom. She was free.

After breakfast and our beach walk, Dave and I return to the empty Love Nest for the last time. Not one piece of furniture or fabric or piece of art animates the place. It feels like a corpse.

We roll out our yoga mats onto the tile floor of our vacant living room, facing the long windows and redwood deck, the trees displaying like peacocks this last day of May. The mats unfurling resurrect the room. It is now an airy yoga studio, a place where we can be present with the ethereal. The emptiness that is fullness. The eternal present.

Yoga. Showers. And then it is time to say good-bye.

I gently turn my attention away from good-bye, toward hello. Every good-bye is a hello. Hello to the next thing. Hello to us in Chitty Chitty Bang Bang. Hello to heading toward a new adventure. My mood drifts from melancholy to eager. Dave takes a selfie of us in the car as we pause at a stoplight before heading out of town. I am wearing my heart-shaped sunglasses. I adore the corny, over-the-top symbolism of looking at life through the eyes of love.

*

The first time I tried yoga was in high school P.E. in the mid-1970s. I remember the teacher's soothing demeanor—and that her pregnant belly didn't diminish her flexibility. She dimmed the lights, played soft music, and spoke in a mellow voice. I associated the peacefulness of being in that class with the baby inside her body. A womb. A respite from the frenzy of high school bells and books and loud voices and slamming lockers.

When she taught us the tree, she had us imagine that roots flowed through our bodies and spread into the floor, keeping us grounded. Ever body conscious, I relaxed into my interconnection with the Earth. Once, in a shoulder stand, someone farted and the class laughed. Calmly she said, "It's natural for the gasses in our bodies to rise when we're upside down." She'd said this so matter-of-factly, as though the body were nothing to be embarrassed about.

Years passed before my next yoga experience. I was twenty-nine and still dating moody Michael. I had finished my Master's program and was hired as a lecturer at the university. To supplement that income, I was a freeway flier, teaching two more classes at a community college and tutoring elementary kids. I also worked a few hours a week at Gabriele's house. I felt honored when she asked me if I'd help her with her writing projects. When I first saw her house, I was floored. In her best-selling book *Writing the Natural Way*, she developed the technique of clustering, a brainstorming technique that involves writing down a word in the middle of a page and free-associating other words in around it, circling and drawing arrows from one to the next to create a visual constellation on the page. Her very house was a cluster: rooms branching off from other rooms in what appeared to be a chaotic mass that, upon closer inspection, revealed a pattern of interconnected space. Surrounded by trees and decks, the house was perched on a canyon and had a beautiful koi pond. The interior was filled with Modern furniture, sculptures and paintings and, of course, books.

When I arrived, Gabriele might be in the front yard digging holes for planting. Or in the living room, doing floor exercises to music on the stereo. Or lounging on the back deck and tanning her gorgeous legs. Or at her computer in her office that bulged with books and papers.

She asked me to help with a textbook project. I was to write sample answers to end-of-chapter questions. The answers would appear in the teacher's manual of the textbook she was co-authoring with Hans Guth, another San Jose State professor. Like Gabriele, Hans was German. But unlike Gabriele, he spoke with a thick German accent. Gabriele's voice was melodious, without a trace of accent. She told me she'd worked conscientiously on her diction. She told me I should, too, implying that by tending to drop my "-ing"s (as many Californians do) that I sounded, well, not very smart.

I was learning that there were two sides to Gabriele. She was an open-minded celebrator of the human spirit, but she was also status conscious. As a child, she'd lost her mother to a bomb attack on the family home in World War II Germany and then—after coming to California as a girl who couldn't speak English—eventually earned a Stanford PhD, of which she was rightfully proud. Although many students at San Jose State revered her, some conventionally minded students and colleagues disdained her. Dismissing her student-centered, creative pedagogy as "airy fairy," they discounted her revolutionary development of clustering by calling her "the bubble lady." Were they jealous? She was the only faculty member in the department to have written a bestseller—and she was in high demand as a speaker all over the world. She believed in everyone's genius; this threatened the hierarchies of traditionalists who deemed that education was about dumping their knowledge into students' naïve minds. Sexism was probably a factor as well; she may not have been taken seriously because she was so beautiful.

Gabriele talked to me about these conflicts. Clearly they affected her at times, perhaps fueling some of her anxiety attacks, which she openly discussed and wrote about. No matter, she appeared as the consummate, caring professional. She shrugged off criticisms with these words: "I've learned it's best to stay out of departmental politics. I just focus on my teaching and my writing."

As part of my job writing sample answers to student questions, I had to read Ibsen's *A Doll's House*. I'd listlessly read the play as an undergrad, when I was nineteen, but re-reading it at twenty-nine was illuminating. I deeply identified with Nora's desire to spread her wings. The way that her husband Torvald treated her condescendingly reminded me of Ray, especially when he'd told me that reading so much made me too idealistic. When I next talked to Hans on the phone, I enthused: "Wow! *A Doll's House* is a great play! And Torvald is my ex-husband!"

"Torvald is *everyone's* ex-husband," he said. "That's why it's a great play."

I knew doing this work was an incredible opportunity. However, I often found myself mentally drifting off as I tried to work in Gabriele's guest room. There was something wrong with me.

I couldn't focus. I felt pulled in so many directions: battling with Michael, teaching at three different campuses, trying to stay on top of all the lesson-planning and paper-grading, driving all over the place, papers and books and pens flooding to the floor when I braked for a stoplight. I couldn't figure out how to slow down my pace, reflect, and take it all in. I was frantically treading water.

Recalling the peace of my high school yoga class prompted me to seek a yoga studio in town. At the end of the class, we were lying on our mats, eyes closed. The teacher directed us to notice our breath. Cars whooshed by outside.

"Accept any sounds or sensations," she said. "Let them pass, just like your thoughts. Let them float by like clouds. Keep coming back to your breath."

I was anxious, lying there doing nothing. As much as I resented having a hectic life, I didn't know how to be at peace when motionless. It was as though I were a passenger in a speeding car that suddenly halted. The car had stopped, but my body continued its forward momentum.

The teacher said, "Everything is fine, everything is perfect, right here in this moment. If you feel anxiety or worry or stress, you're thinking about the past or the future. The past and the future don't exist. Only now does. Just keep coming back, right here, to this present moment."

Wait a minute! Anxiety, stress, worry…they were rooted in my *thoughts*? The past and future were *mind tricks*? I noticed that, indeed, as thoughts came into my mind about my relationship with Michael, or the lesson plans I had to do, or the fact that I was turning thirty this year—tension grew in my breath and body. I was *embodying* my very thoughts.

If I could hold myself in the present moment without judgment, I'd feel better, less erratic, less at the mercy of my emotions, good or bad. The problem was, my mind bounced around frantically like a ping-pong ball. Maybe I wasn't living life, but life was living me.

I felt true peace only when drinking a beer or a glass of wine, or while reading a captivating book, or when I was at the movies. I loved the dark womb of a theater. I loved the way I could lose myself in buttery popcorn and a story-come-to-life.

One afternoon I went alone to see a new movie, *Thelma & Louise*. By the time I left the theater, I was a changed person. I'd never before seen a movie focused on two strong, complex women. They went on a road trip, two women, no men! They killed a rapist! Thelma transformed from a meek housewife with a domineering husband into a gun-toting badass! Louise's heart transformed from bitterness to gold. And that ending—oh, that ending. They chose to fly off into the freedom of death rather than be forever confined by patriarchal authority. They held hands and soared away, united.

I was dying to see the movie again. I asked Michael to join me, but he declined. I was furious. This was important to me! I'd been talking to him for months about how frustrating it was that women's stories were so rarely told in movies. He listed all the movies we'd seen that had women's roles.

"But they're all the wives or girlfriends! Or prostitutes with a heart of gold! The movie isn't the woman's story!"

He didn't understand or didn't care. I was irate. The next thing I knew I would segue to the lack of women on the Supreme Court and boards of major corporations, the fact that women's sports didn't get the TV airtime of men's, the fact that women made sixty-two cents on the man's dollar, the fact that popular seventies rock bands featured mostly men. I could hear myself ramping up. He squirmed, not sure if he should take all of this seriously or personally. It felt personal. I was sleeping with the enemy.

Then again, I adored that he thought me beautiful and sexy. I loved to wear short skirts, and to wait for him at a bar while other men flirted with me so that when he walked through the door he'd claim me as his.

But all of that pissed me off, too. I was objectified. I could never live up to the ideal. All those billboards and TV ads featuring perfect women, not to mention *Playboy* and *Penthouse* taunting me from behind the counter at 7-Eleven. Even in fine art, why were women's bodies idealized? Didn't he realize that women developed eating disorders and self-loathing because of this societal inequity?

In the car, in the apartment, at a restaurant, we could be having a genial conversation, and abruptly something would trigger my anger about the status of women. I'd want him to agree with me.

He had his own way of looking at the world, a version of social Darwinism whose key substantiations involved the world's oldest profession and hunter/gatherer societies. When he invoked these points—calmly, earnestly—I'd dissolve into furious tears. Didn't he see that I felt like a second-class citizen and that his refusal to empathize rubbed salt in the wound? What about the Salem witch trials, for God's sake?

He looked befuddled. What was he supposed to do about historical patriarchal abuses? He respected me as a person. He didn't treat me like a piece of meat.

Soon I began to listen solely to music by women and to read books only by women. I subscribed to *Playgirl*. But as hard as I tried to even the score, I couldn't relax. My anger wouldn't let go.

I was unhappy with Michael yet I wanted him to want to marry me, to be exclusively desired by him. He was quiet on the topic of marriage except once when he said he wasn't sure he could marry a non-Jewish woman. As a shiksa, I took offense. I asked him to explain why that mattered when he rarely went to temple. He said his grandmother would never accept his marrying outside of the faith. His *grandmother*? What about what he wanted?

While Michael wouldn't see *Thelma & Louise*, Faith jumped on the offer. She loved the movie as much as I did. Since I'd first met her, Faith had pulled further and further away from the Mormon church and was deeply involved in writing poetry. She attended a weekly writing workshop at the home of a professor—a lesbian in her sixties named Georgia Constantino. Georgia was a powerful figure, a formidable presence. She kind of scared me, but Faith was drawn to her.

Months later, when *Thelma & Louise* was released on video, I threw a *Thelma & Louise* party at my house. Faith and Emma came. Mary, too, with a scarf wrapped around her neck and dirt on her face, like Louise in the second half of the film. I'd invited Gabriele but hadn't expected her to come. Yet she did, bearing a bottle of wine.

Around this time, I heard a song on the radio that lit me up. It was revolutionary: two women's voices in gorgeous harmony with acoustic guitars and wise, poetic lyrics. The words from the Indigo Girls reached over the airwaves and spoke directly to me.

It felt like a call to claim my power. No more bemoaning Michael's moods and the state of our relationship. Time to buck up, to stop—as the song's lyrics say—thinking myself into a jail.

I held a yard sale. Most of my clothes were spread out on the lawn beneath the big elm, along with my bookshelves, my bed, boxes of books and magazines, my stereo, and various tchotchkes. My rusty silver Honda, parked in the driveway, had a *For Sale* sign taped to its windshield.

It amazed me that two years after my post-divorce Goodwill giveaway, I'd collected so much stuff. Did living really require so many *things*? I intended to get rid of it all but for three boxes stored at my parents' house crammed with journals, photos, books, my baby book, and four fat high school yearbooks. The only other items I kept fit into a suitcase and daypack. Those would come with me to Japan.

After seeing an ad in the local paper for a teacher wanted in Japan, I applied on a whim. A few days later, I interviewed in San Jose with a couple whose daughter and son-in-law ran a small language school in Yokohama. The next day they called and asked me if I could be in Japan in three weeks.

Three weeks? I didn't even have a passport. I'd traveled with my parents to Canada and Mexico, and taken a cruise of Caribbean, in the days before a passport was required. My parents had fostered the love of travel in me. We'd taken road adventures, camping excursions, trips to the homes of friends who lived in various states. Traveling created a palpable sense of freedom where time and place were fresh and malleable.

But now, at age twenty-nine, I'd done more fantasizing about traveling than actual traveling. Michael was tied to the lab, and so we rarely went anywhere—except camping, occasionally. I had jumped from high school into college, and every summer I held a job as a waitress, camp counselor, or lifeguard. In college I fantasized about tramping through Europe, but that felt like the auspices of guys—the Jack Kerouacs and Jack Londons of the world. And then I married Ray right after graduation, at age twenty-two.

Ray had not been the traveling type, but he'd agreed to honeymoon in Hawaii. I'd thought it the ideal honeymoon spot, the place my parents loved.

A private pilot, Ray had been only on small planes. His first day on a jet was the day after our wedding. I wore a blue and white sun dress and a wide-brimmed hat on the plane. I imagined us in a *From Here to Eternity* embrace on a pristine beach. Inspired by my parents' stories of the elegance of island hotels, I saw us on a lanai feeding each other macadamia nuts and champagne.

It turned out Ray didn't like macadamia nuts, and beer was his beverage of choice. He didn't like to recline on the sand (too scratchy and messy), and we hadn't brought the right shoes for trekking over lava. He vetoed my suggestion that we rent horses for a romantic ride on the beach because of the expense. Taking a helicopter ride in Waimea Canyon was out because didn't I know that helicopters are the most dangerous, unstable air vehicle?

He found Kauai boring. This offhanded critique of what I'd imagined would be the most romantic adventure of my life was made worse by the fact that he hated flying on the commercial jet. He squirmed for most of the five-hour flight, white faced.

Something happened to me on that honeymoon. I began to develop claustrophobia. Seeing my new husband—the secure, stable man—drinking beer after beer on the flight home to calm his nerves unsettled me to the core. If Mr. Stability was fearful about flying, then I certainly needed to dread it. He knew a lot about planes. He knew this flight from Hawaii to California on this big, unwieldy jet was unsafe. I swallowed his belief system like an addict swallows a handful of pills. I thought about the doors of the plane, how they'd been hauled shut and locked down, how I couldn't get out if I wanted to. I gripped the armrest. I tried to channel the blasé attitudes of the flight attendants who walked the aisles as though the plane were firmly planted on the ground.

That was the first and last flight I took with Ray. Because he worked (on the ground) for an airline, we could fly free. But we never did. And then, before the divorce was final, I realized I had one last chance to fly somewhere before I'd lose my free flying privileges.

I decided on Hawaii. I wanted to experience paradise by myself. I would ride a horse on the beach. I would dig my toes in the sand. I would snorkel for hours and hike a volcano. In my carry-on, I packed a couple pairs of shorts, a bathing suit and running shoes. I wore a casual sundress with sandals. I didn't have a hotel reservation. With my new Bohemian outlook, I'd figure out where to stay when I got there. I was traveling as light as possible—nothing I had to do but step on the plane, alone. Yet I felt heavy with remnants of fear: could I really do this all by myself?

When the doors of the plane shut, I was gripped by anxiety. The overweight man next to me was hogging the armrest, his flesh overflowing into my space. No matter how I leaned, I couldn't escape his touch.

I tried to focus on the fact that I was now free. I could make my own life choices. The divorce was my decision. I had outgrown a marriage that was making me prematurely old, at age twenty-seven.

The plane began to taxi. It had been cold in the Bay Area that early spring; I reveled in imagining myself basking on a warm beach. As the aircraft lifted, the blue bay appeared below us. The whole planeload of people tilted back, the plane pushing hard, fighting gravity.

We were at six thousand feet when liquid started to pour out of the ceiling of the plane, spurting onto us. The passengers most affected jumped out of their seats, panicked. I watched, oddly detached, a light watery spray on my face. People struggled out of their seats and staggered down the aisles on the floor still angled, still ascending. Some screamed, some cried, some stood there in shock. Flight attendants appeared, throwing blankets over the wet seats, encouraging people to calm down.

Astoundingly, I became calm. Relaxed. Accepting. My eyes swept the blue bay, and I wondered if this was how I'd go, encased in metal, buckled in, plunging into the water. The press of the fat man's flesh morphed from irritating to comforting. I relished the touch of another human being. My breath was the fullest and most relaxed it had been since I'd stepped onto the plane. Even the most it had been in months. Here I was in a situation over which I had absolutely no control. And I felt a deep, profound sense of release.

In a few minutes, the liquid stopped streaming. The plane leveled out. Over the loudspeaker, the pilot told us that we were returning to SFO. We couldn't land with the tanks full so they'd have to jettison the fuel out over the ocean.

"You'll see what looks like flames shooting out the wings," his disembodied voice reported. "Not to worry, that's the fuel being discharged."

Gold and blue flames fluttered out the windows. Even that didn't worry me. I was curious about the process. I wondered how much of the fuel evaporates, and how much ends up in the water.

When the plane landed, the passengers clapped. I smiled at the fat man, whose tiny eyes gleamed with relief. Back in the airport, we learned two things. First, the liquid had been water pouring from a broken drinking water line. Second, we wouldn't be able to get on another plane for ten hours. I had to be back to work in two days. No solo Hawaii adventure for me.

I headed back to my apartment. My body felt oddly light, as though my bones were the weight of a bird's.

The next time I boarded a plane was for my flight to Japan. I was able to expedite a passport. The yard sale was a success. I sold everything, including my car. It had been a fun day. Emma, Mary, and Faith had hung out and helped. They expressed awe at what I was doing: selling everything I owned to move for an indeterminate time to a foreign country. They said I was their hero.

It didn't feel heroic to me, though. It felt necessary. I couldn't break up with Michael, and I couldn't be with him. He supported my decision to accept the Japan teaching job, and we had a vague agreement that we'd remain a couple even with five thousand miles between us. I thought he was probably relieved. A long-distance girlfriend would allow him to indulge in his dark moods and to work hours on end in the lab. He thought going to Japan would be good for me. He thought I hadn't experienced enough of the world. He'd spent months traveling Europe as a young adult and could speak French fluently. I'd never been to Asia or Europe. I spoke only a little high school Spanish. Part of me had decided on Japan to prove that I wasn't a bumpkin.

The morning I was to take off, I woke early in Michael's apartment. I poured Baileys Irish Cream into my coffee. I'd bought a bottle for that purpose, to take the edge off as I faced boarding a plane for an eleven-hour flight, only to land in a foreign country I didn't know much about.

Michael took me to the airport and lugged my massive suitcase. When I checked in, the airline official behind the counter scanned my documents and said: "You need a return ticket." I'd bought a one-way because I didn't know when I'd return. Now I was told this wasn't allowed. For the sake of the visa, I needed proof of intent to return. Purchasing a return ticket now would cost $1,300—as much as a round-trip ticket. Since the school wasn't paying for my lodging, I needed my extra money for my first and last month's rent and a deposit. I had barely enough and was counting on my salary to pull me through.

"Why wasn't I told this when I bought the one-way ticket?" I asked the woman behind the counter.

"I don't know," she replied, helpful as a brick wall.

Because my employers wanted me to get to the school immediately, there had been no time to go through the proper channels to get me a work visa. The school would take care of that once I got to Japan. I wasn't sure what getting a work visa entailed, but I'd agreed.

Maybe this was my out. Maybe I wasn't meant to go to Japan. But the thought of turning around and going home made my stomach churn. I didn't even have a home. In some strange way, I'd already moved on from my life in the Bay Area where I'd cobbled together different teaching jobs, where I'd worked at Gabriele's, where I'd discovered *Thelma & Louise* and the Indigo Girls. That felt like my old life. It was time for the next thing. I was standing on the precipice, wings unfurled. To pull in my wings and walk away from the cliff was unthinkable.

Michael paid for the ticket. I promised I'd pay him back in installments when I received my first few paychecks. He said I didn't have to but I insisted, even though I wasn't sure I could.

When my flight was called to board, he hugged me tightly and handed me a sealed envelope. He told me not to open it until I was on the plane.

Buckled into my seat, my breathing tightened. I tried to recall the lack of fear I'd felt on the plane that had never made it to Hawaii.

I put on my Walkman headphones to listen to the Indigo Girls. As the plane taxied, I opened Michael's first envelope. In the letter, he told me to embrace the adventure but not to forget about him.

As the plane rose, within me nestled an unsettling paradox: he loved me. Yet he hadn't asked me to stay.

I wanted him to want me to stay. I wanted him to let me go.

Like my roots spreading through the ground in tree pose, I wanted to be grounded. And like a bird, I wanted to fly.

7

The Gold Lizard

Loneliness is the poverty of self; solitude is the richness of self.
—*May Sarton*

"It's not your job to keep yourself breathing. Your body automatically does that. Even if you fell unconscious, you'd still be breathing."

A hypnotherapist once said this to me. I think of his words as the airplane doors slam shut. I lean back in my seat, holding Dave's hand. I think, *Being on a plane is an adventure, like riding a roller coaster.* That thought loosens me while kicking up a prickle of excitement. Here we are, starting our odyssey.

Our first flight is a short one, only an hour. We are picked up at LAX by my high school friend Natasha and her husband Floyd. All those years ago, Natasha was the one who led me to my first husband, Ray, because of her desire for margaritas in spite of a broken blender.

They take us to a bar in Venice Beach, where our friends' band is playing. We haven't told our friends we are coming—and when they see us, they throw themselves at us, thrilled by the surprise. We start our home-free life dancing, surrounded by friends.

Guarding Natasha and Floyd's house is a ten-foot-tall silver robot, one of their many quirky pieces of modern art. Smack-dab in the largest city on the West Coast, the neighborhood is surprisingly quiet. After our night of dancing, I sleep deeply. When I wake, I walk downstairs to see Dave, Floyd, and Natasha reading *The Los Angeles Times* and drinking tea. I'm in a bit of a haze. I have a sensation I'm living in an alternate universe where, after our visit, we will be returning to the Love Nest, even though I know full well we are headed out into the world to experience other homes, other lives.

This is one of the aspirations of our odyssey: to immerse ourselves in the ways others live. Since I was a kid, I have been intrigued by how humans do this thing called living. My whole life I've read books for this reason, scouring stories for insights into how people spend their hours and minutes and days.

It's comforting to be launching on our journey from the home of a longtime friend. We spend a couple of days together. Then, in her living room on the afternoon before we are to board our plane to Brisbane, Natasha opens a bottle of Prosecco. We toast thirty-five years of friendship.

"Well, thirty-three," I say, "since there were a couple of years in there when we didn't talk."

"I know, right?" she says.

"What was that about?" I say.

"I don't remember," she says. "But it must have been bad since you didn't invite me to your wedding."

"I didn't?" She nods. I'm shocked. I remember she hadn't been at Ray's and my wedding, but I can't believe I didn't invite her. She introduced me to him. She was my best friend.

I try not to be too hard on my younger self. Besides, I wasn't at her first wedding, which took place at a drive-through chapel in Vegas. At her second wedding, though, when she married Floyd, I was there. We danced with abandon at the reception. And when Dave and I married in Hawaii last year, she and Floyd flew across the ocean to us.

"Well," I say, "at least we were at each other's most important weddings."

*

Six four-year-olds each grasped one of the knots spaced out in intervals along a length of rope. I led, clutching the front of the rope. This was required procedure. The rope minimized the danger of taking the kids outside. The small language school sat in a busy Yokohama neighborhood teeming with screaming motorcycles, fast-moving cars, bicycles, and pedestrians. And six little Japanese kids being led around by a tall, blond *gaigin*. I smiled at how strange it must look.

We walked three blocks to a convenience store, where each child picked out a snack. I enjoyed this change of pace, getting outside the one-room school. I wasn't used to teaching kids with their short attention spans. They were so in the moment and as changeable as the moment. I enjoyed them best when we were moving, which is why I liked taking them out on the rope. Another favorite activity involved playing a scene from the animated *Peter Pan*. We'd run around the classroom, arms outstretched as we sang, "I can fly, I can fly, I can fly!"

Sometimes we'd kneel at the table with crayons and paper. I'd say, "Draw a flower." As they drew, the kids repeated in English, "I'm drawing a flower." Then I'd say, "Color it pink." And they'd color, saying, "I'm coloring the flower pink."

Once I told them to color the sun yellow.

"Eehh?" they said and began jabbering to each other in Japanese. A boy held up a red crayon. In their culture, the sun is red.

Another time I told them to color a tree purple. The kids looked at me like I was crazy. I smiled and told them to imagine a purple tree. Most of them paused but then, giggling, began to color the tree purple. One girl refused. She didn't want to color a tree anything other than green. I tried to tell her she could do whatever she wanted, but she cried. I felt horrible. My boss, Naoki, said I shouldn't ask the kids to do anything strange anymore.

In my favorite classes, I taught "housewives" and teenagers. The teenagers loved American culture. They enjoyed pictures I brought in of my family and home, and they peppered me with a million questions. Their potty humor surprised and delighted me, dissembling my stereotype of proper Japanese girls.

Once I asked them to answer this question: "What would you do if someone called for your mom, and she asked you to make an excuse about why she couldn't come to the phone?"

Hiromi, a spitfire who was sure she'd get to America one day to become a movie star, said, "I'd tell the person my mother was on the toilet."

I said, "You mean that she was in the bathroom."

"No!" she insisted. "That she was on the toilet, pooping!" And she pantomimed her squatting mother, straining, face red. The girls howled, hiding their mouths behind their hands.

For the housewives class, I spread out cards on the table with question words on them: *who, what, would, why, does.* A woman drew a card and asked a question using that word.

One woman asked the group, "Does your husband help with the housework?"

The ladies tittered. "No, my husband does not do housework," said one woman after another. The last woman in the circle, Naoko, said, "My husband do the dishes."

"My husband *does* the dishes," I corrected.

"My husband *does* the dishes," repeated Naoko.

"*Ehhh?*" said the others, sounding like the children I'd asked to color a tree purple.

"Yes, my husband *does* the dishes," Naoko repeated, blushing a little. That sent the women off in a flurry of Japanese. I asked them to speak English.

"She so lucky," said Mika, the woman in the group whose English was most advanced. "Most husband never do anything around the house. She very very lucky."

I hated the deep-set notion that wives were supposed to create a domestic shine and pamper their husbands. I never forgot what Ray's mother once said to me. A dental hygienist, she was disturbed at the amount of plaque she encountered during Ray's latest cleaning. She said, "I think Ray sometimes forgets to brush his teeth before bed. If you put a little toothpaste on his toothbrush and set it on the counter, that might help."

I responded, "Ray is a big boy. He can take care of himself."

Maybe I wasn't cut out to be a wife.

Adjusting to Japan was hard. As if the language and cultural differences weren't enough, I'd never before lived in a major city. I'd never been on a subway. It was daunting and dizzying trying to navigate the maze of Yokohama's and Tokyo's underground systems, miles and miles of train platforms and stores and scurrying crowds. One day I couldn't figure out how to get out of the subway and onto the street. I didn't have the right ticket to insert into the stile so it would open and let me out. People rushed by, bumping against my backpack. I didn't know how to ask for help. I stood there and cried.

An official in uniform looked startled and opened the gate for me. I emerged onto a vast plaza with thousands of people dwarfed by mountainous skyscrapers. Huge video screens projected surreal faces and bodies. Colors and sounds blared. Dizzy, I slumped to a bench. My body and mind froze, assaulted. It was hard to breathe. *So this is culture shock.*

A month later, I could navigate the train stations like a pro, appreciating the low-cost public transportation. On my days off, I enjoyed riding trains and disembarking wherever I wanted. I explored city streets, neighborhoods, parks, and vast department stores. I never worried about getting lost. I knew I'd always come across another subway stop. I couldn't read Japanese, but I could match the symbol on the station sign with the one on my subway map. From there I could figure out which trains to take to get home.

Wandering was one thing. Trying to get something done with intent was another. Simple things like grocery shopping could take hours. I couldn't read labels, and often I was unclear about what the items were. Once I thought I'd purchased cooking oil and didn't discover it was actually *sake* until I tried to cook with it.

Even though I was working on my Japanese, I didn't know enough to do a simple thing like open a bank account. I went to the branch across the busy street from my apartment. When I entered, the first thing I saw was a sign that said, in English, "No Guns Allowed." After a pitiful attempt at trying to explain what I needed, with the teller bobbing her head but obviously comprehending little, a woman next to me in line said, "I speak English. Can I help?"

Her name was Azumi. She asked me if I could teach her private English lessons twice a month, which I did in my apartment where we kneeled on the floor at my low table. She was in her fifties and loved to travel. She'd been to the U.S. many times, as well as Europe and Australia. She traveled with friends because her husband didn't like to fly. She loved to laugh and had quite a cackle. Once we saw a spider crawling up the wall in my apartment. I rose to squash it and she said, "No, don't kill it."

I said, "Do you not kill spiders because you're Buddhist?"

She said, "No, because it's messy!" Her laugh filled up the room.

Eventually she invited me to her house. Her husband greeted me with a slight bow and then disappeared into another room. Azumi was a young fifty-something; her husband looked twenty years older. He never joined her group of friends.

Azumi proudly showed me her bedroom, with its Western canopy bed and flowered bedspread and curtains. Her husband's bedroom, she said, had a traditional tatami mat floor.

Her dinner and karaoke parties were usually for four, the two of us plus two of her other friends: Yumi and Mr. Ishiburu. Yumi was in her twenties and very shy, or maybe she seemed that way because she didn't speak much English. Mr. Ishiburu, on the other hand, was outgoing. It amazed me how much this small man could drink. As he poured more beer into his glass, he joked that drinking beer was the national pastime. I wondered what Azumi's husband thought of her hanging out with a charming, funny man.

Mr. Ishiburu was a music teacher at a middle school and played the flute in the Yokohama Symphony. Once he brought along his *shakuhashi*, a traditional Japanese flute made of bamboo. When he put his lips to it and blew the first note, it resonated through my bones. It sounded ancient yet oddly familiar. I was unexpectedly moved. Later I learned that these flutes are used in Zen Buddhist monasteries for meditation purposes. The sound of the *shakuhashi* is known to penetrate the soul.

Walking the streets of Yokohama one day, I noticed a guy following me. I crossed a bridge. He crossed after me. Finally, I stopped, and he approached me.

"Stop! Following! Me!" I yelled into his face.

Startled, but without a word, he turned and walked the other direction. My power surprised me and, apparently, him.

Another time I was walking along a canal, enjoying the rushing water and trees that dotted the levy, talking into a tape recorder to my friend Laurel. We liked sending tapes to each other in addition to letters. I heard a coughing noise and looked over, only to catch a glimpse of a man openly masturbating, gazing at me. I gasped and turned away, then said, laughing into the recorder, "Oh my God, Laurel, you are not going to believe what I just saw!"

When I was eleven years old and walking home from school, I heard a gate latch click. I looked over, and there stood a man stroking himself. I didn't understand what he was doing, but it felt wrong to me. I ran home and told my mom. In order to better understand what I was saying she asked me, "Did he have an erection?" I didn't know what that meant. Mom called the police. A cruiser picked us up and asked me to point out the house. A few days later, we learned that as a result of my complaint, the third in a month, the guy was arrested.

On the one hand, I could laugh at the stories. On the other hand, they felt like an assault of sorts. I was angry that as a woman, I couldn't be at ease like the men in the world.

I'd met other foreign women who complained about being groped by men on trains or in crowded elevators. This put me on alert, but it never happened to me. Once I saw a guy on the train reading a pornographic comic book. I scooted away but was, at the same time, curious. The next time I walked by a comics stand, I flipped through page after page of racy scenes, trying to look casual. I bought a few, avoiding the eyes of the guy who sold them to me.

I realized it was a contradiction to be offended by men's

objectifying women and yet get turned on by porn. For his birthday, Michael's best friend had sent him a subscription to *Playboy*. I was pissed. How was I to compete with these airbrushed beauties? And what did that say about Michael that he liked to look at them? It was one more strike against him. I was angry that he didn't understand—or didn't care about—the oppression of women.

Michael kept the magazines out of sight, in a drawer. Every once in a while I'd peek at one and find myself turned on. Now I didn't have to hide my hypocrisy. Alone in my apartment, I could look at pornographic comics, vibrator in hand.

I found myself savoring the freedom of living alone in a place where I knew few people. I walked a few blocks to work, taught six hours a day, and had no lesson plans to do or papers to grade. There were a lot of days off, festival holidays.

For the first time in my life, I was master of my own time with no one to report to. Sometimes I'd sleep for ten or eleven hours, waking disoriented until my eyes focused on my dinky blue refrigerator, my tiny low table, and the sheet over my body on the futon. More than once I thought I could die in my sleep and no one would discover me for hours, if not days. There was something surreal about so much solitude. These were the days before email and cell phones. I wrote long letters to family and friends, and would sometimes pause during the day to imagine the letter buried in a bin on an airplane over the Pacific, or in the hand of a letter carrier sliding it into a mailbox. Were my words yet in the hand of my sister or Mary or Michael or Gabriele? What did they feel when they saw that blue, thin, airmail letter folded to create its own envelope? Every day I went to the post office to pick up my letters and packages. On the days my box was empty, anxiety slithered through me like a snake. As the months passed, the serpent of loneliness became less threatening; it would disappear as quickly as it arrived.

Usually when I called Michael he was happy to hear from me, but sometimes he'd be in a dark mood. Once he told me he felt like dying, quickly adding, "But I'm not suicidal." He told me he needed to hang up, that my trying to connect with him right then was not a good idea. "I've been through this before, and I will go through it again," he said. "I'll call or write when I'm back in the light, back in the land of the living. Bear with me. I love you."

On days I didn't work, and didn't feel like going out, I might lie around and write in my journal, then read for hours. I liked following my own rhythms and not justifying my life to anyone, not even myself. Yet at times I had to grapple with a sense that I was doing something wrong. Should I be doing so much "nothing"?

Life felt like a mystery. What did people do moment to moment? Especially when no one was looking? What was *allowed*? I became insatiably interested in books about the lives of women: May Sarton's memoirs (I re-read *Journal of Solitude* many times over), Natalie Goldberg's books about writing, Anaïs Nin's diaries, Virginia Woolf's letters and novels. I envisioned Virginia in bed, pen poised over paper on a laptop desk. I saw May Sarton walking in the wilderness with her dogs and cutting flowers from her garden. I imagined Goldberg's New Mexico landscape, the sun goldening her skin.

Goldberg inspired me to start writing regularly, what she called "writing practice." Her techniques were similar to Gabriele's. She called the left brain the "monkey mind"—that over-critical editor who nosily scrambled around. I went to a corner cafe where I'd order coffee and point to a picture of a tuna sandwich on the menu (*kōhī to sandoitchi, kudasai*). After eating, I looked at my watch and told myself I was going to write for thirty minutes: *go!* And no matter what, I kept my hand moving. When I stalled, I restarted myself with a question or a phrase like, "What I really want to say is …"

Sometimes Ella—my Canadian teacher friend—joined me for a writing session. We wrote nonstop for thirty minutes and then read aloud to each other. It wasn't a time to critique but instead to talk about impressions and to share thoughts about the most promising nuggets.

I met Ella at a *gaigin* party, a gathering of foreigners. It took three trains and a bus to get to the large house. After having lived for months in my tiny apartment and working in a one-room school, I was surprised at the size of the house. It reminded me of the California home I grew up in, built of wood and glass and surrounded by decks. As I walked toward the front door I could hear raucous voices and loud music. A mountain of shoes was heaped in the foyer. I removed my boots and entered. People in their twenties and thirties were gathered in every room. I floated around, glass of wine in hand, and eventually homed in on a conversation. People told drinking stories, detailing places they barfed in Tokyo.

One woman talked about learning Japanese, and another said, "Don't bother. They'll never say anything you want to hear anyway."

I overheard a guy making a case for Hemingway as the best

writer who ever lived. A woman with a mass of red curls argued for Virginia Woolf, whom coincidentally I'd been reading earlier that day. There was something mesmerizing about the redhead. She had a sensual beauty, a vibration that warmed me. I wanted to lean into her. I had the irrational thought that I wanted to touch her skin. She said hi to me, introduced herself as Cheryl. She told me she taught literature at a university. She had turned one of her classes into a women's studies course. She wanted to raise awareness of gender issues.

"I'm thrilled when I see a woman's mind work and light up," she said. "A lot of men don't get it, and I don't care. If I can reach just one or two of my female students, I'm thrilled."

We talked about Naomi Wolf and Toni Morrison and Alice Walker. She asked me if I knew H.D. When I told her I had read H.D.'s biography, she squeezed my hand. Electricity shot up my arm.

"Cheryl, honey, enough of the feminist blather," said the Hemingway guy, whose name was Terry. "You should tell her about your night job, your hostess work."

"Hostess?" I asked.

"You know," he said, "at a men's club. They light the guys' cigarettes, pour their drinks, that kind of thing. And the guys bring them presents. Cheryl, honey, what have you gotten? A diamond pin? A leather coat? Things like that."

She tucked her red curls behind her ears, but they popped right back out. "Things like that," she said.

The conversation veered to travel. Terry, Cheryl, and a few others chatted about their recent forays to Thailand and Malaysia and Korea, as though they were trips to the mall. I yearned to do such travel myself, but I didn't believe I could pull off such a thing. Even though I'd found my way to Japan, I didn't see myself as a freewheeling adventurer. How to live that way felt as mysterious as Cheryl's hostess job. I was curious if "hostess" really meant "prostitute." Discreetly, I asked the woman next to me that question. That woman was Ella.

"Probably not," she said. "There are some hostesses who cross that line, but most of them just let the guys do a little groping. It's a strange cultural thing, actually. The guy pays the woman a lot of money to act like his girlfriend."

A Canadian, Ella had lived in Tokyo for three years, teaching at a university. She could speak Japanese and lived with her boyfriend. We found common ground with our desire to be writers.

I went back to my apartment that night happy to have met a new friend in Ella. But for some reason, Cheryl haunted me for a few days. I thought about her and her red mane of curls, the touch of her hand, and my spine quivered. What a curious reaction.

In addition to meeting for writing practice, Ella and I hung out at her favorite bars and restaurants in Tokyo. Her friend and colleague Val, from Boston, often joined us. Inevitably we'd get drunk and talk about men. They pushed me for stories about Michael, curious about the fact that I'd be faithful to a long-distance boyfriend. Michael wrote me long, loving, funny letters and called me every week. It was hard to fault him. I swung wildly from missing him horribly to being pleased to be by myself.

Once at a bar in Shinjuku, Ella said, "Kate, look up."

A huge gold lizard—at least twenty feet long—clung to the ceiling, shining brightly in the otherwise dim bar. I was learning it was important to consciously look around wherever you were in Tokyo or you might miss something. You never knew what you might see on a busy street: a group of teenagers with shaved heads wearing tutus, a mother teaching her son how to pee in the gutter, a walking vending machine advertising a new energy drink, a forty-foot sculpture of a robot leaning up against a building. The fact that such things existed in the world amazed me. Sometimes my head ached as though my brain pushed against my skull, expanding from so much new input.

I admired Val's elegance. A martini in hand, she had flawless pale skin and shiny ebony hair that ran down her back. She wore a short silver dress and thigh-high black boots. She was impossibly stylish, having spent a couple of years in Manhattan before coming to Tokyo.

"I don't know what's happening," she said, "but I'm finding I'm attracted to some of the girls at the university."

Wait a minute ... Val had a boyfriend, a Korean guy who'd moved to Tokyo to work as a D.J. What was this about being attracted to women? And her students, besides?

"I like their style," she said, sipping her martini. "Some of those girls are so creative, and sweet, and funny. I was surprised when I realized I hopped into bed with one of them in my mind. I lost my place in my lecture."

Ella chimed in that she'd been attracted to women, too. She thought it was natural. Cheryl, the redhead at the party, crept into my mind. And another vague memory surfaced: a year before, I'd gone to Planned Parenthood for a urinary tract infection. The doctor who treated me looked like she climbed mountains in her spare time, yet there was a softness to her, too. She sat and talked to me, taking more time with me than any doctor ever had. When she took my hand to shake it at the end of my visit, my body buzzed in the most pleasing, surprising way. The next day, she called to check on me. Her deep voice spread that same feeling under my skin.

Had I felt a sexual attraction to a woman? Whatever had happened, I shoved those thoughts aside as anomalies. I wasn't a shy person, by any means, but I felt a little intimidated by Ella and Val. They spoke Japanese, they'd traveled to many different countries, they navigated city life with ease, and they openly talked about an aspect of sexuality that was daunting. I didn't say a word.

My employers sent me to Seoul, Korea, for a few days so I could secure a work visa. Before boarding the flight, I downed a few beers to ease my anxiety. I was seated next to a Spanish guy about my age. On the flight, we ordered beers and then pieced together a conversation with his limited English, my limited Spanish, and our limited Japanese. He said, I think, he was a businessman from Madrid who traveled a lot to Asian countries. I told him I would love to travel in Europe some day. As we disembarked, he gave me his card, which creased up and gathered lint at the bottom of my backpack until one day I threw it away.

Now that I'd experienced Tokyo, the Seoul airport was not intimidating. I hailed a cab and showed the driver a piece of paper on which was written the name and address of my hotel in Korean and

English. The cab driver stared at me in the rearview mirror, averting his eyes when I glared at him. A hangover was gathering storm clouds behind my eyes. The waistband of my tights dug into my stomach. My backpack looked ridiculously infantile compared to the sleek briefcases and designer purses carried by the chic Asian women in the airport. I thought about one woman I'd seen, with her perfect navy blue dress and heels, a fashionable scarf twisted expertly around her elegant neck. She knew exactly what she was doing and where she was going. For a moment I pretended I was her, and suddenly I felt more confident.

As the cab poked its way through traffic, the taxi driver said something to me I couldn't understand. I asked him to repeat it. After a few attempts, he made himself clear: he was asking me if I wanted to go to a bar with him. My heart skipped a beat. Was I in danger? In my new incarnation as the woman with the chic scarf, I decided that I was safe. All I had to do was sternly turn down his offer, and he'd zip me right to my hotel.

He did. I didn't want to tip him, but he claimed he had no change. I didn't belabor the point because I wanted him to go away— so he got a tip of who-knew-how-much because I was unclear about the money conversion.

The hotel looked Victorian, with lead-pane windows, vintage furniture, and a fluffy comforter. I collapsed on the bed and turned on the TV. It had been a while since I watched TV because I didn't have one in my Yokohama apartment. The screen filled with the news from America: Bill Clinton had been elected President. Was the Reagan-Bush era really over? I cried happy tears.

That evening, bundled up, I walked out into the cold streets teeming with people. Hot food for sale steamed in carts up and down the street. I bought a sweet waffle made on a griddle by a wrinkled man with a knit scarf bunched up around his neck. I thought about my sister in San Diego with her husband and two little boys. I thought about my other sister, recently graduated from college and living the single life in L.A. I thought about my parents, the two of them alone in the big family house. They were probably having an election party or were attending one. Or maybe they were in bed. I wasn't sure what time it was in California. I thought about Michael in his dark apartment or under the glare of fluorescent lights in the lab. I wondered what my graduate school friends, Mary and Faith and Emma, were doing at this very moment. I even thought about the school in Yokohama, the students, my boss. No one knew exactly where I was, here on the night streets of Seoul. I had the sensation of being insignificant yet expanded, increased yet diminished. I was a grain of sand one moment, a vast beach the next.

The following night, a guy approached me in the hotel lobby and asked if I wanted to go out dancing. He was from Qatar—a place I'd never heard of—handsome, olive skinned, dark haired, in his thirties, adorned by a gold necklace and bracelet.

At the disco, girls in sparkly bikinis danced in cages suspended above the huge dance floor. A massive bar lined the side and back walls, and a covered passageway led to yet another enormous dance floor. I was dazzled by the scope of the place, by the scope of the world. Like the night before, an Alice-in-Wonderland sensation buzzed through my body. There I was, in a colossal building set amidst other colossal buildings in a colossal city in a colossal country on a colossal continent of this colossal Earth…that in reality was a pinprick of a planet amidst billions of stars in an infinite universe.

A big screen TV hovering over the dance floor beamed images of Bill and Hillary Clinton with Al and Tipper Gore, clenched hands raised to a cheering crowd, confetti and balloons flying. The disco music flipped off, replaced by "We Are the World," the supergroup song recorded a few years before. Young Koreans, Americans, Europeans, Middle Easterners—all decked out in our slick urban best—held hands on the dance floor, forming a circle, singing along.

That night the guy from Qatar asked if he could come to my hotel room. I said no, and thanked him for the evening. I didn't want to betray Michael, even though our relationship was slippery. I collapsed in bed, only to be awakened by a sound at my door. I had no idea how much time had passed; it was still dark. I lay there like stone, listening to the scratching and jiggling of the doorknob. My heart raced at the memory of my apartment being broken into last year. Glancing at the phone next to my bedside, I realized I probably wouldn't be able to communicate with whomever picked up. I could scream if I needed to. That was universal communication, wasn't it? Fortunately, before I'd gone to bed, I'd secured the thick hotel door with the deadbolt and safety latch. As the noise continued, I crawled out of bed and put my eye to the peephole. There stood the guy from Qatar. He must have sensed my presence on the other side of the door because he said softly, "Kate, let me in."

"Go away," I said.

"Please, come on, just for a few minutes, let me in. You are beautiful. I won't touch you."

"Go away!" I said loudly, hoping that drawing attention to his behavior might force him to leave. He whispered a few more beguiling words to me, and I continued to insist, louder and louder, that he leave.

"Fucking whore," he hissed as he turned to go.

As my birthday neared, I didn't tell anyone. I wanted to spend it alone. I'd never spent a birthday alone.

After a slow morning of reading, I bundled up in a sweater and tights and threw my backpack over my shoulder. I took a train into Tokyo and walked through Ueno Park amongst its thousands of trees. Ducks and grebes proliferated beneath the low, sweeping branches. Israelis displayed jewelry and fans for sale. I walked by the lotus pond and gazed at a shrine to the goddess of fortune. I paused to listen to Peruvian musicians playing drums and pipes. I stopped at a little restaurant for soba noodles then went to a café for coffee and to write in my journal.

Afterward, I walked through Tokyo streets, finally boarding a train as dusk approached. When I disembarked at my station, I bought a tall can of Asahi beer in a vending machine. Then I went to the nearby KFC for chicken and coleslaw, comfort food. Across the street I rented a movie at a video store, an American film with Japanese subtitles. I walked the four blocks to my one-room school. Using my key, I entered the dark school and flicked on the lights. Putting the movie in the player, I sat on the floor, losing myself in its world. When the movie ended, the credits rolling over the screen, my eyes blinked back to the present.

I'd spent my birthday not speaking to another soul. I was thirty. Maybe there wasn't a right way to do life. Maybe it was about figuring it out as you went along.

8

The Key

So oftentimes it happens that we live our lives in chains
That we never even know we have the key.
　　　　　　　　　　　　　　—The Eagles

On our flight from L.A. to Brisbane, Dave and I have the row to ourselves. One of our flying tricks is to reserve a window and an aisle seat. That way, if the plane isn't full, we'll likely be alone in the row. If someone is assigned to the middle seat, that person has no problem exchanging with us so we can sit together.

I'm happy to be able to stretch out in the hopes of sleeping on the fourteen-hour flight. I've never been good at sleeping on planes. This time I plan to follow Dave's lead and pop an Ambien, prescribed by our travel doctor. Comfortably seated as the plane is ascending, Dave hands me the pill. We take them at the same time like we are involved in a cult suicide pact.

When I awake six hours later, Dave is still asleep, his head leaning against the window, cushioned by his sweatshirt. He's talented at many things, and I put sleeping high on the list. He probably didn't even need the pill. He's the kind of person who can fall asleep at will.

While I'm glad for the six hours, I wish I could sleep more. In the dark of the plane, a shard of light bounces. As my eyes adjust, I see a flight attendant coming down the aisle balancing a lit-up tray holding cups of ice water.

The plane hums peacefully. I stretch out my cramped legs beneath the seat in front of me, lift my arms above my head and take a few deep breaths. I think about how flinging off possessions and heading out on the open road is a time-honored dream, an embodiment of freedom. And here we are, doing it. Invariably when people learn about our plans, they get a dreamy look in their eyes and say, "I wish I could do that, too." Then they launch into elaborate explanations of why they can't: money, jobs, mortgage, kids, elderly parents, credit card debt, health insurance, health issues. Some say you have to be brave to do it.

I don't feel brave. I feel like I'm doing what I'm compelled to do. Maybe it's brave to stay in one place for many years. Maybe I'm trying to outrun death.

I had a former colleague who despised her job. Every time I saw her, she ranted about the horrors of the university. She calculated the years, months, days, and hours until she could retire. Finally, well into her sixties, she reached that coveted retirement date. Literally days later, she was diagnosed with cancer.

I don't want that to be me. Yet on the plane my mind begins chattering, swinging nervously like a monkey from branch to branch.

We're in middle age and don't have a retirement plan. We don't know how we'll make money when our savings dwindle. Will we end up destitute in our old age? And is leaving our friends and family selfish? What if they need us? Will our nieces and nephews forget us? Will we miss out on too many important life experiences? We aren't spring chickens anymore. What if one of us falls ill in a developing country where medical treatment is sketchy?

I catch myself. These thoughts aren't much different than the obsessions of my colleague who ended up with cancer. They are rooted in fear.

How about coming back to now? How about appreciating what's right in front of you? Don't you remember, as the song says, the footholds will appear?

Silently in the dim light, a flight attendant offers me a cup of water. I take a cool sip in this cocoon thirty-thousand feet above the Earth, speeding across oceans and continents.

*

"These drugs are even better than the ones we had in college!"

My former dorm pal, Oscar, may have been withering, but his wisecracking personality was not. From bed, he held out his arms for a hug as I entered the room.

I'd been back in California from Japan a week when I drove up to San Francisco to see him. He'd written me several letters the year I was gone, filling me in on his latest drug trials, and the ups and downs of his battle with HIV, which had developed into AIDS.

"Well, those must be some great drugs," I joked back. He was stationed downstairs in the house he shared with his lover Gary who, as an R.N., was taking good care of him. It was late spring. The room was flooded with light. Beyond the French doors, a tree wore pink blossoms with a feather boa flourish.

I sat on the chair next to the bed.

"I'm having a lot of dreams," he said. He looked a little thinner, but his skin was ruddy and his eyes shone. A sliver of his fine strawberry blond hair smudged his forehead. It was hard to believe he was so sick.

"Yeah? Dreams about what?"

"Every single one of them takes place in the house or neighborhood where I grew up. The weather is always beautiful—no fog or cold."

Oscar grew up in San Francisco. I thought about the time more than ten years ago that we cut class and hopped on a Greyhound bus to venture to the city. Growing up, I went to San Francisco a few times a year with my parents to visit relatives, see stage musicals, and walk through Fisherman's Wharf, where my dad always bought a big loaf of sourdough bread for us to share. But Oscar wanted nothing to do with tourist traps. Instead, he took me to the spots featured in Hitchcock's film *Vertigo*: Mission Dolores. Nob Hill. Lombard Street. Fort Point. Oscar laughed when I told him I'd never taken a city bus. He bought me a MUNI card and showed me how to use it. We hopped on and off public transportation, walking for miles around the city on a cool, blue-sky day. At the base of Fort Point, beneath the Golden Gate Bridge, he played both Jimmy Stewart's and Kim

Novak's roles by pretending to hold himself back as he struggled to fling himself into the crashing surf.

In college, I had a crush on Oscar. We'd experienced a few drunken fumblings in the dark on his dorm bed and mine. When his sister and brother-in-law visited our college town, he brought me to dinner as his date. I loved his quirky sense of humor. We played backgammon all night long. He knew everything about the Rolling Stones and the Beatles. He introduced me to the longest, most intense song I'd ever heard: *In-A-Gadda-Da-Vida*. We'd get stoned or drop acid with his roommate and my best friend, listening to that seventeen-minute orgy of a song over and over and over.

I adored how he saw the world at a slant, that he'd do things like dream up a Hitchcock tour of the city. In the dorms, he'd blast into my room quoting wealthy, beautiful Daisy from *The Great Gatsby*: "Let's do something. What *do* people do?" He'd hold up a thick textbook and quip, à la Dorothy Parker, "What fresh hell is this?"

At the end of our *Vertigo* tour of the city he took me to the Castro. We walked through stores featuring gay books and racy memorabilia. I had a vague understanding that this world was familiar to him, but I was so naïve that I didn't connect the dots. Gayness as a concept, as a sexual identity, wasn't consciously on my radar. I knew Oscar seemed different from most guys, but I couldn't (or didn't want to) put my finger on why. In the early 1980s—pre-AIDS, pre-*Will and Grace*, pre-*The Ellen Show*, pre-same-sex marriage—such naïveté was possible.

At a sidewalk cafe, he ordered beers with such confidence that the waiter didn't blink at my underage face. As we drank, a Harley pulled up to the curb. Aboard were two bearded, muscular guys clad in black. They wore black bands studded with silver spikes around their wrists.

"Look at the leather daddies," laughed Oscar.

I watched him watch the men disembark from the motorcycle. I wondered what he knew, what he saw. It was like he stood on the other side of the shore, and I couldn't quite make out his features or words. He couldn't have been more obvious, but to me it was like he was standing in fog.

Later, Oscar left the dorms and moved in with an older guy off campus. He invited me over and I met his "roommate," yet the obvious truth still didn't click in. It wasn't until another friend told me she thought Oscar was gay that all the pieces fell into place.

We lost track of each other for a few years after college and then reconnected when I moved to the Bay Area. We met for dinner. I went to parties at this house. He played me Whitney Houston records; her incredible voice and beauty enthralled him.

One day we met at a bar. Uncharacteristically, he didn't order a drink. He looked pale. I asked him if he was okay. He told me he'd been tested HIV-positive. He talked about his fears, about friends he'd seen deteriorate and die. Soon, though, he was reading Louise Hay, a pioneer in leading support groups for people living with HIV. When I saw him again, the pink had returned to his face, and he ordered a martini. He told me that his diagnosis was a wake-up call to do the things he always wanted to do, primarily travel. Bursting with idiosyncratic humor and enthusiasm, he told me all about his "bar and man tour" of England and Ireland.

And now, as he lay in bed and talked about his comforting childhood-home-based dreams, I detected no fear in him. He said, "Some people go out on the ten o'clock. Some people go out on the ten-fifteen."

And then he closed his eyes and said, "I'm not dying. I'm transitioning."

His voice tapered off. He held my hand and faded in and out of sleep.

A few months later, he died.

Years afterward, I wrote an autobiographical novel in which one of the characters was based on Oscar. It was incredibly pleasurable to reanimate him, to keep him alive on the page. As I wrote the book, the development of his character flowed with ease and grace. I had the sensation he was there with me, his energy flowing through me. I ascribed that feeling to my love for him and my delight in reliving our friendship.

About twenty years later, though, he would make an undeniable re-appearance in my life. So would my dead father. As would Gabriele. As did Wes at his funeral. The message is always the same: you are safe. You are taken care of. Death is not the end.

A convergence of forces had propelled me to leave Japan five months after my thirtieth birthday. When I got offered a teaching job at a Tokyo university, I gave notice to my employer at the one-room school, and she freaked out. She said I had no right to leave the school. I was used to the American fluidity of job switching. Even if you had a contract, there were ways around it. Most American employers seemed simpatico with climbing the job ladder, even if that meant their employees would leave. But my employer was angry. She told me I was way out of bounds. Through some mysterious channels, she arranged to have me kicked out of my apartment, even though I was the one paying the rent. So I moved in with friends, trying to decide if I wanted to sign a two-year contract with the university. Did I want to stay in Japan another two years? Mired in indecision, I woke one morning yearning for California.

I walked to the nearest phone booth and called Michael. I knew coming to California probably meant living with him—perhaps temporarily, perhaps permanently. He'd sent me a dozen long-stemmed red roses on Valentine's Day. Maybe we had a chance.

"I want to come home," I said.

Without a pause he said, "Come home."

Michael still lived in the apartment complex where we met. He still had the couch where he'd first rubbed my feet. I was exhilarated to be back. Compared to the smoggy congestion of Tokyo, Palo Alto felt like paradise with its blue skies, clean air, and wide quiet streets where I'd ride my bike or walk for hours. I was hired as assistant director of a tutoring center and was able to buy a new car: a red, sporty, convertible Nissan.

After a year of struggling to learn Japanese, I cherished being able to talk easily to anyone: a waitress, a person on the street, a friend on the phone. Experiencing my familiar world in a fresh, new way was an advantage of having travelled. I wanted to enjoy the opportunities now available to me, things I'd taken for granted before. I took a painting class where I learned about oils, acrylics, watercolors, and pastels. I enrolled in a yoga class. I wanted to find a writing group.

I called Faith and asked if I could join hers. When I returned from Japan I learned that Faith had not left her Mormon husband, as I'd imagined she would—especially after the declaration that she now wore black lacy lingerie that he knew nothing about. Instead she lived in the same house with him, along with a couple of her young adult children. It seemed that she and her husband had developed a kind of truce. Faith spent a lot of time doing her own thing: hiking in the hills, reading the literature she loved, hanging out with the women in her writing group, and committing herself to developing her poetic craft.

She told me her writing group was full but that I should consider taking a poetry class with her friend, Professor Georgia Constantino. Faith and Georgia had been close ever since Faith took classes with her in our grad program. I'd never taken a class with Professor Constantino. She intimidated me. There was something serious about her countenance, as though gravity bore more heavily on her than on the average person. She couldn't have been much older than her colleague—Gabriele Rico—but they were absolute opposites. An open lesbian, Georgia chain-smoked Shermans and was rooted in a strong squat body. Her long silver hair and fingers curved at odd angles. I'd never seen her wear anything other than jeans, a jean jacket, and silver bracelets embedded with turquoise.

"Do you think she'd let me audit the class?" I asked.

"Let me talk to her and call you back," said Faith.

When she returned my call she said, "Georgia's open to letting you audit the class, but she wants to see some of your poems first. She said, 'How do I know she doesn't write Hallmark cards?'" Faith laughed her quiet, throaty laugh. "I assured her you don't. Still, she asked that you show her some of your work."

"Thanks, Faith," I said. I found it vaguely curious that she had become so close to one of her former professors. They had developed a kind of buddy intimacy, a different quality from the mother/mentor relationship I had with Gabriele. I couldn't put my finger on it—that is, until one day Faith casually told Mary and me that she thought she might be a lesbian. Mary and I took it in stride. There was something that seemed right about that for Faith. She was very woman-oriented. Perhaps being a lesbian was the next logical step. Still, I wondered what that was like for her, to be a Mormon mother of seven on the exterior and a lesbian deep down. Was Georgia her friend or her lover? Just as Faith wouldn't tell us her secret name, she held back on the details of her love life. Her glowing face and her radiant poems, however, conveyed her happiness.

I wanted to feel that way. Living with Michael had its sweetnesses. I enjoyed the intimacy of sex, and reading side-by-side on the couch, and going out to dinner, and hiking or camping. But he was still subject to dark moods. I'd never know from one day to the next if he'd be okay. I'd spent a year away in a foreign country. So much had changed but nothing had changed. He still worked late at the lab and then would watch TV with headphones on until late into the night. He'd sleep with a pillow over his head. Irritably, he asked me not to make noise before 11 a.m. As I got ready for work in the mornings, I'd sneak around as quietly as I could, blow-drying my hair in the kitchen.

Working in the learning center was fine, but I knew I could last only so long in the corporate world. I felt boxed in by arbitrary regulations. No jeans except on Fridays? Inflexible hours putting in "desk time" when I didn't really need to be there? Following a script rather than being encouraged to draw on my expertise?

I was restless. Even though years had passed, my life felt too similar to the days I taught high school and was married to the wrong person. I wanted to break free, to move forward.

One afternoon, I brought a few poems to Georgia's office. She took her rough hand in mine and shook it. Then she sat at her desk, silently reading my poems and blowing verboten cigarette smoke out the open window. She looked like the Blood Indian chief depicted in the famous nineteenth-century George Catlin painting, a print of which hung in my family home. Although her long hair was silver instead of black, she had the chief's same chiseled face, thick neck, hooded eyes and stately comportment. I sat on a squeaky wooden chair, palms sweating, scrutinizing her deadpan face for hints at my fate.

What a contrast to Gabriele, whose eyes—when reading my work—would widen then narrow. She'd stop every few lines to enthuse over a juicy image, or to proclaim a phrase unneeded, making a case for the elegance of "less is more."

Finally, Georgia sat back in her chair, perching an ankle on a knee and stubbing out a dark Sherman butt in a ceramic ashtray.

"These'll do," she said. "Although there are a few lines you should throw off a small cliff."

I smiled nervously.

"Class starts next week. See you then."

I was dismissed.

Driving home, I vowed to write poems with no lines Georgia would want to toss from a cliff. The idea of writing poems again, of sitting in a classroom surrounded by others who cared about art and the written word, thrilled me. The academic and creative world promised to put its lips to mine, to resuscitate me, to kiss me awake like a prince.

9

Tinker Bell

All the world is made of faith, and trust, and pixie dust.
—Peter Pan

Dave and I wake to a symphony of birdsong. Sun deluges the bedroom. It's our first morning in Brisbane. I pull one of Quentin's bathrobes off the door hook and slide it on.

In the living room, I take in the whimsical décor: lime green shag rug, miniature multicolored glass animals, and a handmade purple-and-blue chandelier shimmering with white crystals. I open the sliding glass door and walk onto the deck. The morning is bright and cold. Here, from the house's upper story, I take in a view of treetops and a thriving garden.

I don't dawdle because I have a job to do: make a cup of espresso for Lilian, Quentin's ninety-year-old mother who lives downstairs. Even though Quentin, a concert pianist, is away performing concerts in England, he offered his place for us to stay. We'll spend time with him when he returns in three weeks. In the meantime, his apartment is ours. Such generosity is remarkable considering we don't know Quentin that well. We met him two years ago on an Alaskan cruise.

One morning on the cruise, while Dave slept, I'd decided to go to the gym. On the way, I stopped in the cafeteria for a cup of coffee. In line, Quentin and I struck up a conversation about the consciousness-raising seminars offered on the ship, and he asked me if I'd like to join him at a table. As the vast ocean drifted by and we sipped our coffee, we dove into talking as though we were picking up on a lifelong conversation.

Quentin told me that after decades of living and teaching in Oxford, England, he was planning to move back to his Australian childhood home to be near his aging mother and to start a new chapter of his artistic and personal life. We talked about major life transformations that had brought us to this point in the journey. He'd had a lot of, as he put it, "contrast" in his childhood, a father as cruel as something out of Grimm's fairy tales. Quentin said his childhood had brought him unexpected gifts. He was a big believer that every experience is an opportunity, that we create our reality, and that the universe is abundant and fundamentally good.

Meeting each morning to talk over coffee became our ritual. At the end of the cruise, he gave Dave and me a CD of his piano performances and said he'd love for us to come visit any time.

Now I feel like Dorothy plopped down in Oz. We were with Quentin in Alaska, and suddenly we are in his house in Brisbane. We left L.A. on a Tuesday and arrived on a Thursday. Wednesday disappeared into the mist, although we'll regain it on the return.

What if we never return? Will that Wednesday hover over the world, never to be reclaimed?

Heightening the time-traveler feeling is the daunting espresso machine on Quentin's kitchen counter, a chrome monstrosity. The directions to operate the machine rival a Microsoft Word user's manual. After struggling to understand why the appliance won't turn on, I realize that in Australia you can't merely plug things in. You have to turn on the electrical switch next to the outlet.

Eventually I coax two cups of coffee out of the machine, one for Lilian and one for me. Dave and I take them downstairs, along with a cup of tea for him. She's thrilled we are visiting. She greets us with hugs. We sit in front of her fish tank, watching the watery creatures scurry about and waiting for her favorite, whom she calls Silky, to come out of hiding. I've never before seen a person her age sit on a pillow on the floor and then jump up when excitedly exclaiming something, again and again. It seems her years of gardening have kept her nimble. I see Quentin in her enthusiasm for life—and her round face and blue eyes.

Gardening isn't her only passion. She loves making jewelry. Until her eyesight began to fade, she painted and drew. The house is filled with her framed artwork. She shares stories about her garden, her neighbors, her world travels. We learn that during World War II, she lived in Papua New Guinea with her husband, who was stationed there. When the war was over, the Americans took off, leaving behind a vast array of unexploded ordnance, tanks, and jeeps. She laughs at the memory of Papua New Guinea natives haphazardly driving American military jeeps around their island.

Over the next few days, she is always grabbing something to share with us: a book, a photo album, or a behemoth, juicy pawpaw (better known to me as a papaya, my favorite tropical fruit). Dave spends time working in her garden with her. She jokes with me that she wants to keep Dave, that she'll trade him for Quentin.

"Sorry, Lilian, you can't have him," I say. "I married him just last year."

"Too bad you didn't marry him ten years ago," she says dryly, "or you might be willing to hand him over."

Lilian doesn't bemoan her failing health or live in the past. She doesn't talk about how much better everything used to be in the good old days. Dave says he intuits a symbiotic relationship between Lilian and her garden. There is constant change in nature. Maybe someone who embraces gardening is less likely to begrudge change.

One morning, I plug my American curling iron into the Australian outlet using a handy electrical adapter. When I wrap my hair around the curling iron's barrel, the plastic end pulls off into my hand, melting and stretching like taffy. When I yank the iron away, the hot barrel takes a chunk of my hair with it. I scream and drop the iron. Dave comes running, rattled, only to find the emergency is, as he puts it, nothing.

This sends us straight into an argument. He thinks I overreacted. I think he's being an insensitive bully. According to him, I always overreact about everything. Come to think of it, I add, he's often an insensitive bully.

My face burns. My heart races. He turns his back to me. We retreat in silence to opposite ends of Quentin's apartment. I feel sorry for myself, for my poor scorched hair. I could have hurt myself. Dave apparently doesn't seem to give a shit. So I screamed. Was that a crime? I was scared; I was shocked. I was the one in peril. He should have coddled me, not gotten angry.

I'm stung. I try to distract myself, think of other things. I can't stop the churning thoughts, so I do my best to let them be, like bad weather. I fold clothes in the bedroom, smooth the bed covers. I walk into the living room. He's lying on the couch. We avoid eye contact.

I go to the refrigerator, open it, close it. I stand at the kitchen window, gazing at all that green. So much change in the last year. Our wedding, my mother and Gabriele dying, my retirement, our leaving the Love Nest to come here, to the other side of the world.

I hear Dave rise from the couch. I keep my eyes on the surreally green yard. I hope he's coming to me. If he's not, I will give him a little more time and go to him.

I feel him approach. His chest presses against my back, his lips at my neck. I lean into him.

That afternoon, Dave takes pictures of a koala in my arms at the Lone Pine Koala Sanctuary. Her name is Tinker Bell. She's cuddly and dignified. The trusting weight of her compact body rests in my arms, as though they are limbs of a tree. Eater of eucalyptus leaves, she smells faintly of cough drops. She reaches out across my chest and stares into my eyes.

*

The first day of Georgia Constantino's poetry class, I saw my future but didn't know it. Two mysteriously alluring women with spiky hair, jeans, and leather jackets sat across from me in the circle of students. I couldn't take my eyes off them. Clearly Georgia, the professor, thought they were enthralling, too. She welcomed them, watched them as they settled into their seats. I figured that like Georgia, they were lesbians, but I couldn't be sure. To my knowledge, I'd never known a lesbian before—except for Faith, who had recently come out.

At first I couldn't distinguish between them beyond their names, Emily and TJ. I didn't know if they were friends or lovers. I discovered they were art students who shared a studio on campus. After a few classes, I began to discern differences, taking special note of Emily's elegant neck and dark brown eyes. It felt odd to think of her as pretty since she was vaguely masculine. Her very presence challenged my gendered ideas. I also began to see that Emily's poetry was narrative and focused on her childhood, whereas TJ's was more lyrical and abstract. Their energy was quite different: Emily was softer than TJ, who had a badass edge.

Every class session we passed out copies of our new poems. I loved taking home a stack of poems to read and respond to. I'd find myself digging Emily's and TJ's poems out of the stack to read first. Sitting on Michael's couch, I wrote long, effusive responses. I couldn't wait for Tuesday nights. I eagerly anticipated what TJ and Emily penned on their copies of my poems. My life felt alive again because of poetry, because of the class, because of these women. My learning center job and home life with Michael felt gray compared to the vivid, three-dimensional world of poetry, art, and iconoclastic writers.

By mid-semester, I was having conversations with Emily and TJ, reveling in their flirtatious energy. One day after class, we went out for beer, the three of us. There I sat in my corporate work outfit of black nylons, black skirt, and fuchsia blazer across from two women in black boots, jeans, and T-shirts. They both seemed enviously at ease, as though their bodies were to be inhabited, not gazed upon.

TJ wasted no time in asking me if I lived with anyone. I shyly admitted I had a boyfriend. I thought I must seem like a child to these women who, I presumed, had experienced things I couldn't imagine. I asked them how they knew each other. Turned out they were buddies who'd been lovers ten years ago, in their early twenties. I was in awe that they were talking about their lesbianism like it was an everyday thing. Like it was a given. It became real, concrete. Women who loved each other? They didn't have to think about what men thought of them. They didn't have to care about men's judgments. Like outlaws, they created their own rules. And they'd been lovers and now were friends? Talk about breaking the rules. I was enthralled.

I asked them both the same question they'd asked me: who do you live with? TJ volunteered that Emily had a partner of three years.

"Look who's talking," teased Emily. "What about Fran?"

"You know we broke up," said TJ.

"But you still live together," Emily countered.

"She's moving out soon," TJ insisted. TJ seemed irked by Emily's taunting, as though she didn't want to claim her girlfriend. They teased each other like sisters, like fraternity guys. TJ looked at her watch, a thick black band with a silver face. My small gold watch, which suited me, would look silly on her. It crossed my mind that they weren't playing dress-up any more than I was. What were typically men's garments worked on them. They weren't acting like men. They were women who just happened to be more masculine than most. I thought about how I'd sometimes feel over-feminine in a dress and over-masculine in pants. What was the real me? Perhaps Gloria Steinem was right when she said, "All women are female impersonators."

"Damn, I've gotta go," said TJ, looking at her watch again. "I promised Fran I'd take her to the airport."

Fran, the ex-lover who still lived with TJ? They remained friends, too? The world of these women was so foreign, so fascinating. What was I doing here with them? How did I belong? Whatever was happening, I didn't want to be anywhere else than right there.

"Okay, see you later," said Emily.

"Why don't you walk me to my car?" TJ asked.

"Nah," said Emily, smiling faintly, "I think we'll stay here and have another beer. What do you think, Kate?"

I was nervous about, and thrilled by, the thought of being alone with Emily. I said I'd stay. TJ turned and left abruptly.

"Is she mad? I asked Emily.

"She'll be fine, trust me," she said.

I noticed Emily had a small scar that looked like a dimple puckering her cheek. A cowlick in her short, dark hair highlighted her boyishness. It was like she was part girl, part boy.

Emily and I settled in for extra beer and conversation. The more we talked, the more I was drawn to her. Poetry, politics, art: we touched on my favorite subjects. I liked the way her mind jumped around, weaving connections. In spite of the boots and jeans and spiky hair, there was absolutely nothing aggressive about her. Her words, her hand movements, her long eyelashes—all gentle.

She was enrolled in an interdisciplinary Master's degree combining poetry and visual art. I asked her about her art, imagining vast canvasses splattered with paint, but she talked about ceramics and sculpture. In Japan I had immersed myself in writing, literature, and spontaneous exploration. But now I lived with a scientist who believed men and women were biologically programmed. I was tutoring children in reading and math, following a script and wearing required corporate garb. And now here, before me, sat a woman who blurred gender lines and whose life was devoted to aesthetics and artistic expression—promising another way to live.

We decided to walk back to campus so she could show me her studio. First, though, she excused herself to make a phone call. When she returned, I could tell she had called her girlfriend. Did she tell her she was with me? I doubted it. I had no reason to call Michael. He was probably still in the lab. He never kept tabs on where I was or when I'd get home.

Emily and I walked out into the cool night. A sliver of moon hung low in the sky. Other students walked across the shadowy campus to and from the dorms and night classes. For the first time I became viscerally aware of Emily's curvy body, her slim waist and round hips. The beer had warmed me. I was buzzing on it, on life. Before reaching the studio, we stopped at a bathroom.

"You don't happen to have a tampon, do you?" She laughed. For a brief moment I was taken aback. She had her period? I caught myself. Had I been unconsciously categorizing her as a man? I was attracted to her so she must be a man, right? Because I was straight. Oh, the machinations of the mind that thrives on categories.

I did have a tampon, buried in my purse. I pulled it out and handed it to her. We giggled like teenagers. She seemed like the best of both worlds: firmly rooted in herself like a man, yet completely simpatico with my concerns and interests as a woman.

This late at night, the dimly lit studio space exuded a weird magic. A pile of women's high-heeled shoes slumped in the corner. Emily told me a grad student was using them for an art installation. That was the first time I'd heard about art made from found objects.

Emily showed me some of her small ceramic sculptures. One was a colorful box embedded with a plump goddess on the lid, surrounded by phases of the moon. A beautiful thing, made with skill and heart.

"This is a fertility box," she said. "It's meant to help someone who wants to conceive."

"Do you want to have children?" I asked.

"I would love to have a daughter someday." Another vista opened up: two women raising children.

"What about you? Do you want children?" she asked.

I was ambivalent about having a child, mainly because I didn't want to be the one to have to do it all, as mothers usually did: nurse a sick child in the middle of the night, make all the pediatrician appointments, keep track of homework and activities.

"I like the idea of having a daughter, too," I said. And we began to riff on girl names we loved, like Megan and Lilly, a flight of fancy, of fantasy, baby-sweetness warming the space between us.

At that moment, we were startled by a noise at the studio door.

"Maybe it's the janitor," said Emily. But TJ appeared, her loud boots clomping.

"Hey, what's going on?" she said. If she were a cartoon, jagged spikes representing anger would have shot from her eyes.

Emily leaned back on her stool and crossed her arms.

"Not much," Emily said, "just showing Kate some art."

TJ looked from Emily to me and back again. The silver studs on her black leather jacket glimmered. Then she turned abruptly and left, slamming the door like a cannon blast.

"Whoa, what's wrong with her?" I asked, intuiting the answer.

"Well," said Emily, pausing to choose the right words, "she's attracted to you, too. And she's used to getting what she wants."

She's attracted to you, too... The phrase shot through me to the core. Two women desired me? Two strong, smart, attractive, artistic women? We sat on stools, drenched in the smells of paint and glue, amidst wax and clay and pieces of armature, our knees nearly touching, lit up by our connection. Emily was attracted to me. I was dizzy. The moment felt surreal, hyper-real. Was I really in the dark art studio of a lesbian, as drawn to her as she was to me?

As though her words had burst a dam, we launched into a topic we'd avoided all night: our partners. We were both in three-year-long relationships, we both lived with our lovers, and we were both unhappy. Her lover was controlling. Mine was morose. I launched into my concerns about Michael, and she into hers about her partner, who was a minister. They had been joined in a commitment ceremony at the church last year. Emily regretted it. She'd felt pressured. Even as Emily sat there with me, she felt burdened. She knew her partner was home, waiting for Emily, keeping tabs on her. I laughed and said that my problem was exactly the opposite. I felt I could drop off the planet and Michael wouldn't notice.

The energy between us grew as we bonded over our miserable relationships. It was thrilling to believe that someone—this amazing woman—totally understood me. It was thrilling to identify a gap in my life and imagine that it would finally be filled. I leaned into this thrilling newness. It promised complete and utter fulfillment.

That night, I drove home in a daze, hardly noticing the dark night, the road, the other cars whizzing by. Emily and I hadn't touched or kissed, and as much as I was enthralled with her, I had a hard time conceptualizing crossing that line. I turned on the Indigo Girls. It was a few years before they would publicly come out, but right then it came to me as though the information was downloaded into my brain: they were lesbians! I thought about them on their videos, the way they owned their music, their guitars, their bodies. How strange it had never before crossed my mind. I thought about Amy singing the Dire Straights song "Romeo and Juliet." It was code! She wasn't just covering a classic song in the role of Romeo, begging Juliet for love. She was singing *as a woman in love with a woman.*

And what about Melissa Etheridge? I knew there were rumors about her. I totally dug her deep raspy voice and raging guitar, the masculine within the feminine. And May Sarton? Even though she didn't feature it in her writing, she was a lesbian, too. No wonder she conveyed such independence! She didn't *need* a man. Then there was

Virginia Woolf's affair with Vita Sackville West. I'd read *Orlando* in college but no one had clued me in that the book was a love letter from Woolf to West. I discovered that fact later. There were lesbians everywhere.

That night, I didn't consider what kind of mood Michael might be in when I walked through the door. It didn't matter to me. He looked up from the couch, headphones and TV on, and waved hi. He didn't ask where I'd been even though I was hours later than usual.

After climbing into bed, we had sex. Something shifted. For the first time, I fully inhabited my body and mind. I looked *through my eyes*. Usually I was stuck on what Michael was seeing, hoping he found me desirable. Sex had been an act of projection: *what was he seeing? What was he thinking? Was I enough for him?* I'd been objectifying myself!

That night, I took my pleasure without worrying about his. I wasn't thinking from his imagined point of view but purely, wholly, and fully from mine.

Latent possibilities bloomed before me. Life became something new, something I'd never imagined possible. It was now thinkable to live in a totally new way, outside of the constrictions of patriarchy. An alternative life filled with women and art and poetry.

One afternoon, I sat in a cafe writing about these ideas in my journal. I was on fire in a liminal space, living with Michael yet falling in love with Emily. I was a straight woman with lesbianism abloom in my heart. Words flowed from my hand, creation pouring through me uninhibited.

My pen paused. I stopped and looked up.

Everyone around me glowed. Every person sitting at a table with coffee or tea, writing or reading or talking, was surrounded by a bright light. More than surrounded by. Emanating. Dazzling white light radiated from every person.

Was I seeing auras? I'd always thought auras were an idea, a symbol for human vitality, not a literal thing.

I stared, frozen, not wanting to blink my eyes.

The moment I did blink, the mysterious light disappeared. Everything reverted to its regular state. Yet the tenuous link between the seen and unseen remained.

10

Paradise

Certainly paradise, whatever, wherever it be, contains flaws.
If it did not, it would be incapable of drawing the hearts of
men or angels.
—Henry Miller

After a plane hop from Brisbane, Dave and I arrive in Cairns, Australia. The seaside town displays its seedy side, bordered by bars and strip clubs. The room we reserved in what had appeared online to be a heavenly resort turns out to be cheesy and isolated. Greasy Chinese food at a strip mall across the street is the only alternative to crappy, expensive resort meals. The huge waterfall-laden swimming pool that appeared so inviting on the resort's website looks tacky and dirty up close, and the Jacuzzi isn't heated.

After a day of traveling from Brisbane to Cairns, we're exhausted. It's late afternoon. We lie on the hard bed in our hot room beneath a ceiling fan, me in a tank top and underwear, Dave naked.

The air is sticky. As though to add insult to injury, it's raining. My skin crawls with irritation. I can't find a comfortable position on the bed. The pathetic pillows are lumpy. Where is the promised luxurious, blue-sky perfection? I have terrible period cramps. I am fifty years old. Why the hell am I still getting a period—and on the day before we are to snorkel in the Great Barrier Reef?

I know what's happening. The more I entertain thoughts of dissatisfaction, the more reasons I find to be bummed out. I've become what T. Harv Eker calls a "living, breathing crap magnet." I know the best way to deactivate the crap magnet is to drift off to nap, or to ease my mind with a few better-feeling thoughts. My watching self notices how my ego is digging in, finding reason after reason to be miserable.

My inner voice counters: so what if Cairns doesn't live up to my idea of perfection? What exactly is the issue with staying in a cheesy hotel for a few days? It could be fun in its weirdness. I'm in Australia, for God's sake. I'm fortunate to be here. *Something good is going to come from this.*

Lying next to me, Dave is reading *A Short History of Everything* by Bill Bryson. Every once in a while he shares a tidbit about atoms or elephants or Elvis. There we are, on other side of the world, half naked and reading in a humid hotel room beneath a whirling ceiling fan like Jane and Paul Bowles in the Sahara.

Suddenly a cacophony of bird sounds rushes at us from outside, an uncanny explosion of animal noise.

Dave jumps from the bed to grab his camera, pulls on his shorts and shirt, and shoves his feet into his flip-flops. He is not one to miss out on an animal spectacle. I throw on a sundress and follow him to the mall parking lot adjacent to our room.

There, amidst asphalt and parked cars in the orange light of sunset, hundreds of sulphur-crested cockatoos are dropping from the heavens. Filling the sky with feathers and shrieks, they descend—one after the other after the other—on a stand of trees. The treetops come alive with vibrant yellow-and-white bodies, a marvel in an unlikely place.

That night I dream of Gabriele for the first time. It's been three months since she died. I am walking down a brightly lit hallway, at ease, strolling. I look to my right and there behind a plate-glass window stands Gabriele, so vibrant her skin emanates light. She smiles and waves at me from behind the glass. She doesn't say a word but her presence transmits the fullest, most complete, most profound sense of joy. An electric, ecstatic tingling rushes through my body. A rush of bliss.

When I wake, the intense body charge remains. My skin, my bones, are abuzz. The feeling is so heavenly I don't want it to dissipate. I can recall every detail of the dream. The bright hallway. Gabriele on the other side of the window. Her empathic, telepathic, visceral message of beauty and perfection. *Death isn't what you think. It isn't the end.*

The waters of the Coral Sea are rough. The day before, when I was in crap-magnet mode, I would have felt disillusioned; what kind of paradisiacal boat to the Great Barrier Reef makes you feel like you're on a bucking bronco? Instead, I accept the boat's movements as part of the adventure. A pale Brazilian woman stares at the horizon. She tells me she tends to get seasick, and moments later she rushes for the railing.

My first time on a cruise ship, years before, I felt nauseated. Later, a friend told me that motion sickness is a control issue. Instead of fighting the movement of the boat, she started to think of it as comforting, like being a baby rocked in a cradle. The next time on the water, I relaxed into the swaying of the boat, conceptualizing it as comforting. I was never seasick again.

Until now. Perhaps I am focusing too much on the Brazilian woman. Perhaps I am overthinking the idea of being coddled. But the next thing I know, I too am running for the back of the boat. I make it to the bathroom to retch. One of the crew members gives me a seasickness pill.

I sit back next to Dave and lean into him. He wraps his arms around me. I don't say anything. I don't want to create drama. *Relax*, I think. *Be happy*. And I do, I am.

When the boat stops at Hastings Reef, my nausea has abated. In wetsuits and snorkel gear, we plunge into the water. The corals and fish are extravagantly variegated. We float over a giant clam, open to reveal its pulsing siphon and purplish-blue scalloped edges pixilated with countless eyes. A shoal of translucent squid drifts by.

When we glide over the edge of the reef, the sea opens out into indigo infinity, creating the sensation of flying off into the abyss. Nothingness and everything-ness converge. I hang there, suspended, thinking of Gabriele behind the glass, of the ecstatic electricity pulsing through my body during and after the dream, of embracing of the fertile void. The night before, I read a line from Alan Watts that echoes through my mind:

"The now-moment is eternity, and one must see it now or never."

*

Tension built between Emily and me. I felt that if I kissed her, I'd cross a line that would carry me away into a whole new world, saying good-bye to the one I knew so well. It was alluring and frightening. Michael must have felt me pulling away because for the first time in three years, he asked me if—during spring break—I'd go with him to New York for seder with his family.

I told Emily about the trip. She asked me if after the last session of poetry class before break I'd go out for a drink with her. She took me to a gay and lesbian restaurant and bar. I hadn't known such places existed. Men in cowboy getups crowded the dance floor, line dancing. Women with piercings and multicolored hair draped their arms around each other. Years ago, I'd explored the Castro with my college friend Oscar, but I'd never seen anything quite like this. A covert society disguised as a regular hamburger joint. I was being inducted into a thrilling underground world.

We sat in a booth, drinking beer. Emily slid close to me, her thigh pressing against mine. Her leather jacket squeaked as she reached over and caressed the top of my hand with her pinky finger. My pulse quickened and my breath tightened. I looked over at her and she bent her face toward mine. The softness, the velvety skin—

what a lovely surprise. No wonder so many men loved it. I leaned into the kiss like it was natural, like I knew exactly what to do.

She pulled away. "Easy," she said. "You must be used to kissing men."

She placed her lips lightly on mine.

"Let's get out of here," she whispered.

We climbed into her car—actually, the minister's car. The windows fogged as we kissed and pressed our bodies together. There was the wonderful surprise that she was warm and wet, that she was responding to me as I was to her. Touching her seemed familiar and foreign.

Me? I'm someone who gets to do this? I marveled.

I was in awe of the taboos I was breaking, of the stone walls liquefying before my eyes. Life's boundaries were an illusion. Anything was possible.

At the Seder meal in Michael's family home, I sat like a ghost sipping matzo ball soup. His father was a well-known professor, his mother an eminent economist. His sister was a brilliant musician, his brother an antiquarian book collector. Everyone was a product of Ivy League schools. It was all so weighty and traditional in contrast to my bright and light California redwood-deck-and-glass-house, state-university upbringing. And so staid, in light of the fact that I'd just made out with a woman a few days before.

I didn't fit in Michael's world. In the gay bar, I'd felt at home. The outsiders were my tribe. For so long I'd wanted Michael to do what he was doing: invite me into his world and desire to marry me, to let me know he wanted me forever in his life. But it was too late.

I was grief stricken, ecstatic, crawling out of my skin. When Michael went to the store with his dad, I felt a deep urge to talk to someone. Who could I confide in? Who wouldn't judge me because I'd been with a woman? I pulled out my credit card and picked up the phone to make a long-distance call to Japan. I exhaled when Ella picked up. I wasn't sure why I'd thought to call her. Maybe she seemed like the safest friend to talk to because she lived on the other side of the world.

The line crackled as I told her the story of how I met Emily in the poetry class, how I'd been drawn to her, and how we'd made out in the car. I said it felt right to be with her but I was deeply torn. I loved Michael, but I felt I'd crossed a line and couldn't go back.

"Well, when I was with a woman—" said Ella.

"You've been with a woman?"

"Yes, don't you remember? I told you that time when we were with Val at a club in Roppongi?"

"I remember Val talking about being attracted to her girl students," I said.

"Yes, that was the conversation. And I said I'd been with women."

"I'm sorry," I said, "I just don't remember that." Deep down did I, though, since I chose to call her?

"That doesn't surprise me," she said. "I actually brought it up a couple of times, and each time you seemed totally uninterested— even a little disgusted. You quickly changed the subject."

"Oh my God, I can't believe this," I said. "You brought it up a *few times?"*

"Yes."

"And I changed the subject? I didn't want to talk about it?"

"It seemed that way."

What was going on? Was I in some kind of deep denial? Was I really a lesbian? Had my subconscious fought against it? But how could I reconcile that with thirty-one years of loving men?

"Anyway," Ella went on, "what I'm trying to say is this. I was with a woman. And it was a good experience. But I decided I didn't want to live that life. It's not easy. There are lots of homophobes out there. It's hard not to be able to be totally open about your relationship. It's much easier to move through life as a straight person, as a straight couple. Kate, are you asking my advice?"

"Yes," I said, not sure that I was. I may have wanted empathy more than anything. But I clung to her words. I had to hear what she was going to say.

"Stay with Michael. It will be a much easier life."

On the plane on the way back to California, I cried and cried. Bewildered, Michael held me. He didn't ask me what was wrong. I didn't say a word. I didn't know who I was. I didn't know what I was going to do.

When we got home that afternoon, I was deeply fatigued. After pulling our suitcases into the bedroom, Michael left to check in at the lab. I picked up the phone to call Emily. We'd spoken briefly twice when I'd been in New York, but it wasn't easy for her to have conversations with the suspicious minister lurking about. Emily answered the phone and told me in a hushed voice she'd call me right back. I knew that meant she'd leash up her dog and go to the pay phone down the street to call me, under the pretense that she was walking the dog.

When the phone rang ten minutes later, I was jolted from a half-sleep. It was reassuring to hear her deep, calm voice on the other end of the line. She asked me to meet her in an hour at a bookstore cafe.

"I'd love to, Emily, but I'm totally exhausted. Let's meet tomorrow." It was only four o'clock, but I had thoughts of crawling into bed.

"I have to see you now, today. It's been a week. You're telling me I have to wait another day?"

The idea of getting up and driving somewhere seemed impossible. But she begged, and I relented. It felt good to be deeply desired.

I'd been so caught up in travel and seder and my conflicting emotions that I'd forgotten it was Easter Sunday. Downtown, people milled about in suits and spring dresses. Emily hugged me when we met at the cafe, and my blood flooded with warmth.

"I don't have much time," she said. "I'm so glad you met me. I just had to see you, to know what's been happening is real."

Real? My head was spinning. I wasn't sure what was real anymore.

"I got you an Easter present." She handed me a box. I pulled out something smooth and compact that fit perfectly in my palm. A crystal egg. I held it to the light. Thin fissures in its thick, clear middle made it shimmer. Its beauty radiated from its imperfection.

"What are we going to do?" I said.

"I don't know," she said. "What are we going to do?"

We sat with the table between us. I stared into her brown eyes framed by thick eyelashes. We were both in committed relationships. As far as I knew, I was a straight girl.

When she walked me back to my car and hugged me good-bye, I was dizzy. Everything glittered like the crystal egg.

Driving away, I felt relief. It was good to be alone, to have no one—not Michael, not Emily—expecting anything from me. I needed space to breathe. Ella's words echoed in my mind: *stay with Michael. It will be a much easier life.* I didn't care about easier or harder. I just wanted authentic. One person's paradise was another person's hell. And for three years now, the truth had been that I loved Michael, and I wasn't happy with Michael. Was Emily the answer? I didn't know. But I did know one thing. I wanted to be free.

11

Any Direction

You have brains in your head, you have feet in your shoes. You can steer yourself in any direction you choose.
—*Dr. Seuss*

It's dawn. Dave and I stand on a vast beach in Cape Hillsborough, Queensland, Australia, bundled up against the cold. Lingering near a massive time-sculpted volcanic rock, we watch the sky brighten at the edge of the dark sea. The only sound is the whistling of the wind.

Then, a thudding noise.

Thump, thump, thump.

Before I can say, "What's that?" a gangly kangaroo hops by not fifteen feet away on clown-shoe feet. That one is followed by a second one, then a third. The trio whizzes along the gently lapping water line.

Dave and I look at each other with the excitement of children.

The kangaroos fly across the wide expanse of beach, frolicking in the water. We follow them. Even while keeping a respectful distance, we are able to see them clearly. Dave takes picture after picture.

Tears spring to my eyes. The answer to my unasked question has emerged: *why are we doing this again? Why have we left our home and family and jobs and beloved seaside town?*

This is why.

The kangaroos cavort and run. They stop and sniff the sand. Two of them face each other and began to box playfully. Abruptly they stretch up high on their back legs, using their tails to balance like tripods, and spar. They look seven feet tall, maybe more.

They don't seem to notice we are their audience. That is, until they pause mid-action. On their haunches they look over at us, sniffing the air. Then they start hopping directly toward us.

Closer and closer.

Are they charging us?

I've heard kangaroos can hold their prey with their front legs and use a rear-leg claw to slice a belly top to bottom. My nerves get prickly, and I position myself behind Dave, just in case.

Dave isn't concerned. He's kind of a Dr. Doolittle. He has had lots of encounters on sea and land with wild animals, and domestic pets are drawn to him. He thinks the kangaroos are merely curious. And maybe they are hoping for a free lunch. Earlier we saw one kangaroo and six wallabies on the beach run up to a guy who fed them barley.

Dave rolls the video camera as the beasts hop at full speed toward us. When the front-runner reaches Dave, he laughs and says,

"What do you want, buddy?"

The beast sniffs Dave's feet instead of KOing him with a spring-release foot. Satisfied, the three turn and bound back toward the waves.

Later we are eating at a picnic table, shared with strangers. A weird trilling fills the air, morphing into what sounds like hysterical laughing.

"What's *that?*" I say.

A young guy sitting next to us says, "That's a kookaburra. Look, you can see it up there." On a limb sits a squat, large bird with a white chest and black wings. A black mask covers his eyes.

"It's adorable!" I say. It seems that Australia has the quirkiest animals on the planet.

"Common as crows," says the guy, whose name turns out also to be Dave. He and his wife, Courtney, who are in their twenties, are drinking beer and eating greasy fries. Like us, they got rid of their possessions and took off. Unlike us, they are traveling Australia in their camper van and don't have a plan. They are going wherever the winds blow.

*

Our first summer together, Emily and I spent a lot of time in bed. There were so many new things to try, it was like we were inventing sex. I couldn't get enough. I felt powerful, limitless, unashamed.

I didn't have the idealized woman's body. Nor did she. I didn't care. Her body was an extension of her artistic self: fluid, playful, expansive. She worshipped my womanly curves. There was no implied criticism of the flow and overflow of meaty thighs or bellies.

Finally, I could truly celebrate myself as my hero Walt Whitman urged. I stopped shaving my armpits and legs. I stopped plucking my eyebrows. Whereas most of my life I wouldn't even go to the store without mascara on, I stopped wearing makeup altogether. No longer an object to be gazed upon, I was liberated from obligatory adornment. It was incredible to not worry what men thought about me. What a relief to wear whatever I wanted to wear, to say whatever I wanted to say, to eat whatever I wanted to eat. I was natural. I was free.

We called the apartment our cocoon. Some days we'd eat breakfast in bed then sleep for a while more, waking to make love and talk for hours and hours. From the bedroom window, we had a view of a tree in the yard, its limbs and leaves sculptured to a perfect round green like a child's crayon drawing of a tree. We told each other stories of our childhoods, of what we loved in the world and what we mourned. We scrutinized our former relationships, picking them apart for all that had gone wrong. We reveled in the magnificence of us. We were destined to be together forever.

With an artist's eye, Emily helped open up my vision of the world. Whether we were lying in bed, or walking through the woods, or hanging out in a cafe writing and sketching in our notebooks, she'd draw my attention to a slant of light, the shape of an object, a juxtaposition of color. The apertures of my eyes and mind and heart were expanding.

At the women's bookstore, we bought matching rings. They were designed with a female body stretched out, hair flowing, as though she were gliding through water. In her hands she held a gemstone: indigo for mine, lavender for Emily's.

That night we went to the beach. The moon spread golden light over the sea, the amniotic fluid of Mother Earth. Everywhere, womanly energy greeted me, enfolded me, celebrated me just as I was. In the company of barking sea lions, we exchanged rings and offered extemporaneous vows. We promised to always love one another and to never betray that love.

Emily, fresh off a dominating relationship with the minister where she'd cowered and lied in order to not ruffle feathers, added this: "I promise to never squelch you."

I promised the same thing back.

I loved our little basement apartment, the downstairs of a large Santa Cruz house. Our upstairs neighbors were three techies who watched a lot of movies, played a lot of Dungeons and Dragons, and smoked a lot of pot. We had all we needed with one bedroom and a small bathroom. The kitchen was bright and large, the living room narrow and long. One wall of the living room was embedded with built-in bookshelves, which we filled with literature, poetry, and art books.

Our sliding glass door opened out to the yard. Next to an expanse of lawn sat a picnic table, where we held dinner parties on cool, salty-air nights. Mostly the guests were lesbians: TJ and her former partner Fran, who'd remained friends; Fran's new partner

Lisa; and our new Santa Cruz friends Kiki and Vera. Georgia—who'd become our friend now that she was no longer our professor—also came, accompanied by Faith. They never proclaimed they were lovers, but we suspected they were. They didn't hold hands or touch, but they finished each other's sentences and took sips from each other's drinks.

TJ and Emily had remained best friends in spite of undergoing turmoil as Emily and I fell in love. According to Emily, TJ was angry that Emily had scooped me up. Soon, though, it became clear that TJ and I would have been a disastrous match. We were both strong personalities who would have butted heads. The realization that TJ hadn't missed out helped heal the rift between best friends.

Besides, they had a business to tend to. They washed windows for elderly people in mobile home parks. They laughed at how some of the old people thought TJ was Emily's husband. They didn't bother to correct the misperception. Every few days, Emily left our cocoon to do a window-washing job. It was hard for us to separate. We wished we could take the other with us wherever we went. Apart, something was missing. Together we were whole.

I had the summer off. I'd quit my job at the learning center and been hired to teach fall classes at the university. I'd also been hired to observe and support student teachers in public high schools. I was out of the corporate world and back in academia where I belonged. And, most thrillingly, I was living a woman-centered life.

When Emily left for work, I'd shop, clean the house, and walk the dog. Emily had brought a dog into our relationship, Mazie—a huge black Lab. I found her pack nature endearing but also suffocating at times. Did she really have to follow me everywhere

I went? We had such a small space, and it could be awkward with a 110-pound animal underfoot. That didn't bother Emily. A dog glued to her side pleased her. Sometimes the two of them would sit quietly in the living room, staring out the sliding glass door, or in the back yard listening to birds. I wasn't a person to be still, doing nothing. If I was sitting, I'd be reading or writing, or perhaps talking on the phone.

Every day I needed to do something physical: take a walk, ride my bike, or complete a Herculean whirlwind of domestic tasks like vacuuming and laundry. It had been a few years since I'd meditated, and I'd never gotten the hang of it. Emily, however, didn't have to *do* meditation. She was a meditative person. I admired her gentle, serene quality.

I soon learned that Emily had a pattern of leaving her relationships for new lovers. She had left the minister for me. And she had left someone else—a twenty-year-old piano player—for the minister. Emily had been living with the piano player, and the minister was their neighbor. Before that, Emily had been living with a car mechanic. They'd been together for five years. Miserable with the car mechanic, she'd started up with the nineteen-year-old piano player.

Emily and the mechanic were still friends. Every so often we'd stop at her shop to say hi, or drop by her house. The mechanic—a sprightly woman—laughed when she told the story of their breakup.

"So can you believe this? Emily just disappeared! We'd been together for five years, and one day she was gone. She even left Taz behind!" Taz was the golden retriever puppy the mechanic had bought for Emily. "Wow, I mean Emily took off without so much as a word. She took the car I bought for her, but I took it back. I didn't know what to do with Taz, but I kept her, and I'm so glad I did because she's my best friend, aren't you girl?"

Taz, lying at the mechanic's feet, looked up and thumped her tail against the linoleum.

Emily smiled at the story, good-naturedly deferring to this version. Later, she explained herself. Their relationship had been withering for years. It had been a long time since they'd had sex. They were more like friends than lovers. The piano player had been a quick fling who served as impetus for Emily to finally break free from the mechanic. Emily and the piano player lasted only a few months. The piano player was immature. She had slumped into a depression and hadn't played the piano for months. She ate donuts morning, noon, and night, glued to the TV. When Emily met the minister, who lived in the same apartment complex down the hall, Emily was attracted to her adult seriousness, her philosophical thoughtfulness. The minister had her shit together. Shortly, Emily moved down the hall into the minister's place. Of course later Emily discovered the minister's controlling nature.

Emily could dish it up, too. In TJ's presence, Emily tauntingly told the story of TJ's betrayal. When they were in their early twenties, TJ and Emily had been living together for a few years. TJ started taking a class at the local community college, where she met and started courting Fran with conversation, poetry, and little gifts. TJ neglected to tell Fran she was living with Emily. One day Emily came home to discover Fran and TJ in bed.

Fran and TJ stayed together for years. After they broke up (in the shadow of some of TJ's apparent infidelities), Fran's new partner was welcomed into the group. This complex web of lovers and former lovers created a circle of lesbian comrades.

The first time I heard the women—the mechanic, Fran, TJ, Emily—sit around and josh about the others' betrayals, I couldn't believe it. I was entertained by their jovial ribbing and the way they'd interject and talk over each other, butting heads over competing versions of the stories. Yet I was unnerved. What happened to the jealousy, the hurt feelings, the pain of rejection and lying? Had those feelings really disappeared? Sometimes I detected an underground tension, as though the joking were a way to get in a dig or to non-threateningly air grievances.

It niggled at me, Emily's past. As I met her women friends—some of them lesbians, some of them not—she'd eventually reveal that in the past there'd been a flirtation between them, a sexual tension, a few sessions of hand-holding or kisses. It seemed she had no women friends who weren't also potential sexual partners. Is that what happened as she jumped from relationship to relationship? Friends had morphed into lovers?

But who was I to talk? I'd ridden out of my marriage to Ray on the wave of Harry's allure. I'd fallen into Emily's arms while I still lived with Michael. Maybe we were alike. Maybe people who jumped from relationship to relationship were drawn to each other.

I couldn't imagine, though, that Emily or I would deceive each other. Things were different now. We'd broken the pattern. Before the moon and the waves and the sea lions, we'd exchanged rings and vowed never to betray our love. We were fated to be together.

Unlike the group of former lovers who could laugh at past fiascos, Michael and the minister were in a world of hurt. When Emily had left their shared house, the minister denied Emily access to many of their things and battled with her over financial issues. Michael had no interest in revenge. He wanted to understand why I'd disappeared from his life. And I'd literally done that—vacated our apartment to start staying in hotels with Emily for a couple of weeks before we moved to Santa Cruz.

I'd called Michael a few times to let him know I was okay. He implored me to tell him what was going on. I wasn't ready to tell anyone that I was falling in love with a woman. I told him I was sorting out some things, trying to figure out what I wanted. His reaction surprised me. He'd been so emotionally distant for so long that I was convinced he didn't care much about me. I'd thought his taking me to New York had been an unconscious reaction to my emotionally pulling away—and that perhaps if I finally broke up with him, he'd be relieved. When he told me the contrary, though, that he was devastated and could hardly eat, sleep, or work, I decided to meet with him and tell him the truth.

We met at a trailhead on a warm afternoon. Tall oaks cast shadows over the golden foliage, emblematic of California summer. He looked thinner and paler than usual. We hugged. I could feel his ribs. How could I tell him what was really happening?

"I've been so worried about you," he said. In his understated way—I'd never heard him raise his voice—he talked about how he'd been thrown off center. He'd never felt so confused or distressed. It was deeply ironic that he was finally offering what I'd wanted: emotional connection. I still cared about him, felt tenderly about all of our strengths and inadequacies as a couple. I didn't want to hurt him. It was too late for that, though.

In the back of my mind I thought about Emily, how nervous she'd been that I was going to see Michael. If I was gone too long, she'd be beside herself. I needed to get back to her. But how to tell him the truth? Just spit it out, I guess.

"Is there someone else?" he asked, offering me the perfect segue.

"Yes, but it's not what you think."

"What do you mean?"

I hesitated. This was a monumental moment. I hadn't told anyone yet, except for Ella on the phone across continents. If I said it out loud, the split would be real and permanent. Saying it meant saying good-bye to my straight life.

"Well, I'm with a woman."

He blinked. Blinked again. Staring at me.

"What do you mean, with a woman?"

"I've fallen in love with a woman."

I could see he was incredulous. "You're a lesbian?"

I didn't have anything against that word, but I wasn't sure it fit me precisely. *Lesbian* wiped away all my years of loving men.

"I guess so," I said.

His Adam's apple slid up and down his long neck.

"Kate, I must say, that's the last thing I expected to hear."

"Tell me about it," I said, half smiling. His face remained

downcast. "It's the last thing I expected to happen," I said.

Beneath a tree in the warm afternoon, I offered him a few details about where Emily and I met, and about my journey to this moment.

"A lesbian," he said, as though to confirm it. "Wow. I don't know what to say."

I took his hand. I wanted to comfort him, but that didn't seem possible.

"I didn't want to hurt you," I said.

He squeezed my hand. We walked back to our cars in silence. As he drove away, a sweet sadness spread through my body. It had been time to say good-bye to Michael for a long time. And now, it had happened. I thought of Emily at home, waiting for me, Mazie at her feet.

12

A New Adventure

The answer is in dreams.
—Haruki Murakami

Powdery sand. Calm aqua waters. Dave and I walk along what feels like the edge of the world, a pristine beach abutted by a steamy rainforest. Shadows reach out from drooping trees rooted by ancient trunks.

We are in the northern reaches of Queensland at Cape Tribulation in the Daintree National Forest. When I tell Dave there's an antediluvian vibe to the place, he says this is the oldest living rainforest on earth.

It hits me that this place is heaven, not only metaphorically but literally; it's exactly like the afterlife in a dream I had as a teenager. In the dream, I fell from a cliff and died. Next thing I knew, I stood on the most beautiful beach I'd ever seen. People lay on the sand and swam in the tranquil water. In an instant, they began to telepathically communicate with each other. *How about a little snow?* They agreed snow would be lovely. Snowflakes began to drift down, and the people looked up, smiling, welcoming them. At that moment, I saw a man holding a clipboard walking toward me. He seemed to be in charge. I knew he had all the answers. I knew I could ask him who or what God was.

But the minute he stood before me, I was flooded with such a feeling of wellbeing that I lost my desire to ask questions. The clipboard man welcomed me. He pointed to a distant glass-and-wood building and told me in it were books that detailed every day of everyone's life.

I entered the building, which was packed with tables displaying thousands of scrapbooks. I easily found mine and flipped it open to a random page: November 26, 1974, my twelfth birthday. The page was filled with pictures of me, my parents, my sisters, candles, a cake, and presents. I didn't feel sad or nostalgic, just pleased that everything had been recorded and therefore, somehow, mattered.

*

As she worked to complete her degree, Emily took a class with Gabriele. One day, as Gabriele and I sat on the back deck of her house overlooking the canyon, I told her that Emily and I were a couple. She took the news of my leap from a man to a woman gracefully. She told me she liked Emily and thought she was "handsome." I smiled.

I was sure things would not go as smoothly with my family. My parents were liberal, but I had a feeling they'd take it hard. As a school nurse, Mom worked with kids and families, serving as a kind of social worker. Dad was a licensed marriage, family, and child counselor and had been a college counselor, teacher, and administrator. He was among the first group of educators to undergo counseling training in the early 1960s at a San Diego institute, where he studied with Carl Rogers. Still, I intuited they wouldn't be happy with a lesbian daughter. As it was, they perceived me as compulsive and headstrong in my untraditional ways. They were proud of—yet often exasperated by—me.

How to tell my parents had been weighing on my mind when Emily and I attended my first pride parade in San Francisco. What an awesome sight, thousands of people gathered in a show of celebration. Crazy, colorful costumes! Sparkling beads and floats! Hundreds of dykes on bikes! A contingent carrying the PFLAG (Parents and Friends of Lesbians and Gays) banner walked by: parents pushing baby carriages and holding the hands of toddlers and teens. They threw out Mardi Gras beads and candy.

I saw a woman wearing a T-shirt that read, "My daughter is a lesbian. Get over it!" I started to laugh and cry simultaneously. If only my mom would one day wear such a shirt.

As though someone heard my wish, in the midst of the bellowing voices and thunderous music and thousands of people, the woman walked right over to me.

She said, "You look so much like my daughter." Then she hugged me and disappeared into the crowd.

I started slowly, telling my parents I had a "roommate." Then I brought Emily to my parents' house for a visit. I'd never had a friend who was such a gender bender. I'm sure we weren't fooling anyone.

My parents were friendly to her. They were taken with her kind, gentle nature. Soon after, they came to visit me in Santa Cruz. Emily made herself scarce. I took my parents to a downtown cafe, determined to tell them. I was tired of censoring myself. If I was going to have a relationship with my parents, they needed to know the truth. I figured breaking the news in a public place was a good idea because they'd be less likely to freak out around other people.

Sitting across from my parents with cups of coffee between us, my heart racing, my head roared. I finally spit it out.

"You probably already figured this out," I said "but Emily and I are together. We're a couple." Tears smeared my vision. "I was scared to tell you because I thought you'd disown me."

My dad reached across the table and squeezed my hand. My mom said, "We'd never disown you."

This loving response served as a strong foundation that would be harshly tested. They loved me—no matter what, I would always be their daughter—but they thought my choice was a bad one. For months we had long, teary phone calls. They worried what other people would think. They worried that I'd be treated poorly. They worried I'd be a target for violence. They thought I could just as easily choose to be with a man, that I wasn't "really" a lesbian, that this was a phase.

I argued back that living my authentic life was most important. I objected to the word "phase"; it diminished my life experience. It might not work out, but I had the right to try. We all grow and change—and, ideally, learn as we go. I also emphasized that there are lots of perfectly happy gay and lesbian people in the world. In fact, one of my father's colleagues was a lesbian. Why accept her and not me? I agreed I had a choice about my actions but not my feelings. I didn't want to live a false life. As far as violence, all women were potential targets. I refused to walk around living in fear.

Being generally reasonable people, they knew my arguments were valid. But their reaction was not logical; it was emotional. I sensed my father felt I was rejecting men. I tried to reassure him that wasn't true, although deep down part of me felt it was.

The more time they spent around Emily and me, the more they calmed down. But certain events triggered a new round of arguments. My parents wanted me to spend more time with them, to come for a weekend, not just a day. Emily was welcome, too, but we'd have to sleep in separate beds.

"You know that's always been our policy," said my mom. "Only married couples can share a bed under our roof."

"Well that's fundamentally unfair to Emily and me since we aren't allowed to legally marry," I countered, knowing full well that their discomfort had nothing to do with our unmarried status. Eventually, my parents gave in. The next weekend, Emily and I slept in my parents' guest room.

One day my mom said, "I think I can understand why you'd want to be with a woman. It seems more equitable." In the 1970s, my mom had supported the Equal Rights Amendment. She wore a denim, unisex apron with "E.R.A. All the Way!" emblazoned across the chest. When the amendment didn't pass, she was disconcerted. My father had also been influenced by the women's movement and for the most part was gender enlightened for a man of his generation. He reminded me of the older, gentler Alan Alda. He even looked like Alan Alda but with a handlebar mustache.

Still, my parents had unquestionably fallen into prescribed gender roles. It was expected that my dad would do the yard work, and my mom would cook, clean, and iron. Mom resented the relentless nature of domestic tasks. Even though my dad had been a cook in the Navy, he didn't cook at home, other than manning the barbecue. Often he was unhappy with my mom's meals, saying she didn't make enough food. He'd reach across the table and grab the bones off our plates, sucking out the marrow and nibbling around for any last shred of meat. Dad was always ravenous. If Mom ate like a bird, Dad ate like a lion on the veldt, digging into his first antelope in weeks.

My father was a fairly genial person, but he could also be a bit of a bully, asserting his masculine authority at will. Mom grew quiet, steaming at his intimidating tactics. Watching the way Emily and I operated as equals nudged her to imagine what married life might be like *sans* a man.

Emily and I had been together two years when my younger sister got engaged. While the wedding was being planned, my mom called and asked me to not dance with Emily at the reception. My father was on the extension, breathing softly, saying nothing.

"On the very day we're celebrating love, I'm supposed to deny the person I love?" I all but yelled into the phone.

"Your sister's wedding day is not about you," said my mom, her voice tightly controlled. "It's about her. If you draw attention to yourselves by dancing together, you might create a problem on your sister's special day."

"What kind of problem? What, exactly, do you expect people will do?"

"Kathleen," she said, "everyone is not like you. It will make some people uncomfortable. And don't say anything to your sister. I don't want an argument to spoil her wedding planning."

"All I have to say is if I'm not allowed to dance with Emily, I'm not dancing at all."

"Well, that would be selfish," said my mom. She may have been a lapsed Catholic, but she was good at guilt.

The wedding was lovely. My sister asked me to read a poem. My other sister was a bridesmaid. With so many friends and family gathered, joy was in the air. Yet at the reception, I sat there boiling at the hypocrisy of my sister and all her girlfriends with their arms around each other, laughing and dancing together to the gayest of gay paeans, the Village People's "YMCA."

When a slow song came on my father, looking handsome in his tux, turned to me.

"Can I have this dance?" he said, standing and taking my hand.

"Dad," I said, gesturing to Emily. "I'm not dancing."

He squeezed my hand, let it go, and guided my mom to the dance floor.

A few years later, my father told me that a middle-aged lesbian couple had moved in down the street. One of his neighbors snidely said, "Get a load of those dykes." My father, outraged, responded, "Don't ever use that word in that way around me again. My daughter is a lesbian." He also said he'd told his men's spirituality group about me, opening the door for one of the other men to reveal he had a gay son. My mom, too, made huge strides. In their small conservative town, she helped co-found a PFLAG group.

Emily had been out to her mom, Louise, for years. I first met Louise at her house in San Jose. With thick dark hair and brown eyes, there was a striking resemblance between mother and daughter. However, their dispositions were poles apart. Louise was direct and opinionated. She said she was concerned that I'd never been with a woman before. Did I know what I was getting into? I assured her at age thirty-two, I did.

Later, at holiday time, it was clear I'd received the stamp of approval when Louise said she would *not* crochet a Christmas stocking for me. She had a tradition of making elaborate stockings adorned with the names of family and friends. Emily's hung on the mantel. Louise was beginning to think the stockings were jinxed. Every time she made one for one of Emily's partners, they'd break up. She didn't want that to happen with us. So, no stocking for me.

When I taught, I sometimes shared personal stories to illuminate points. In those accounts, I might mention my husband or boyfriend in an offhand way. But now it felt awkward to do the equivalent. If I mentioned "my partner," most people knew that was code for same-sex partner and I'd be outed. I didn't mind people knowing one on one about my sexuality, but it felt awkward, if not threatening, to come out in front of a class. This was the mid 1990s, the days before active LGBTQ student organizations, the days when same-sex marriage was barely a dream, the days before public figures commonly came out.

Sometimes students asked me if I was married. How was I supposed to respond? I experimented with various replies. "No" felt like a betrayal of my relationship. "Yes" felt like a lie. My favorite was, "If I was legally allowed to, I would be." That seemed a bit alienating, though. The last thing I wanted to do was to make a student feel attacked.

In the English Department, everyone knew that Georgia was a lesbian, but she never overtly mentioned it in class. As a young woman, Georgia had been married to a man and had kids. At times she would mention her children who were now adults. She shared her poetry with us, but there were no direct references to her love life. No student poems mentioned homosexuality, yet many overflowed with references to heterosexual attraction, love, and sex. Many of my straight colleagues displayed pictures of spouses and families in their offices that made public their heterosexual lives. I became more and more aware of a double standard. "There's no need to share your personal life" was targeted at the non-mainstream life.

Once when Georgia and Faith came to our house for dinner, Georgia stressed that life had vastly improved for gays and lesbians.

"You have no idea how bad things used to be," she said in her gravelly voice, eyes boring into me. Almost five decades earlier when Georgia was an undergrad at an Ivy League school, she got called into the dean's office. The dean accused her of being a lesbian. Georgia hadn't even known what the word meant. She and a friend had been reported holding hands and kissing. Georgia was kicked out of college.

Things may have changed, but not enough for me. I was used to being my authentic self as a teacher. I was used to holding hands with my lover wherever we went, kissing hello and good-bye, snuggling at a movie. Emily had reservations about public displays of affection, even in Santa Cruz, where gaggles of lesbians roamed about. She said, "There are people out there who would rape you and kill me." The likelihood of that happening seemed slim. I was supposed to give up my pleasures in life? I was supposed to deny in public who I was? The irony struck deep. Living as a lesbian meant living my truth, but I was supposed to hide my truth in public? I'd lived with heterosexual privilege for more than thirty years. How insulting that I was expected to relinquish it.

At the local bookstore, I found a book called *From Wedded Wife to Lesbian Life*, a collection of personal stories profiling women like me who'd fallen in love with women later in life. I hunted down similar books and read ravenously. I wanted to understand how other women handled the transition, the tensions at work and with their families. I was on fire about the fundamental unfairness of it all.

For some time, I'd considered pursing a PhD, but I'd been unsure of my focus. I loved American Literature, but I'd heard getting into such programs—much less getting a job in the field afterward—was nearly impossible. Now I knew. I would apply for graduate programs in education, with a focus on gay and lesbian equality.

Emily supported my applying to programs but didn't want to

move away from the Bay Area. Emily had lived her whole life in San Jose. She liked the ease of dropping by her mother's and TJ's, of going to the queer hamburger joint, of hanging out at her campus art studio. Her window-washing clients were in San Jose. She told me, after the fact, that moving to Santa Cruz had been a big deal for her. In my mind, Santa Cruz meant easy to access to San Jose as needed, while living in paradise. In her mind, she had sacrificed her home, her place of familiarity and comfort—for me.

Trouble brewed in other ways, too. Once, as we were making out, I passionately whispered, "Fuck me." Emily recoiled.

"Please don't say that," she said. "It sounds like you're thinking of a man."

Shame flared in me. Had I been thinking of a man? Actually, no. I was just loving the way we were going at it. Sex was sex in my book, no matter the equipment. Then again, I could understand her concern. Our first few weeks together, while we were drunkenly making love, I called out Michael's name. It was purely out of habit, although a Freudian lens would insist on something else. Besides, I'd been drunk. Really drunk. The minute Michael's name erupted from my mouth, Emily jumped from bed. I curled in a ball and cried and cried. Eventually we talked about it, and she seemed to be assuaged by my explanation, that I didn't miss Michael or want to have sex with him. Calling his name had been a knee-jerk response. Yet I wondered if the experience would leave a scar.

Sex toys and porn were out. To her, the lesbians in porn were male fantasies. Even women-friendly porn was verboten. It was too corny and embarrassing. Besides, it would involve watching other people.

She didn't want us to masturbate. She thought we should save ourselves for each other. She thought she should be enough for me and I for her. I broke that rule early on, and once when she came home early I was nearly caught red-handed with my vibrator in one hand and a lesbian magazine in the other, open to a hot butch centerfold. After that close call, I tossed my vibrator in the trash.

The University of Washington in Seattle offered me a full ride. Emily was devastated. I was asking her to move nine hundred miles away? Leaving TJ and her mother and her friends and her beloved Bay Area was an excruciating prospect. I suggested we try a long-distance relationship. She vehemently rejected that idea. She said if we lived apart, our relationship would be over. Those words shoved a knife into my heart. I was hooked into her, into our relationship, into the *idea* of our relationship. Because of her—of us—I'd found my life calling. Still, I couldn't be persuaded to stay. This PhD program was too important. I was thrilled to be continuing my education and to be focusing on a field I was passionate about. Expansion called to me—and I was compelled to answer.

I promised her we'd live in Seattle for only three years. I'd finish my coursework and then we'd return to the Bay Area, where I'd write my dissertation.

The morning we were ready to leave—my red Nissan packed to the brim, including two cats in carriers and our bikes clamped onto the back, and the U-Haul jam-packed but for a spot in the front seat for Emily and Mazie—TJ dropped by. In her black leather jacket, she hugged me then gloomily leaned in the doorframe, glaring at me with accusing eyes. That characterized our relationship, a friendly enmity. Emily said she needed time alone with her best friend, to say good-bye. I stayed behind and finished shampooing the carpet so we'd get our deposit back.

I was glad we were leaving the Bay Area and shaking up the ties. I was ready for a new adventure.

13

Negotiating the Self

Possibility is not luxury; it is as crucial as bread.
—Judith Butler

It's summer solstice in the U.S. and the first day of winter in Australia. The sun gleams, the air is soft. Dave is driving us down a narrow dirt road, through mud and across narrow, low bridges enveloped in roiling water. We park at a trailhead.

Finch-Hatton Gorge is isolated and super-oxygenated by enormous trees, with well-tended hiking trails. We follow a path up the mountain amidst a dreamy rainforest landscape. Even though it's a blue-sky Saturday, we are alone. As we near the top, we hear the song of a rushing waterfall. There it is, Araluen Falls, a glittering stream dropping from granite into a lucid pool.

We bypass the observation platform and inch down to a flat slab of rock. We sit enveloped in the ionic buzz of water splashing upon water. The pool sparkles like a disco ball. Mist tingles our sweaty skin.

The top of my head feels like it's opening. All of golden life flows, both entering me from an outside source and being generated within.

Later, we head to Noosa, where our lodging is a room in a pink five-bedroom house, dubbed the Pink Palace. We found the spot through a website where people offer rooms in their houses as alternatives to hotels. The owners—Lila and Phil—have traveled widely, including a two-month stint in China. They entered via Vietnam with no reservations or specific plans. Even though they spoke only English, Lila said they ate good food, always found places to stay, and met great people. China? I like their daring.

Like Santa Cruz, Noosa is a beach community surrounded by mountains. We hike through Noosa National Park. The curly, animated branches towering over the path look like the trees that threw their apples at Dorothy. We see magpies, herons, and a pair of colorful lorikeets.

In the dirt, someone has written "koala" with an arrow pointing left. We go that direction into a grove of gum trees. Perched high in the branches is a dozing koala. He looks gruffer than gentle Tinker Bell.

Our walk winds up and out of the forest. Suddenly we are edging cliffs with a dramatic, drop-down view of the sea. To our right, exotic flora. To our left, infinity.

Wait a minute. Did that round, spiky plant move?

Dave and I notice it at the same time and peer more closely. A head appears from a thorny lump, a face with a long gray beak and little half-mast eyes.

"It's an echidna," Dave whispers.

About the size of a rabbit, the creature is a sleepy cross between a porcupine and a miniature anteater. Like the platypus, it's an enigmatic creature, a mammal that lays eggs.

We're thrilled that this elusive creature has made an appearance. Many Australians have never seen one in the wild. Dr. Doolittle snaps pictures until it waddles off into the brush.

*

In a small community north of Seattle, Emily and I rented a dream house on the Puget Sound. Out our bedroom window, fishing boats and container ships drifted by, as well as the occasional bald eagle and whale. The snow-capped Olympic mountain range hovered in the distance.

Because rent was cheaper in Washington than California, we could afford a two-bedroom beach pad with a low-slung ceiling, fireplace, office, and large basement with high windows for Emily's art studio. The big back yard, strewn with fruit trees, had room for a vegetable garden. At the end of our block was a bar where salty characters hung out, playing pool. We could walk two blocks to a rocky beach, or up the street to a little neighborhood park, small store, and Greek restaurant.

When we met the landlords, a couple in their forties, I sensed they liked us immediately. I wondered if they had lesbian friends or family members. There was something about the way they treated us that made me feel extra welcome—not only accepted but esteemed.

Being a lesbian could be like being a celebrity. Some people admired our status as social outlaws. Occasionally strangers smiled at us in public, implying that they admired us, or that they were fascinated by our special club. Some straight people who were appalled by homophobia went out of their way to let us know so. They'd ask our opinions about politics, about the fight for same-sex marriage. They'd want us to meet their lesbian friends or sisters.

The flip side was bad vibes projected our way. At times we were thrown dirty looks. Now and then, people would assume Emily was a man. When they realized their mistake, or when we corrected them, most people became flustered or embarrassed, but some expressed annoyance or veiled anger. We were like Geiger counters. We knew whom to gravitate toward and whom to avoid based on people's vibes.

Once on a road trip from Seattle to the Oregon coast, we stopped for food in Aberdeen, Washington, the backwater hometown of Kurt Cobain. As we sat in a restaurant booth near a window, two leather-clad women—one with long hair, one with short—drove into the parking lot on a motorcycle. At that moment, two lumberjacks next to us started laughing. One said, "Ugh, dykes," and then proceeded to lift an imaginary machine gun and rattle off rounds in their direction.

"Oh my God, Emily, did you see that?" I said. "Assholes."

"Shhh," she hushed me. "Don't you dare say anything. Let's get out of here." She grabbed the bill and rushed to the register. I followed her, my heart pounding, my eyes keeping track of the dudes through the back of my head. I wanted so badly to put those guys in their place. What would I say? I didn't know. Something about how fucking uncool it was to pretend they were committing a hate crime.

As we stood paying our bill, the two women walked in, holding hands. Holding hands? In Aberdeen? So bold. The guys in the booth shrunk in my estimation to petty, silly middle-school boys exerting their squeaky masculinity through name-calling and dim-witted pranks.

I shared my insight with Emily as we drove away, how the guys were insecure dorks, and the women beautiful and powerful bad asses. They did not live in fear. They were being themselves, damn the torpedoes.

A few years earlier when Emily, TJ, and I first started hanging out, we went to the campus pub after poetry class. From a group of beer-drinking football players in the corner came laughing and, harshly, *Dykes.*

TJ marched to their table in her black, steel-toed boots. Towering over them she said, "Do you have something to say to me?"

Their smiles disappeared. They looked shrunken, pale, alarmed.

"Well?" said TJ.

"No," squeaked one of the guys.

"I didn't think so," she said.

I'd admired TJ's bravado and wanted to do something similar to the Aberdeen guys. I thought they might be taken aback to be confronted by a woman, especially a feminine white woman with long blond hair. But Emily said we shouldn't mess around in a small town like that. You never knew what would happen. Worse things than you could even imagine. The world was a dangerous place.

Once I'd suggested we apply for the Peace Corps. Or what if

I got a job overseas? She wasn't comfortable with that. She knew I wouldn't be happy pretending we were sisters or friends. You never knew how people in foreign countries would take the lesbian thing. Best to hang out in places where you knew you'd be safe.

Sometimes I thought she was her own worst enemy. She said I didn't understand because I was raised as a gender conformist in a middle-class household. I had an inborn sense of safety. She, on the other hand, had endured times in childhood with no food or electricity. Her mother had left her at her grandmother's for weeks, months, at a time. Emily's childhood haunted her. She knew the world wasn't a safe and beautiful place. To top it off, as a gender nonconformist she had a more difficult time navigating the world. Even using public restrooms was stressful because when she walked into the women's room, strangers did a double take.

I realized the fact that I visually fit into my gender category made things easier for me. Still, it seemed crazy to make concessions to a homophobic society. We were in a position to change the world. If we were following the truth of our love, shouldn't we go for broke? If we died in the line of fire, at least we were fighting for what we believed in. I knew the abomination of hate crimes occurred. But the likelihood of a hate crime directed toward us was statistically much less than getting in a car accident. I wasn't afraid to drive a car. Why be afraid to live out loud?

Besides, things weren't so black and white. There was something about Emily's sweet boy-girl quality that drew people to her. We laughed about how strangers would offer her candy as though they intuited she loved sweets. I'd never seen anything like it—a grocery store clerk pouring M&Ms into Emily's palm, an old lady behind us in line at the post office offering her a stick of gum.

And her difficult, poverty-stricken childhood made her sensitive to others' plights. Once, at a taqueria, Emily noticed a disheveled guy rifling through half-eaten discarded food. She walked across the room and asked him if she could buy him something. He thanked her and asked for a burrito.

She chatted with him while his food was being prepared. When it came, she returned to our table and told me about him: his name, where he'd been working, how he was down on his luck. My heart felt so tender toward her. I hadn't even noticed the guy. It had never crossed my mind that rifling through dirty tables at a restaurant was a strategy for getting free grub. Emily's life experiences had created compassion in her.

That day I began to see the world a little differently. When I came across a woman who stood begging, her child on her hip, in front of Walgreens, I invited her inside to pick out what she wanted: diapers, baby wipes, baby food. If not for knowing Emily, I don't think I would have thought to do such a thing. Emily was more powerful than she knew.

Her compassion and unconventionality made her an excellent teacher. Not long after we moved to Seattle, she was hired to teach art at a middle school. The students loved her. Still, the kids—being kids—wanted to know more about her. One day, a kid in class raised his hand and asked:

"Are you a lesbian?"

She'd been around the block enough to catch the vibe of the

question. She had a good relationship with this kid. He wasn't being cruel. He was truly curious. Her answer was brilliant.

"Is this school a place where someone can answer 'yes' to that question and feel safe?"

The kid thought for a moment and softly said, "No."

A few of the other kids talked about how often they heard the words "fag" and "dyke" at school—and how the word "gay" was used as a universal pejorative for everything from bad cafeteria food to stupid homework assignments.

"Well, once that changes," said Emily, "perhaps people can freely answer such a question."

I thought it was a skillful way to come out. Instead of coming out as a lesbian (although that was certainly implied), she came out as a person for justice and equality. The school, like most, was a homophobic hotbed. It wasn't up to one lesbian to change that. It was up to everyone.

I became engrossed in my doctoral program and was hired as a research assistant. I loved being expected to spend most of my time reading, writing, and talking about juicy ideas. I fell in with the queer theory and educational philosophy crowd. We drank beer for hours in a local pub, arguing the fine points of Foucault, Bakhtin, Butler, Sedgwick. Post-modernism and critical theory blew my mind. Reality is a human construction? Gender is performed? Emotions are relational? It all struck a deep chord, as though these theories intricately explained things I knew intuitively but didn't have the language for. I was learning how to look below the surface. So much squirmed in the soil like earthworms.

Lights turned on in rooms I didn't even know existed. I learned there was a word for what had bothered me so much as I tried to navigate the tensions of being a lesbian teacher: heteronormativity. The notion that heterosexuality was "normal" was a societally controlling mechanism! Language revealed our assumptions: that heterosexuality is *natural and normal*, and homosexuality is *unnatural and deviant*. These human-constructed ideas served to form and control people's ideas and behavior. When marginalized people were duped into buying the beliefs of people in power, they developed internalized racism, internalized homophobia. Emily's fears? Internalized homophobia!

No wonder some arguments against homophobia felt like running in circles. Saying that homosexuality was "just as natural" as heterosexuality meant attempting to use the master's tools to disassemble the master's house. Audre Lorde proclaimed such dismantling impossible. New tools were needed. How about saying, "There's nothing wrong with homosexuality. So who cares if it's natural or not? Who cares if it's a choice or not? It doesn't matter because people are free to do as they wish!"

That was a revelation for me. In the stories I'd read about lesbians who came out later in life, most proclaimed they'd been in denial their whole lives. Even if they'd loved men, dated men, been married to men, and had children with men, they claimed they could look back now and see that, really, they were lesbians all along. Upon retrospect, their love for their first-grade teacher was a homoerotic attachment, or their curiosity about another girl's body in middle school proved their suppressed lesbianism. That was the primary story: *I fell in love with a woman in my thirties, but really I was a lesbian all along.* Certainly this was true for some women. But it didn't feel that way for me. Sure, I could look back at the attraction I felt toward the redhead in Japan and toward the Planned Parenthood doctor as indications of my "true" sexual identity. But to feel I must claim a truth about my sexuality denied the complexity I felt.

The question isn't, "What is the truth?" The question is, "How is this story told, and whom and what does this story serve?"

When I discovered the Kinsey Scale, it was a revelation. Sexologist Albert Kinsey developed a scale to reflect an array of sexualities possible beyond the homo/hetero binary. The six-point scale delineates "total heterosexuality" on one end and "total homosexuality" on the other. Those on the extreme ends of the scale have never experienced the minutest homosexual or heterosexual attraction or fantasy. Kinsey's research showed that most American men and women could be placed somewhere along the middle of the scale. He also concluded that at different times in our lives, we can be at different points on the scale. That rang true for me.

When I asked Emily where she thought she sat on the scale, I expected her to give herself a "six": complete and total homosexuality. She said "five." I was immediately intrigued.

"Why not a six?" I asked.

She smiled. "Well, I think Denzel Washington is pretty hot."

She also told me about a short-lived liaison she'd had with a guy when she was a late teen. They'd meet and kiss in dark corners of the building where they worked. It never went beyond that, but she'd enjoyed it. I was stunned! I'd put her into a box and hadn't realized it.

The social justice philosophies I encountered—and made use of in my dissertation—spoke eloquently to my strong feelings about fairness. Yet I didn't buy victim narratives. I was beginning to believe in radical freedom. I salivated over Foucault's *Discipline and Punish*, as best as I could understand it. While he argued that systems such as prisons, schools, factories, and the military used constant observation and physical control to exert power, he also spoke of how power is not uni-directional. The term "those in power" always irked me; was there really such a thing as a group in control? Foucault argued for flux. For every exertion of power, there is a reaction. Like language, power is slippery. Cracks are created, and people slip through. That is how change is possible.

Gay pride came about because of a response to prejudicial laws and crackdowns on queer people. Without an attempt to control gays, there would have been no counter fight for gay rights. Attempts to control created new strength. The American peace movement of the 1960s would never have come about without governmental attempt to exert power over so many young men who didn't want to go to war. Fundamentally, I believed that every exertion of power had a freedom response. Attempts to control were doomed to fail at some point because we all have the potential for power, power that we are often unaware of until we are prodded, pushed, pulled, or plundered. As Foucault said, "We are freer than we think."

Learning about transgender people enhanced my understanding of freedom and fluid identity. My first encounter with a trans person occurred before we moved to Seattle. My college friend, Cynthia, came out to me as a lesbian. How cool that one of my friends was also falling in love with a woman! Then Cynthia told me that her partner, Vicky, used to be a man. I didn't quite know what to do with that information. I wondered if that meant Cynthia was not really a lesbian. I discovered I wasn't the only one with such a reaction. Trans people and their partners are often met with misunderstanding and prejudice from gay and straight people alike. Any challenge to what is "natural" raises hackles. After meeting Vicky and reading *She's Come Undone*—Jennifer Finney Boylan's wonderful memoir about her transition from male to female—I began to better understand such a journey. I began to believe that everyone should have the right to be whatever version of whatever gender they wanted. What if there weren't two genders but three, four, five, six, seven? Who could say? Trans, gender-queer, post-op, non-op—whatever someone wanted to claim, wasn't that their right? Weren't they still a person to be afforded dignity?

I was deeply moved by a French film, *Ma Vie en Rose*, about a boy named Ludovic who wishes to be a girl. In one scene, Ludovic tells his grandmother that he's going to marry his friend Jerome when he's "not a boy." Instead of arguing with him that he will always be a boy, the grandmother says, "You have a lot to teach me." That was my ideal: to turn toward what I didn't understand so that it could teach me.

My doctoral program was opening my mind in new and exciting ways. Yet the method of talking about ideas around the seminar table and pub table leaned toward combative. In those contexts, verbal sparring was fun. We were playing an intellectual game.

This disposition didn't transfer to my life outside of school. In talking to my friends and family, anything less than a rigorous examination of an idea seemed naive. I made use of my developed intellectual muscle to insist *everyone* see *every* nuance of homophobia, heteronomativity, sexism, and racism; that everyone become aware of the tensions between social justice and radical freedom; that everyone examine their unquestioned beliefs. If they refused to see the light, heat rose in my chest. Sometimes, to my chagrin, what I'd hoped would be a civil discussion developed into an argument. I knew I was on the attack but couldn't seem to help myself. Was it my calling to force others to face the truth of these crucial matters?

My friends in the doctoral program were the only ones who "got it." I loved sitting around a seminar table or in a pub booth as we deliberated our way into intellectual ecstasy. My impatience grew with those who hadn't learned these concepts and the specialized vocabulary. Ironic, given that my studies focused on fairness, compassion, flexibility, and freedom.

As much as I loved my academic life, I felt agitation with something fundamental. Was this disturbance rising in the contrast between school and home? I didn't know. I began to feel overwhelmed. Everything got to me. The dog had to be walked. The cat boxes cleaned. Groceries shopped for. Dinner made. The garden planted. Calls returned. Emails written. Books read. Notes taken. Papers written. Grad assistant work done. Interviews completed. Data analyzed. Dissertation proposal written and defended. When would I get it all done? While arguing about Foucault's notion of "docile bodies" in a pub was fun, I'd arrive home afterward sparking with edginess.

To ease my agitation, I began listening to meditation tapes and reading books on Buddhism. Not that I didn't have more than enough to read for school, but I needed something to provide relief. My yoga teacher's invitation, years ago, to reside in the *now* still resonated. I thought wisdom from the East might soften the restless workings of my mind.

Pema Chodron spoke directly to me. Ease up on myself. Release aggression. Don't fixate on the past or the future. Come back to the breath. Pema told me there's wisdom in acceptance: "We can spend our whole lives escaping from the monsters of our minds." The knife of my mind scraped at me. I didn't want to fight with myself.

Still, I couldn't quite get a handle on making peace between my philosophical ideas and my life. There were times I sank into the couch, the tranquility of our cocoon, and was seduced into believing *this* was all that mattered: a glass of wine, bread and cheese, a good TV show, a tree out the window bending in the wind. Sometimes I wanted to burrow into a domestic hole and forget about the rest of the world.

When I finished my dissertation proposal, I had to undergo a proposal defense. I was led to think the defense was a mere formality. My four committee members had read the proposal and guided me with feedback. Now the goal was to support me in the next step of gathering and analyzing my data, and of writing five chapters of my project, a study of gay and lesbian teachers called *Negotiating the Self.*

I walked into the room and sat at the seminar table, ready to engage in a conversation with my greatest allies: four professors who believed in me. Surprisingly, one of my committee members began attacking my project. She asked me to define my key terms and then played devil's advocate, aggressively stating that I might not understand exactly what I was doing. I had it all wrong.

I was shocked. She had been the one person on my committee who'd been most supportive of what I was doing. In her fifties, she herself had fallen in love with a woman for the first time after years of marriage to a man. She'd told me this in confidence, making clear she hadn't come out to many people. She gave me excellent advice about how to proceed with my project. She urged me to call it not a "dissertation" but a "book" so that I could visualize it as a finished, published project.

But now this professor whom I'd discerned as my greatest ally was filled with enmity. What happened? Why was she out to get me? Shaken, I did my best to stay detached and answer her questions when all I wanted was to crawl under a rock.

The committee dismissed me so they could deliberate. I stood in the hallway, trembling. When they called me back in, the attacking professor smiled broadly and told me I had passed. She reached forward to shake my hand and then gave me a hug. I stiffened.

Later I talked to a friend in the program. What the hell had happened?

"Oh, Kate," he said, "she's a trained analytic philosopher. She's softened a lot over the years as she's become more focused on humanism, but in a situation that involves a defense, she is trained to attack ideas rigorously. That's all. Don't take it personally. It's all a game."

14

Special Delivery

What if rather than being disheartened by the ambiguity, the uncertainty of life, we accepted it and relaxed into it?
—Pema Chodron

Dave and I wake to Vivaldi's *Four Seasons*. Quentin is on the piano downstairs, accompanied by a violin. We rise, roll out our yoga mats, and stretch to the music. We have a week left in Brisbane, and it feels like we are perched on the edge of leaving home.

We've become settled into Quentin's apartment. Sometimes we go out to dinner with Quentin and Lilian. Other nights, they join us upstairs. We drink champagne, Quentin's favorite, and have a dessert of Lamingtons, a white cake with chocolate and coconut crust.

We play cards, spend afternoons reading while Quentin teaches piano lessons. Some mornings I sit on the couch writing in my journal near the portable heater while Dave cooks breakfast in the kitchen. From my perch I watch him drop rice and leftover veggies into a fry pan, cracking a couple of eggs over the top like he used to do at the Love Nest.

At times I become awash with the feeling that I should be doing something else, like grading papers, preparing to teach a class, volunteering at a literacy center, writing a grant, planning the future...

I think about how yesterday, we hiked through nearby Toohey Forest, then up to the top of Mt. Gravatt. There at a little cafe, overlooking the distant panorama of the city, we drank ginger beer. A hearse came winding up the road, the silhouette of a casket visible through the smoky windows.

One voice judges me, tells me, *Be productive.*

Another voice says, *Just be.*

In a private concert for ninety people in a palatial Brisbane home, Quentin sits at a grand piano that once belonged to Victor Borge. He is joined by an oboe, clarinet, horn, bassoon, and flute from the Queensland Symphony Orchestra.

They play the weirdly eerie and sublime music of an early twentieth-century French composer named Francis Poulenc. Poulenc was both a devout Catholic and a gay man. Quentin calls Poulenc and his music "half priest, half clown."

When the crowd leaves, Quentin sits at the piano and spontaneously plays a grand Schubert. Centuries collide. Time folds over, touching at the edges. Tomorrow we will be on another continent.

*

Emily and I were vegetarians who consumed mounds of comfort food. Salt-and-vinegar potato chips. Cartons of chocolate-peanut butter ice cream. Pasta soaked in melted cheese. Bottle after bottle of wine and beer. There was nothing more soothing after weeks of gray skies and windy days than snuggling on the couch with something warm descending into our bellies, wrapped in the haze of wine and TV.

I loved the feather comforter on our bed, our maroon couch and big chair, a log in the fireplace, a cat curled between my legs. We had three cats by this time, and they piled on us every night in bed. I loved waking to the view of the water, birds drifting by. I loved reading for hours in our warm cocoon. I loved my little office with its comfy chair and computer. Out the window I watched the cats and squirrels play chase in the rain-soaked yard.

Even when it wasn't raining in Seattle, the sky was usually gray. Emily and I laughed the first time we heard a weather reporter alert us to a "sun break" expected in the afternoon. As native Californians, we were used to living in a perpetual sun break. One morning when I woke to yet another sallow sky, my eyes searched and searched for a ray of sunshine. I missed the sun terribly. Where was it? A wave of claustrophobia clutched at my chest. I lay there, trying to catch my breath. I was shocked. Even though I was safe in my own home, I had the sensation of feeling trapped in an airplane or an elevator. When the feeling dissipated, I wondered what the hell had happened.

Still, the air was fresh and the Cascade mountain range stunning. I liked the feeling of being under an umbrella, rain pattering away, as long as the wind wasn't whipping. When I took a walk to the beach, I was always happy I had. Cruising down the hill was like rambling through a charming fishing village. Mazie pranced on her leash. When I let her off, she bounded along the water's edge, sniffing at driftwood and dead creatures. The cold, the movement, revived me and Mazie alike. After trudging back up the house, my skin tingled at the contrast between frosty outdoors and warm indoors.

For the most part, though, I moved my body very little. Seattle gave me an excuse to sink even more deeply into a resistance I had fostered for years. I associated exercise with patriarchy, with double standards. I had spent too many years running, working out on gym equipment, doing aerobics—all for one purpose: to look beautiful for men. I thought of dieting the same way. I wouldn't strive to be eye candy.

Who needed to focus on the body, anyway, when the world of my mind felt so vast and rich? If I wasn't slung on the couch reading, or sitting before my computer writing, I was perched on a chair around a seminar table on campus. These were the most comfortable places to be while rain drizzled on a cold afternoon.

I'd see people running the stairs in the park, their breath puffs of cotton, and I'd mock their exertion to justify my inertia. With all the eating and drinking, I often felt blurred and lumpy. After one too many hangovers, we'd vow to not drink for a while but by the evening we'd shrug and pull a bottle of wine from the shelf. When most of my clothes became too tight, I'd vow to eat lighter, only to binge that evening on something, anything, thick with melted cheese. Emily would forgo buying ice cream during the weekly grocery shopping but then jump in the car at night to go to the little store up the street to buy Ben & Jerry's.

The fatter we got, the more we lost interest in sex. Or was it the other way around? We cuddled. Kissed. Snuggled in bed. Gave each other foot rubs and skin tickles. We talked for hours about school and work, about our dreams and fears, about the past and future. Whenever anything happened to me at school—any interesting interaction, an intriguing insight, a funny thing in class—I'd store it in my mind to tell it to her.

We were so very, very close. But our sexual fire had died.

I'd read about lesbian bed death—a supposedly inevitable regression into a sexless state when women lovers morph into celibate best friends. I didn't buy that bed death was a gendered thing. I'd experienced waning sexual interest in my marriage to Ray. I knew of other straight couples this had happened to.

A friend of mine argued that bed death was much more common in lesbian relationships than in gay or straight ones because men have a stronger sex drive. When a man lost interest in sex, forget it, the relationship was over. Male sexual energy, she said, keeps the sex life alive. Women, though, naturally aren't as sexual as men. So two women together? Vanishing sexual vitality was normal. Lesbian bed death didn't have to mean end of the relationship, she said. Two women could happily live together sexless for a long time. Sex wasn't everything. It was possible to be sensual and not sexual.

I didn't speak to anyone about Emily's and my sex life. Everyone, even my closest friends, assumed our relationship was close to perfect, that we were soul mates, that we were the ideal lesbian couple, and that we had a hot sex life. We both did a lot to foster that perception.

For years whenever people asked us how we met, we launched into the long, sweet, dramatic story that portrayed us as a kind of lesbian Romeo and Juliet. We believed in the story. We clung to it as a balm that soothed the cracked edges of our love.

Almost all of my writing—poetry, memoir, fiction, academic prose—featured lesbian life. One poem about our devotion, titled "First," was sparked from Emily's declaration that she couldn't live without me. We spent a morbid amount of time worrying about who would die first. The poem—which later appeared in my poetry collection *Like All We Love*—perpetuated our status as an iconic lesbian couple. Whenever I performed the poem, it was the hit of the evening. *I have to die first you say…so you think I'm the strong / one, the one who can stand being left…When we were in bed / last night we imagined how we'd go. Our / favorite: I'm 100, you're 104. / Our hearts stop, just stop, gently you said, / in our sleep.*

The poem moved me to tears each time. I'd catch Emily's tender look as the audience clapped. It was a once-in-a-lifetime love. I stashed my unspoken reservations deep down, in a place dark and unvisited.

Emily missed the Bay Area. She missed her mother and TJ and the familiar streets. Even though my longing wasn't as deep, I too missed the Golden State, mainly for the weather. We played Joni Mitchell's song "California" over and over, singing to it and twirling in the living room, intensifying our yearning for home.

Yet the ache went much deeper in her. I'd try to buoy her, encouraging her to work on her art. Art could bolster her mood, and she was capable of making such beautiful things. Yet she was stymied. She talked about *wanting* to make art. She bought a potter's wheel, a kiln, paints, color pencils, and canvasses, but the creative process eluded her. She enrolled in an art class at the community college and completed pieces by the required deadlines. But once the class was over, she abandoned her studio that was packed to the gills with dusty art materials.

At times I'd get frustrated. Why be so glum? There were possibilities galore in a new place. We would return to California one day, a day that would be here before we knew it. Once when she was in an especially foul mood—nothing about Seattle was right; why had I brought her here?—I said if she was so unhappy, why didn't she just go back? I'd join her when I finished my program. She looked at me like I'd slapped her.

"What, and have a long-distance relationship?" She said the phrase *long-distance relationship* like one might say *serial killer on the loose.*

"If that's what will make you happy," I countered angrily.

"That would mean the end of us," she said. "Long-distance relationships don't work."

She'd told me before that she felt this way. As much as I loved her, part of me thought I'd be relieved if we got some space from each other. Space would lead us organically down the path to bring us closer together or pull us apart. Maybe we needed to try something different, something other than forcing out the story, again and again, of the perfect love.

Befriending the neighbors gave Emily a bit of a spark. Across the street lived an elderly couple we'd chat with as they worked in their yard. Next door lived a young Nordic couple with two hearty blond babies. And on the other side lived a couple about our age, Jim and Polly. Emily and Jim became buddies. He brewed his own beer, and she helped out, fascinated by the process. They'd sample the beers in his man cave, listening to music and playing pool.

Emily joined a hiking group. One of the women in the group—Val, the wife of a teacher at Emily's school—lived up the street. Val and Emily carpooled to the trails together. Once I detected a certain energy between them. The way Val glanced at Emily. The way Emily glanced back. It was subtle, but my intuition shouted in my gut. Jealousy flared in me.

I'd seen it before. There was something about Emily that attracted certain straight women—me, for example! Her handsomeness, as Gabriele had called it; the touch of masculinity combined with sweet womanliness. I once joked that butch women were the gateway drug to lesbianism for straight women. We both thought that was hilarious.

One day I asked Emily, "Do you think Val has a crush on you?"

Emily flushed. "Yeah, I think maybe," she admitted.

I don't recall talking much more about it. But when the hiking class was over, they stopped hanging out. I had a feeling something may have happened between them. Not sex but something like a mutual acknowledgement of their attraction. Who knew? It was too painful and verboten to ask.

Then there was me. I was developing a crush on Cole, a student in my program. He was married and had two little boys. His wife was a delicate thing, pale and blond and painfully shy. He confided in me that she was deeply depressed and that their marriage was in trouble. I was sure I was an exciting breath of fresh air in comparison. As my crush grew, I began to take less refuge in food. I dropped a few pounds, started to feel pretty, put on a little mascara, highlighted my hair. I couldn't wait to see him in class and to talk to him after class, just as I'd felt with Emily in poetry class five years before. I wondered if he thought I was safe to befriend because I was a lesbian. In class and at the pub, we'd discuss fluid sexuality, and the electricity in my skin sparked. Intellect met libido. *Would I be a lesbian forever?* I dropped the thought like a searing hot stick pulled from a fire.

Cole and I were invited to a conference in Chicago. I flew in a day early to visit Gabriele, who now lived in Chicago with her new husband, Rich, an orthopedic surgeon and photographer. They lived downtown in a stylish loft, filled with colorful, Piscasso-esque paintings made by a local artist. I arrived late and slept hard. By the time I awoke, Gabriele was in the kitchen, in her yoga clothes, making oatmeal. She'd already jogged a mile in the frosty morning to the yoga studio, participated in a yoga class, and jogged back. I admired the way she—a woman in her fifties—inhabited her lanky, youthful body.

She confided in me that she'd had a rough couple of years. She and her beau, a man she'd been with for fifteen years, had parted. It broke her heart. Teaching became impossible. She had panic attacks. In California, he lived down the street from her. She needed to get away.

So she took a sabbatical and rented out her house, coming to Chicago to be near her daughter, who introduced her to Rich. They'd recently married. Emily and I had been invited to the wedding, but we'd been unable to attend. Gabriele regaled me with stories about the ceremony. At the reception, Joan Baez had entered unannounced, playing a tambourine and singing a love song.

Joan and Gabriele had become friends a few years back. Joan called Gabriele to thank her for her book *Writing the Natural Way*. Joan said she'd had writer's block; working through the book had helped the flow of poems and lyrics return. She began mailing pieces to Gabriele for feedback. Living not too far from each other, they started to visit in person, and a friendship was born.

That Gabriele would draw Joan Baez into her circle said a lot about Gabriele's power as a creativity guru. I thought I'd become a bit jaded about such things in my hyper-intellectual doctoral program. But being around Gabriele again, and basking in her artistic and loving flair, warmed me inside out. I ached to tell her about my attraction to Cole. I thought she might offer words of wisdom. But I'd shoved everything down so deeply that to consider surfacing it frightened me. I was afraid I'd trigger an avalanche. There would be no turning back. I was too invested in my love for Emily. My identity as a lesbian felt intractable.

Cole picked me up in a rental car. Being a passenger with a man at the wheel felt vaguely familiar, like a dream of a past life. My stomach clenched, my blood heated up. As we rode along, as we stopped for gas, as we ate lunch together, did people think we were a couple?

During downtime at the two-day conference, Cole and I

talked for hours in the hotel restaurant. Drinking beer and wine, we dissected papers that had been presented, chewing on philosophical notions, the air between us ignited by desire. By this point, I was pretty sure he had feelings for me, too.

I learned something new: Cole loved to sail. He'd grown up with boats. But his wife didn't like the sea. Cole had a dream to buy the perfect boat and sail around the world. I felt the ache in his yearning, saw the bittersweet gleam in his eye. I understood escape fantasies. I had plenty of mine. The primary one being a man, like Cole, sweeping me off my feet. I would disappear, offering no explanations to anyone.

It was late. The waitress approached and asked us if we'd like anything else. They were closing. Cole walked me to the elevator. He was staying in the first floor on the conference hotel; I was staying on the fifth. In a haze of wine and longing, I stood close to him. His seductive lankiness hovered over me.

"Good night, Kate," he said. His voice sounded different, like we were on an international phone call, far away yet intimately close, his imaginary lips to my ear over oceans and continents.

I stepped into the elevator. As the doors slid shut I watched him slowly disappear.

At times I awoke from a dead sleep, orgasming. The first time it happened I was shocked. I thought only men had wet dreams. When the desire for sexual release became an ache, I'd masturbate when home alone, trying to let the guilt evaporate when Emily returned. Something strange happened in my mind. I could hit the reset button and erase the act. Delete the lie.

At least I wasn't cheating with another person. Resigned to a sexless life, I shelved my libido like a dusty jar of plum jam, sweet and lovingly created, into the dark recesses of my heart.

To make a baby, two women don't need sex anyway. Emily was ready. Her biological clock was ticking. We asked a gay friend of ours if he'd donate his sperm. He was honored we asked. It was perfect: he loved the idea of progeny but didn't want to be a dad. He'd let us raise the baby. He would be the loving, non-meddlesome uncle.

One afternoon, he arrived at our house. He went to the bathroom and took care of business into a cup. He bounded out, smiled, and said: "Special delivery!"

Surrounded by candles, incense and Emily's handmade ceramic goddess box, we inseminated her using a device from a medical supply store. Afterward, we held each other, willing the sperm and egg to join. Our baby would bring new life to our love.

15

Into the Mystic

It's right underneath your fingers, baby. That's all you have to understand—everything is right underneath your fingers.
—*Ray Charles*

On his guitar, our friend Austin plays his sweet and gravelly rendition of my favorite song, "Into the Mystic." With Austin's wife, Fiona, Dave and I recline in their southern California living room, jet lag-mellow after our flight from Australia.

The first time I heard the song, I didn't catch the lyrics, yet I cried, from the yearning feel of it. When I learned the words, I understood its longing—to be free of the fear of dying, to embrace life's journey.

As Austin plays, the fireplace crackles and sea air drifts in through the screen. Today would have been Gabriele's seventy-sixth birthday. This morning I read a piece on her daughter's blog about how as her mother was dying, Gabriele said she was experiencing an awakening. She'd said she felt no fear.

The next day, Dave and I ride bikes through Venice Beach and Santa Monica. I think about how living isn't possible without dying. While we're alive, shouldn't we, as the song implores, *let our soul and spirit fly?*

I think about how often we humans wriggle out of the present by tormenting ourselves about the past, by obsessing about the future, and by harshly judging ourselves and others.

I wonder if riding a bike has any meaning. Is this moment merely about pushing my feet onto the pedals, the sun and sea air on my skin?

Is this really enough? If I'm not going back to teaching, or setting up house, or raising kids, or going to therapy, or introducing bills to Congress...does my life have a purpose? Do we have to have purpose—other than to *let our soul and spirit fly?*

Is every moment an opportunity to wake up?

There is only one now. There are infinite nows. Perhaps grace is this moment. Perhaps grace is the fact that *now* is always here for us to return to.

I think of Walt Whitman, "I loaf and invite my soul."

I think about how when they picked us up at the airport, Austin and Fiona asked, *Is this all the stuff you have?* It's been only a couple of months, but I can barely remember what's in our storage. A small Love Nest's worth of furniture. Boxes packed with a tablecloth our friend Eran brought us from Indonesia, and cloth napkins our friend Cathy brought us from Rio. Purple couch, Tempur-Pedic.

I love the world of things but I don't have to own them. Things I see as I glide by on the bike, shiny cars and blue water and vast white sand. Venice Beach tattoos. Waft of pot smoke. Cleavages, dreadlocks, leather hot pants. Tarot cards, tie-dye. Break dancers, sweat glistening.

Is that enough? To love? Is it enough to just be?

*

It was another sunny Santa Cruz day. I walked, picking up my pace to a jog, reveling in moving my body down the street away from Emily's and my house and toward the beach. In minutes I reached West Cliff Drive. To my left, the Boardwalk. Roller coasters and cotton candy and kids on the beach. To my right, miles of road that snaked high along the cliff, following the shoreline.

When Emily and I moved back to Santa Cruz from Seattle, I was as ashen and rotund as Casper the Friendly Ghost. Most mornings I awoke to a bright room, golden light flooding in. Or, if I awoke to fog, by noon it split open like a gray curtain. California beckoned. I began to move my body again. I hiked, rode my bike, walked. Then one day I felt inspired to jog for a few minutes, just to see if I could. Maybe it was the ionic air. Maybe it was the muscled legs of women who jogged past me. Whatever, I began to run. Or more like scuttle. Or lope. My body wanted to move at a rate faster than walking, so I went along for the ride. A few hundred feet of scurrying and my lungs cried for mercy. My chest heaved. My face burned. I felt something…what was it? Something good.

Soon, almost every day I was outside moving my body. I sucked up ocean air, my lungs blossoming. Potato chips and candy lost their luster. My body craved fresh fruit and whole grains to replenish itself. Pounds melted away. My body reshaped, elongated, muscled up. This was the first time in my life I exercised because I enjoyed it, because it felt good, not as a way to punish myself or to sculpt my body into perfection for what I believed a man wanted. Running long, slow distances, especially near the beach or on a trail lined with redwoods, was my meditation and medication.

Running along West Cliff, I passed a picturesque seaside hotel, the place Emily and I spent our first night together six years ago. As I moved my body out in the world, my libido began to reassert itself, slowly at first, a tiny spider spinning a glistening web of desire. Little things would spark a phantom sexual feeling: a cool breeze through a window, the pulse of my calf muscle as I rubbed lotion into my skin, warm clothes pulled from the dryer.

Cole and I had never consummated what I was sure was a mutual attraction. He did, though, get a divorce after he finished his PhD. Sometimes he'd call me, and he'd share his dating fun and fiascos. I marveled at how my attraction to him had diminished. I enjoyed him as a friend.

Every so often Emily and I would make love. Then we'd drift back to non-sexual touch for months and months. I funneled my libidinous energy into work and the sweet, sunny outdoors. I was making good progress on my dissertation while teaching classes at U.C. Santa Cruz. Emily taught high school art full time. We lived in a little yellow Victorian house not far from the beach.

I picked up my pace on the elevated path, overlooking an expanse of ocean. In the distance, a dog dug like a maniac, scattering sand that glittered like mist. A line of pelicans flew horizontal to me, prehistoric wings outstretched. I imagined I, too, was flying. I passed the surfer statue, a colorful lei looped around his neck. I approached Steamer's Lane, a famous surfing spot. Waves were low. A few surfers bobbed on their boards, their black latex wetsuits gleaming in the sun like seals' pelts.

As I ran, I wondered if a tiny being was forming in the damp, dark recesses of my body. Our attempts to impregnate Emily in Seattle hadn't taken hold. We tried four or five times then decided to wait until we came back to California. Since I was in my late thirties, four years younger than Emily, we thought I was now the better candidate. This time, we used frozen sperm. We perused sperm banks online, examining profiles for smart, creative, healthy men. We wanted tall stature, dark hair, and Western European lineage, so the baby might have some of Emily's looks. When we picked our man, we input our credit card information and hit *send*. The sperm was FedExed overnight in an unassuming box. In goggles and gloves, Emily pulled the container from dry ice and heated it over the stove, while I lay on the bed inserted with the insemination device. With a syringe, she injected the device with semen. We visualized it swimming up to greet my awaiting egg.

Our desire to create life seemed more urgent these days because so much illness and death permeated our world. First, Georgia died. Lung cancer took her in her seventies.

Two of our cats died weeks apart. One slunk under a bush in

the backyard; we found her a few days later. The other stopped eating and drinking. Emily injected her with subcutaneous fluids to try to keep her hydrated, to no avail. Then our black lab, Mazie, began to decline. Toward the end she lay on a blanket in the living room, mute, her eyes dull. Emily agonized over calling in the vet to put down the dog. The living room smelled of dying. One evening, Mazie's body jerked then released. Emily called the vet. *Touch her eye*, said the vet tech, *If she doesn't flinch, she's gone*. The next day, our vet—a gentle, big man who worked primarily with horses—lifted Mazie's body, wrapped in a blanket, into his truck.

As I ran, I thought about how after the vet drove away, Emily and I took a walk along this very place, West Cliff. In her grief, Emily couldn't believe the sun was out, that people were walking around, that it was just another day. I thought of Brueghel's painting *Landscape with the Fall of Icarus*. Dying Icarus appears as a tiny splash in a vast body of water while boats sail, birds fly, and a plowman plows. In the midst of suffering, life goes on.

I, too, felt sad, but also profound relief, though I couldn't say that to Emily for fear she'd be offended. Mazie was no longer suffering. I took solace in the fact that everything that lives, dies. And maybe dying wasn't the end. I'd never forgotten what I'd experienced at Wes' funeral all those years ago, his body a shell in the casket and him hovering in the corner of the church, talking to me, consoling me. At times I also thought about the phantom woman stroking my head when I was a teenager—and that amazing dream I had years ago of a beach in heaven.

Whenever I hiked through the redwoods, I saw how fallen

trees decomposed, creating rich soil for saplings to emerge. As Walt Whitman wrote, "The smallest sprout shows there is really no death; / And if ever there was, it led forward life."

I ran up an incline and caught a glimpse of something dark in the cold and sparkling Pacific. I stopped at a railing to peer out, my breath fast in my chest. As I stretched my legs, I watched the dark spot. It took shape as a sea otter on its back, obsidian eyes shining. Her paws were wrapped around a rock, a tool used to break open a shell on her belly. I loved these creatures. I thought otters were good luck. Was this a sign the insemination had worked? The otter rolled over like a log a few times, cleaning her catch. I watched, entranced, until she disappeared under the water.

Then there were our parents. In one of those life ironies that could be called coincidence or design, Emily's mother and my father were deteriorating with lung disease. Both were on portable oxygen. Louise had emphysema, and my father had a degenerative lung disease called bronchiectasis. Diagnosed at age fifty, he was told he might live just a few years. But he didn't believe it, and now in his seventies, he had proved the doctors wrong.

As happens with chronic illnesses and war, there'd be long periods of routine punctuated by hair-raising emergencies. We'd get calls in the middle of the night: a fall, an intestinal blockage, an irregular heartbeat, a spiking fever. We raced over the hill to her mother's house, or three hours through the valley and into the foothills to my parents' house or the hospital, time and time again. So many moments at the edge of the cliff. So many this-is-it good-byes, followed by exhilarating yet grueling resurrections.

It seemed our parents' illnesses were all we talked about these days. We'd try to steer the conversation another direction, but inevitably it wound back to them. We wrote about worries, our sorrow, in our journals and our poems. Talk of our parents dominated our conversations with our friends who started discussions with "How's your mom/dad?"

I developed breathing difficulties. My chest and stomach felt super-glued together. I couldn't take a full breath. I was dizzy. Exhausted. I was overcome by a hacking a dry cough that wouldn't seem to go away. A doctor gave me an inhaler. It didn't seem to help. I had medical test after test. Asthma was ruled out. Leukemia. Other cancers. Finally it was determined: I had mono. Emily's body, too, was being affected. Her heart skipped beats, picked up its pace, then suddenly slowed down. Hooked up to machines, she walked on a doctor's treadmill. She was diagnosed with arrhythmia, cause unknown.

Even then it seemed clear that the causes of our ailments were related to anxiety. Yet I never considered that our minds might help ease the symptoms or cure us. No doctor talked to me about the mind/body connection. No doctor asked about what was going on in my life or gave me suggestions about how to avoid stress. I was told to drink lots of fluids and rest.

When the mono lifted, I found relief from stress in running. So here I was, encountering lucky sea otters, running along West Cliff, moving my body, a line of sweat running down my back, ocean air on my face. A *V* of pelicans lifted through the sky. I wanted to shake off my fears like a dog bounding from the sea shakes water from his coat.

After my run, I showered and packed then took the three-hour drive to Auburn. I often went to my parents' house on weekends. Sometimes Emily would come; sometimes I'd go alone. Mom needed a break. She was worn down from caregiving. Fortunately, my parents and I had reached a place in our lives where we enjoyed being together. We played cards, watched movies. Mom and I walked the neighborhood. When she retired from nursing, she delved into writing articles and romance novels. We edited each other's most recent work.

Still, I often grew fatigued, drained, after just a few days there. My father's needs were relentless. In the mornings, I helped him out of bed and into the living room, where he inhaled a series of medications while watching the morning news. I'd start the coffee and make the bed and pull the slant board from the closet, unfolding it onto the bedroom floor. I set out the portable suction machine and placed a cup of water next to it. In the garage, I filled up a small oxygen tank by hooking it onto the big tank, an awkward maneuver that took two or three tries.

Because of Dad's incurable, degenerative lung disease, his lungs would not clear on their own. Every day he needed therapy: him lying on the slant board, and someone (usually Mom) pounding his back, sides, and chest so he'd cough up phlegm. Without such therapy, he'd drown. There was a specific routine with his therapy and medications, never to be varied. That precision increased Mom's weariness. Dad insisted on exactness. He believed meticulousness kept him alive.

He lowered his body on the slant board, head at the low point, his feet tucked under a strap. With cupped hands I pounded one spot on his chest until he coughed up phlegm five times. Then the other side. Then he moved to his side, then his back. He coughed, hacked, wheezed. He spit into a plastic wand that suctioned the yellow goop. He examined this bodily secretion, seconds ago nestled in his dark lungs—because if it started to turn green, he knew it was time for a round of antibiotics.

I handed him a tissue. He removed the nose cannula, which fed him oxygen, to blow his nose. He took a few breaths and moved onto the next position.

In his white T-shirt and blue sweatpants, stringently following his routine, sweating and breathing hard, he struck me as a fierce competitor of his disease. I was in awe of his strength, this man whose X-rays revealed ruined lungs. (One doctor said, "It's amazing you're still alive.")

"Dad," I said, "you're like an athlete in training. You do this relentlessly every day, like an Olympian."

He paused, absorbing that notion. "Thank you for that. I'll never think of therapy the same way again"—said the man who'd been doing this routine for twenty-five years.

The process took two hours, including the cleaning of the machine, pouring his fluids down the toilet, rinsing the machine, pulling it apart to dry properly. Afterward he might need help showering, cutting his toenails, applying fungus cream to his feet. Then it was time to make breakfast.

As I broke eggs into a bowl, Dad's cough clattered from the living room. His labored breathing filled the air. Being in the same house with him was like living inside his body.

When I completed my PhD, a tenure-track faculty position opened up at San Jose State in Secondary Teacher Education. For years I'd been a lecturer. Lecturer positions offer low pay and no job security. A permanent position on the faculty of a university is the crème de la crème in academia. Even if a lecturer has been teaching on campus for years, a new tenure-track professor can receive a higher salary, better office space, benefits and retirement package, and a more desirable class schedule. Years of being a freeway flier, piecing together various teaching assignments to make ends meet, had been part of my impetus for pursuing a doctorate.

I was thrilled when I made it through the first round and was called in for an interview. Wearing a new suit, I walked into Sweeney Hall, where I'd be spending most of my interview day. I passed the classroom where, when I was married to Ray, Gabriele Rico floated through the door in a cloud of beauty and brainpower. I also passed the classroom where Emily and I had met in Georgia's poetry workshop. I walked by a few rooms where I'd taught classes. I drifted through my past, toward my future.

The interview was a grueling full day. I presented my research, taught a class, engaged in a one-on-one meeting with the dean, and met with faculty members at lunch. A few weeks later I was offered the job.

If my father was proud of me for completing my PhD, he was over the moon about my new academic position. Dad was a child during the Depression in Cleveland, Ohio. His mother, who worked as a waitress to support four children, had only an eighth-grade education. Because he flunked first and second grades, Dad didn't reach high school until he was sixteen—and still he still could barely read. He remembered as a teenager struggling to decipher the words in comic books.

As soon as he could, he joined the Navy. Once out of the Navy, he didn't know what to do. Following the lead of his friends who were taking advantage of the G.I. Bill, Dad went to college. Still struggling to read, he used his other smarts to get passing grades: listening closely in class, participating in discussions and study groups, memorizing for tests, avoiding classes that involved a lot of reading and writing, and asking friends (and eventually my mother) to edit and type his papers.

He realized that a college education meant moving up the social ladder. He'd not have to rely on manual labor. Dad was strong. He painted houses, built decks, cut down trees. But he liked to do these things on his own terms, out in the open air. One summer he was hired to work in a silver mine. During lunch break, when he was pulled up out of that dark hole, he walked away, not bothering to collect his half-day's wage. That experience hardened his resolve to finish college, get a teaching credential, become a teacher—and eventually go to grad school and become a college instructor and counselor.

Of their three daughters, I was the one destined to follow in my parents' footsteps and become an academic. The fact that I had achieved a higher step up the rung than my parents thrilled my dad. He believed in progress. He believed in the American Dream. He valued education tremendously, and he'd worked so hard—against the odds—to become an academic professional. Of course my mom was pleased, too, but my dad was the one most invested in my achievements.

Dad said he wanted to visit one of my classes. He wanted to see his university professor daughter in action. I had a hard time imagining him doing so. His disease had progressed to the point where it was difficult for him to take a few steps without gasping for breath. He insisted, though, and one day Dad and Mom came to campus. I showed them my office. They met the chair of my department and the dean. Dad's skin looked gray and his blue eyes weak. I asked him if he was still up for coming to class.

"Of course!" he said, a smile breaking out beneath his signature handlebar mustache. He'd had that mustache for thirty years, carefully waxing it each morning.

I introduced my parents to my students. The students said *hi* and *welcome*. My parents sat in the back, Mom helping Dad slide the oxygen tank off his shoulder to rest it on the floor. As I taught and bantered with my students, I was struck by the beauty, the gravity, of the moment. I was literally here on this planet, and here in front of this classroom, because of the two people sitting in the back.

Month after month, my period arrived. The inseminations were not taking hold. After an exam, my gynecologist told me there was no medical reason I wasn't getting pregnant. She added, however, that since I was forty, insemination—especially at home, where we were likely to be not as accurate—was less effective. She recommended I begin fertility medication and be inseminated in her office.

On my way home, an abrupt clarity came to me. I didn't want

to get pregnant. I could drum up all kinds of reasons: we were overwhelmed with care giving for our parents, I liked my freedom, I wanted to travel. But these reasons didn't quite strike at the heart of the matter. It was a sweeping feeling that could not be explained. A feeling not to be ignored.

Emily and I walked to the beach where, under the moon, we'd exchanged rings and vows all those years ago. We sat in the sand, and I broke the news to her that I'd changed my mind. I didn't want to have a baby.

She said, "I'm so relieved. I feel the same way."

"Really?" I said. "You told me from the beginning that you wanted a daughter."

"I know," she said. "But that feeling has been changing lately."

We talked about this surprising turn of events. For years we'd either been trying to get pregnant or planning for it. And now, we were giving it up.

We agreed that if either of us changed our minds, we'd reconsider. Maybe we'd adopt, or become foster parents. There were other options, if we decided we wanted a family after all.

That night, lying in bed, Emily sleeping next to me in the dark, I thought about the baby that never was. It was bittersweet to deliberately, consciously let go of the idea of being a mother. I hadn't grown up yearning for motherhood like many women I knew. Most of my friends, and both of my sisters, had children. Then there was me, always the oddball. I checked in with my heart. Was it broken? No. Something new was forming in my belly. An opening. A desire to do other things. A desire to write, to travel, to live the life of my dreams.

I'd always loved the idea of traveling but hadn't done much of it in my life, other than my forays to Japan and Korea and the trips I took with my family as a kid. Emily and I had taken a few short road trips. And once we went to Mexico to visit her brother and his family. But the two of us, going somewhere new and far away, designing our days in some foreign land as we saw fit? I loved the idea. Maybe such an adventure would reinvigorate our relationship, nudge us from our daily ruts and relieve our obsession with our parents' mortality.

I thought England would be a good place to start because at least we spoke the language. What if we went on winter break? What could be more magical than a Dickens Christmas?

"What if my mom dies while we're gone?" she asked.

"You've been saying that for years," I said.

Every Christmas she'd say, "This might be my mom's last Christmas." And then Emily would go all out, hauling a tree into her mom's house, decorating, making a huge meal. Louise didn't like the way the tree made her sneeze. She didn't want Christmas music on because it interfered with TV. Instead of coming to the dinner table, she wanted to eat in her recliner. Sometimes it felt like we were harassing her mother. Some holiday.

Finally, I talked Emily into it. Ten days in England. We'd leave the day after Christmas, though, so she wouldn't miss her mom's possibly-last-Christmas.

That Christmas night, after the meal at Louise's, I lay in bed, anxious. Was traveling a mistake? Our house was comfortable and warm. What had I been thinking to uproot us, especially in winter, especially to a place where we'd have to take a ten-hour flight? My throat tightened at the thought of being gripped by claustrophobia on the airplane.

I rolled over. Emily was still awake.

"Want to change your mind?" I said, half-joking.

"Maybe," she replied. I could feel her smile in the dark. "We could just not go, you know. No one is making us."

"That's true," I said. "We are our own bosses."

We giggled and snuggled up together.

In London, we stayed at a Victorian-era hotel near Hyde Park and walked for miles every day, through parks and cathedrals and museums. I couldn't believe the museums, filled with incredible treasures, were free. When we got cold and hungry, we stopped at low-ceilinged pubs for pints and surprisingly tasty food. I thought England's food was supposed to suck. But I liked it. We sat by a roaring fire eating a whole fried fish with chips, doused in malt vinegar. Or a savory bowl of soup or a stuffed potato. Comfort foods.

Every day broke cold and bright. We'd pull our jeans over long underwear, and—fortified in coats and boots—ogle medieval cathedrals, squeeze up ancient spiral staircases, walk through antiquated stone arches. At Westminster Abbey I stood before the burial places of Chaucer, Tennyson, Dickens, Kipling, Hardy. Chills ran through me when I read T.S. Eliot's words engraved in stone: "The communication of the dead is tongued with fire beyond the language of the living."

In the National Gallery and the Victoria and Albert Museum we saw masterpiece after masterpiece. Art I'd seen only in books blossomed before my eyes, an orgy of time and space and history. Art students sprawled on the floor and on benches before a Leonardo da Vinci, a Picasso, a Turner, sketching in their notebooks. What would it have been like to grow up surrounded by all of this?

After exploring the Tate Modern museum we bought hot chestnuts in a paper cone, steam rising to our faces. I gazed at the Thames. A scene from Virginia Woolf's *Orlando* came to me, the one that takes place in a frosty wonderland. The Thames has frozen over, and on the ice is held "a carnival of the utmost brilliance." Orlando sees Sasha, a Russian princess, and falls in love at first sight. In this fantastical novel, Orlando's gender is transmuted from male to female as s/he mysteriously lives through several centuries.

That was me, at this moment, overlooking the Thames. I'd transformed from a woman who loved men into one who loved a woman. And I was now experiencing the pentimento of time, as though everything were happening at once: Virginia Woolf walking along the Thames, Shakespeare directing plays in the Globe Theater, William Hogarth sketching scenes of eighteenth-century London street life.

At Stratford-on-Avon, we visited the birthplace and burial place of Shakespeare. I was stunned, walking through William's childhood home. We saw "Shakey's grave," as the caretaker called it. He allowed me to take a picture of it, even though a sign prohibited photos.

When we ventured to Oxford, I gawked at the antiquity of the buildings and gravesites. Time was vast, yet our individual time was so short. I didn't want to live a small life, huddled in a cocoon because it felt safe. Weren't cocoons meant to be temporary? I didn't want to live in fear of the natural order of things, the death of parents, or ourselves. Everyone dies. All the famous people buried in those cathedrals had died. Shakespeare died. It didn't matter who you were. What was the purpose of living? I wasn't sure. But there was something flickering inside me, small but steady, a flame that ignited to a roar the more we experienced England. Emily seemed to feel a renewed energy, too. She was the happiest I'd seen her in a long time.

Although we both felt enlivened, one thing remained the same: we didn't have sex. We slept together in the Victorian bed, side-by-side like nineteenth-century spinster sisters.

Louise did not die while we were on our trip. She succumbed two years later, Emily and her brother at their mother's side. Under hospice care, Louise had lain in a hospital bed in her living room for days, gripping the bars like a hostage. For days Emily watched over her. I came and went, to go to work, to do errands, to walk the dog. One day when I entered the house, Emily looked up from her mother's side and grimly shook her head. Louise was gone.

In the Catholic tradition, the family held a rosary the night before the funeral, a ritual of praying and standing and sitting led by a priest. Even though I'd been raised Catholic, I'd never been to a rosary before. I found it tedious.

Suddenly, just as had happened fifteen years before at Wes' funeral, I heard the dead talking to me. I didn't get a sense of Louise's presence as I had of Wes' up in the corner of the room. But I heard her voice clear as day, as though it were being broadcast from a station I tuned into. She asked me to watch over Emily because she knew she was suffering. She asked me to ease Emily's mind, to tell her everything was fine. She said this abruptly, not softly, as though her personality were still intact.

Emily didn't believe I heard her mother's voice at the rosary. Why didn't she hear it? Because, she believed, it was a trick of the mind.

There was no way to prove it one way or the other. Besides, when it came to my glimpses into life's mysteries, I had no interest in trying to convince anyone of anything. I was pragmatic about hearing Wes and Louise talk to me from the other side, about having once seen auras, and about having felt a ghostly woman stroking my head. The events were as real as using the phone or switching on a light. I couldn't see how electricity or radio waves worked, but they were real.

Also, though I didn't say it to Emily for fear she'd think I was being insensitive—she railed against how much her mother had suffered—I thought suffering must serve a purpose. Fundamentally, we learned and grew from it. Gabriele said we were meaning-making beings. There was meaning to be had, everywhere. We simply had to open ourselves to it.

One weekend when we visited my parents, Dad asked Emily to describe how her mother had died. I thought he might be trying to feel his way into that moment, to imagine what it would be like for him. Emily emphasized that she believed her mother, who was given a lot of morphine, felt no pain. She left out the part about Louise grimacing and gripping the bars of the bed.

Emily also talked about how she missed her mother, how hard it was to fathom that she had disappeared. Dad said, "If an afterlife exists, I'll do everything I can to let you know. How about this: I'll reach out from the beyond and pinch you."

We all laughed. But he said he meant it.

Unlike Louise, who never liked to talk about her illness or impending death, my dad was open about it. He talked to my sisters and me, asking us to take care of Mom after he was gone. He made sure we knew where all the financial documents were. He even wrote his own obituary and asked me to put the polishing touches on it when the time came.

One weekend in March, Mom called and asked me to come. She said Dad wasn't doing well. I figured it must be bad since Mom rarely admitted Dad was struggling. So I packed a bag and took the three-hour drive out of the Bay Area and through the Sacramento Valley. As the car began to climb into the Sierra Nevada foothills, I took in green hills dotted with oak trees and manzanita, the flora of my childhood. I was forty-three years old. I would never be a parent. Ever since our decision not to have a child, I'd occasionally wonder—wrapped in nostalgia—if it was the right decision. Because I didn't have children or a nine-to-five desk job, I had more flexibility to drop everything and drive up to Auburn when my parents needed me. It wasn't as simple for my sisters. My younger sister had three children under the age of eight, and my older sister lived in southern California and had two teenagers. If there was a grand design, perhaps part of my life's purpose was to be unencumbered so I could come to my parents now.

When I arrived at the house, Mom was making tea and Dad was sitting at the kitchen table, sorting through mail. I hugged them both. Dad looked thin but venerable. Sometimes I thought he lived out of sheer will. Even though he'd had his illness for twenty-seven years, I'd never seen him spend a single day in bed.

I settled at the table and drank tea with my folks. We played cards. That evening he ate a full dinner followed by peach pie. We watched *Walk the Line*, a movie about Johnny Cash's life. Afterward Dad asked me how old Johnny Cash was when he died. I looked it up. Seventy-one.

"Imagine that," he said. "I've outlived Johnny Cash."

That night I saw him staring at himself in the mirror. He caught my eye in the glass and said, "I don't understand why I've gone downhill so fast."

I thought about what the hospice nurse had said to me that afternoon. She recommended bringing a hospital bed into the house. Dad was adamantly against it. I was sure a hospital bed symbolized death to him. He didn't want to languish away in a sickbay. He wanted everything to be as normal as possible. When Mom and I agreed with the nurse that such a bed would be good—it would be easier for us to help him in and out of, we could do therapy on it instead of on that slant board on the floor that was harder and harder for him to get onto—he said, hurt and angry, "Why are you all ganging up on me?"

I shut up and let the nurse make the case. Finally, Dad said okay, as long as it was put in a corner of the house, as long as he could sleep in the California King he and Mom had shared for almost fifty years until, and unless, the hospital bed became absolutely necessary.

When I walked the hospice nurse out to her car she said, "I think your father is having a spiritual crisis."

I saw the little gold cross twinkling on her neck in the sun and shrugged off her comment as one offered thoughtlessly by a religious zealot. I hadn't considered asking what she meant. But now as I saw my father gazing forlornly in the mirror, her words came back to me. Was Dad clinging so tightly to life out of fear? Who was I to say I wouldn't feel the same in his place?

I took comfort in what he'd said to me on the phone the other day when I'd expressed concern about his condition: "It's okay, Kathleen. Parents going first, that's the natural course of events."

That night I was awakened at 3 a.m. by a howl. In a daze of half-sleep, I knew it was my father shouting out in the dark. I'd never heard such a sound, and I immediately understood, deep down, what it meant. Yet part of me thought I'd been dreaming. I drifted back toward sleep when my mom shouted out my name. I pulled on my bathrobe and walked to their bedroom. The trip was just a few steps, but I knew it was a life-changing one.

Mom stood next to Dad, a bewildered look on her face. He lay there on his side, eyes closed. I touched his shoulder. "Dad?" He didn't respond. He was taking strange, deep breaths.

"Mom, take his pulse," I said, invoking her skill as a nurse.

She couldn't find a pulse. I sat next to him, knowing he was dying, and in awe that his lungs—his lifelong nemesis—continued to pump, the last to go. I told him I loved him, that he'd been a great dad, that everything would be okay. I had a surreal sense that this was the way it was supposed to be. It made sense that his leave-taking was slow, that I was there with him, assuring him he was loved, assuring him that Mom wasn't alone and would be taken care of. Daughter comforting father. As though I'd trained my whole life for this moment.

I kept thinking the last wheezy breath would be it, but then as though gathering energy from the center of the Earth, another breath rumbled up through his body. I called my sister and then the other sister, waking them, telling them what was going on. I put the phone to his ear, and as they spoke their love, the last breath shuddered out, and he lay still and silent. I leaned into his already stiffening body.

A few days after Dad's funeral, I was home leafing through a book I was teaching, taking notes on the next day's lesson. It had been two weeks since I'd been with my students. My students knew my father had died. I received emails and electronic sympathy cards from them. I had one student whose father had died during summer break. I wondered how she did it, sat in class like a normal college student.

My urge was not to rejoin the hustle. The idea of facing the classroom tightened my heart. How could I face the rushing world? I wanted to hibernate for a few months, to walk by the beach and in the redwoods, to grow my hair long and tangled, to become a thing of the earth.

A few months later, I was sitting at my computer, engrossed

in writing. Out of nowhere a feeling enveloped me that I can best describe as this: Dad came for a visit.

I hadn't been thinking about him. I'd been in that state of flow where time is suspended, which sometimes happens with writing. Then suddenly there was Dad, inside of me, as though he walked into the house of my body. My fingers froze at the keyboard. I didn't want to move. I could feel him fully, wholly. It was an extraordinarily blissful sensation, my skin alive and tingling. I wasn't scared. I was exhilarated.

Hi, I said in my head.

Hi, he said back.

And then he told me all was well, he was fine, and I should be, too. *Don't worry*, he said. *Enjoy your life. It's to be lived and loved.*

Just like that, he embraced me inside out. Then he was gone, back into the mystic.

16

The Web

Let the miracles, even the ones we don't want or see, unfold.
—*Mark Nepo*

A few days ago I was riding my bike along the Pacific and now, on a hot and dreamy day in Cape Cod, I'm swimming in the cool Atlantic. In the distance, Dave and his friend Gordon play Frisbee on the beach with Gordon's two sons. Gordon's wife, Robin, is a speck in a blue bikini, sitting on a low beach chair.

As I swim, I feel how time takes on a different dimension in summer with its long, lazy days. As though you can feel eternity in each moment.

In the salty Atlantic, I'm buoyant. I move through the briny wet, alternating between drifting on my back and moving forward with a breaststroke. I can no longer see the guys playing Frisbee or Robin on her chair. They are lost in the distance. I am out far, alone, cradled in the sea.

We've been without a house more than two months. Mostly, I cherish our rootlessness. When I allow it to be so, I feel rooted anyway. I'm becoming better and better at, as Virginia Woolf wrote, arranging the pieces as they come.

That night, Dave and I go to bed satiated. Our skin is firm from sun and water, our bellies full. We are staying in a cottage that once belonged to Robin's sister, who died in her thirties after a long illness.

Dave drops into sleep. When I close my eyes, my head spins. The swaying water ghosts me. I have the sensation that I am floating on my back in the sea. As I drift off, I think about how tomorrow is our one-year wedding anniversary. Our Hawaii wedding, forty family and friends gathered on a lava-strewn beach, a giant green sea turtle our best man.

The veil between the worlds is thinner than you think, says Gabriele.

She stands before me. I know she's dead, but she's not. She's vibrant, shining. My skin pulsates with energy as she speaks.

When you really look, you can see the perfect beauty of it all. Moving from one state to the next is like lifting a gauze curtain. There's no reason, ever, to be afraid of dying.

I awake to a charley horse in my thigh. No, it's my whole body, hardening, gripped by something beyond my control.

A hurricane screams through my body. I'm sure I am dying.

It's okay. Release, release. No matter what, you are all right.

Dave wakes to an otherworldly sound. Half asleep, confused,

then shocked, alarmed, he jumps out of bed. The clock reads 6 a.m. Is he having a nightmare? Kate—as of this day his wife of one year—is on her side, doubled over, moaning and shaking, her hands curled and clenched. An animalistic, guttural cry comes from her. Is she choking? Can she breathe? It seems the air is being pushed from her body. Most alarming are her open, bulging eyes. Is she having an epileptic fit? Is she in some kind of death throe?

Moments later, a shift happens, a sense she is relaxing into whatever is happening. Her eyes close. The sound eases in her throat. No more panic. A softening. A winding down replaces the winding up.

She rolls from her right side onto her left side and falls quiet.

Dave leans over Kate. He listens carefully for breath, for pulse. She seems relaxed, sleeping. He thinks she needs to recover from whatever has overtaken her. He joins her in bed, spooning her from behind, listening, waiting—for what, he isn't sure.

There is a man lying next to me. A lamp. A curtain. I feel wispy, like a husk blown free in the wind.

I stand from bed. I don't know who I am, where I am. I have little emotion, except a shred of innocent curiosity.

"Where are we?" I ask.

"In Cape Cod," he answers. My sense of him is hazy and formless. *Cape Cod.* That seems vaguely familiar, like a song I heard a long time ago.

"How did we get here?" I ask.

"We flew from L.A.," he says. "We stayed in Boston at Gordon and Robin's for a few days then we all drove here together."

"How did we get here?" I ask again.

"We flew from L.A. Then drove here, from Boston."

We flew from L.A. makes sense in a nonsensical way. I know the words are true, but they don't mean much.

I have no sense of myself as a person, an identity, a separate self. I feel free flowing yet connected to something big. I'm a wave in a vast sea.

A voice in my head speaks. Serenely and matter-of-factly it says: *go to the E.R.*

"I think I should go to the E.R.," I say.

"Okay," he says. He leaves the room. I hear knocking on a door. His voice talks from the distance. Another responds. I somehow know to pull on clothes. He returns to me. We walk out into the kitchen where a blond woman stands, keys in her hand ringing like little bells.

"Who are you?" I ask.

"Robin," she answers. I know I should know that. But it's okay that I don't.

We get in the car. I sit still, no thoughts. The car moves forward. We are going somewhere.

*

"I can't take it anymore," I said on my office phone to my friend Mary. "I feel like I'm losing my mind."

She'd heard it before, how much I loathed my tenure-track

job as a professor of education. There were so many nonsensical and time-consuming bureaucratic rules to follow, forms to fill out, committee meetings to attend. My boss seemed to care more about the typeface of my documents than the quality of my teaching. She lost her temper easily and then, in a bizarre about-face, emailed me jokes more offensive than funny.

Part of my assignment required me to visit public schools to observe and support student teachers. I liked being a mentor. But I found it depressing to walk onto campuses surrounded by locked gates and barbed wire. The crowded classrooms steeped in the stench of sweat recalled my miserable days of high school teaching, sitting in the dark playing a movie, neurotically eating candy meant for the kids, one of the lowest points of my life. It broke my heart to watch teachers who behaved like babysitters or prison wardens. Yes, there were bright moments, meaningful interactions between teacher and students. Overall, though, I was educating teachers how to work within a system I didn't believe in. The hypocrisy was killing me. Yes, I believed in the *idea* of public schools—but not the reality. Thousands of kids herded behind fences, lock-stepping to the buzzing of electronic bells, force-fed material that didn't matter to their lives. I loathed being part of that system, even on the periphery.

Teacher education had undergone a sea change. Suddenly we were to teach and model quantitative and qualitative assessment, student learning outcomes, and pedagogical approaches involving multitudinous acronyms. My syllabi bulged to twenty pages. Where was the beauty, the mystery, the nuance of teaching and learning? Where was the joy and authentic meaning?

Even a major benefit of working in academia had been pulled out from under me: summer vacation. Part of my assignment was to teach in a year-round Master's program. That meant summer school.

A number of my colleagues were miserable, too, professors who had been teaching for years. One woman informed me she had only eight years left before her coveted retirement. She was hanging on by her fingernails. *Only* eight years left? I hadn't done *anything* for eight consecutive years.

Sometimes I felt relief from my disquiet when I was teaching my classes. I could embrace the power and nuances of education when face to face with real human beings. I focused on what I felt to be most meaningful in the moment. I gave time for the teachers-in-training to vent. Together we offered ideas, support, and solutions.

Still, walking across campus to class, I'd begin to hyperventilate. I'd have to stand still before I walked in the door, relax my breathing, take a drink of water. After class, if I had to return to my office or attend a committee meeting, angst rose in me like mercury in a thermometer.

So there I was on the phone with Mary, in my locked office, pouring out a litany of complaints.

"Listen, Kate," said Mary in a firm voice. She sounded frustrated with me. "You know what? You worked really hard to get where you are. You applied to PhD programs, which in and of itself is a lot of work. You moved a thousand miles away. You took all those classes, three years straight. You completed a dissertation, which many doctoral students never do. You applied to that job and went through the grueling interview process. And for two years now, you've worked very hard within that job."

It was true. As though to counteract my despair, I'd become a shining star professor. My student evaluations were strong. My dossier was thick with committee work and a list of published articles, speeches, and workshops. My dissertation, *Negotiating the Self*, had been released by a reputable academic publisher. I'd co-authored a textbook. On top of it all, I won a prestigious campus-wide endowment award that came with a $2,500 check and a plaque. There was no doubt that next year I'd be granted tenure, a secure job for life.

"What the hell is wrong with me?"

"As I said," Mary went on, "you worked very hard to get where you are. Here's the reality: wherever you put your energy, there you are."

If I'd been laying down tracks, I would have frozen in them. She was right. I'd been putting all my energy into being a successful professor of education. And guess what? I was a successful professor of education.

"So the question is," said Mary, "where do you really want to put your energy?"

The minute she asked that question, I understood. She was asking me, *What's your passion? What's your highest excitement?* And I knew right away. No question.

"Writing," I said. Then I broke down crying.

As though watching a film reel, I saw exactly what I'd done. I'd chosen to get my PhD in education, rather than a PhD or an MFA in English, because I believed what I'd been told: there were no jobs in

English. If I focused on education, I'd have a better chance at getting a tenure-track job. While I loved the PhD program, the job was not for me. The plum job had shriveled up into a prune.

I had done the same thing in my twenties. When I met Ray, I'd been majoring in English not because I wanted to be a teacher, but because I loved English. I loved writing poems, stories, essays. I loved reading books and talking about them. What I wanted to do more than anything was to travel the world and write. But that seemed like the province of dreams, or men. I became a high school English teacher so I'd have a profession. So that I'd contribute to my married household. So that I'd be a grownup, not a silly, unrealistic girl who fantasized about living abroad and writing.

When Gabriele Rico crossed my path, I learned to love teaching. Yet writing was my true passion, the thing that seemed like my reason for walking this planet.

"Writing." Mary echoed my word. "Okay, can you imagine if you put the same amount of energy into writing as you have into this professor of education thing? Where would you be five years from now?"

Around this time I was reading *Arrowsmith*, by Sinclair Lewis—and was stunned by the parallels between a book written in 1925 and my feelings seventy years later. In the novel, Martin Arrowsmith, the protagonist, struggles between his passion for pursuing scientific research and being sidelined by the business of science. At one point it looks like he has made a big discovery. He's excited. He receives congratulations from his higher-ups who promise him money and promotions. Arrowsmith begins to realize that their expectations will pull him away from his real work. When another scientist scoops him by publishing similar findings, Arrowsmith's colleagues backpedal. Arrowsmith is relieved. He wants to be "lewd and soft collared and easy, not judicious and spied-on and weighty."

When someone tells him he's selfish to pursue science in the way he desires, he says that conforming turns one into "a machine for digestion and propagation and obedience....Oh, this debate could go on forever! We could prove I'm a hero or a fool or a deserter or anything you like, but the fact is I've suddenly seen I must go! I want my freedom to work, and I herewith quit whining about it and grab it!"

Emily was embroiled in her own professional turmoil. Ever since I'd known her, she was torn between focusing on art or writing. And for four years now, since we returned from Seattle, she'd been teaching high school art. She harbored many of the frustrations with and objections to the public school system that I did. She wanted a change.

She'd heard that San Jose State's English Department was starting a new MFA program in creative writing. As we drove down the freeway one afternoon, she told me she'd decided to apply. She'd take a night class or two and continue teaching art. Eventually, with the MFA, she'd have poured herself into poetry the way she'd always wanted to. After that, maybe she'd teach college.

As she talked and drove, I watched the horizon unfold. What if I, too, applied for the MFA? As a professor at the university, I could enroll for free. Like Emily, I could continue with my job and take a class or two in the evenings. Yes, I already had a PhD. Yes, I'd be a student at a university where I was currently a professor. None of that mattered. Mary's words echoed in my mind: *wherever you put your energy, there you are.*

"I want to do the MFA, too," I said.

At the wheel, Emily reached over and placed her hand on my leg.

"Really?"

"Absolutely."

Emily drove and listened as I talked through my idea. No, it was more than an idea. It was a reality waiting for me to step into it. Twice before I'd surrendered myself to an academic program to become unstuck. First with the M.A. when I'd met Gabriele. Then with the PhD where I'd stretched my mind in ways I hadn't thought possible, where I'd written a dissertation that became a published book. When that book had arrived in the mail, I held it in my hands and ran my finger over my name on the cover. The ache to write another and another surged through me.

"How fun!" I said. "We will do this together. We will be writers together."

She thought I sometimes steamrolled over her. In my excitement, perhaps I was doing that now. I softened my voice.

"Would you mind? I mean, would it be okay with you if I did this? It was your idea first. Am I horning in?"

She assured me it would be fine.

Maybe this change would revitalize us, reconnect us. We first met in a poetry class, after all. Our love of creativity had brought us together. Then we'd veered off into focusing on education. And the illnesses of our parents darkened our skies. Maybe this was a parting of the clouds. I could see us excited again about life, ravenously devouring the same books and talking about them into the night, writing reams of poems and stories, helping each other edit for the best polish and shine. Maybe together, as writers, we'd create a more exciting life, a more meaningful life.

The next semester, we were taking classes. I loved sitting in a circle of desks in writing workshops with other writers. I had a knack for excavating the gems of even the most seemingly worthless pieces. There was always at least one interesting turn of phrase, sonic treat, or germ of an idea.

The greatest feature of the MFA was the distinguished visiting writer program that brought notable writers to the department each spring semester. I studied nonfiction with Simon Winchester, fiction with Molly Giles, and poetry with California Poet Laureate Al Young. Other writers came for a day or two to give a reading. Sometimes they led a discussion with a small group of graduate students. One summer Emily and I took a two-week summer seminar where we worked with poets Mark Doty and Scott Cairns, and fiction writer and memoirist Bernard Cooper. I was in literary heaven.

One day the director of the visiting author program asked me if I would pick up W.S. Merwin from the San Francisco Airport and drive him to San Jose. The acclaimed poet—the Pulitzer Prize winner who in later years would be designated U.S. Poet Laureate—was flying in from his home in Hawaii. I was delighted yet nervous. In his seventies, Merwin was an icon of the poetry world, not to mention the anti-war movement, Buddhism, and ecology. How would I keep a conversation going with such an erudite man?

I needn't have worried. When he settled into the passenger seat of my car, he started talking about his dogs. Now that was something we had in common.

That evening at his public reading, Merwin mentioned our conversation and said as a result he was going to read a recent poem called "Dream of Koa Returning." In the poem, Merwin's speaker feels the presence of his dead dog. He wonders if the feeling is a dream. Or if life itself is the dream.

Emily enjoyed the program, too. She was drawn to creativity but also, somehow, it pushed her away. She was stymied. She wanted to write, but as she toiled to finish a poem or a story, she'd think she should be painting. So she'd go out to her studio in the detached garage and start—then stop. Just as her art supplies piled up dusty and unused in the Seattle basement, the same thing happened in California.

Even as she hit writer's block for MFA assignments, she wrote fluidly, voraciously, in her journal each morning. Either sitting up in bed or in the bathtub, she wrote for an hour or two. When she read her pages to me, I was in awe of the beauty and depth of her writing. Why couldn't she be as fluid and free in her writing for school?

Once, with a deadline looming, Emily begged me to write her American literature seminar paper.

"Just this once," she said. She believed her grief over her mother's death had intensified her writer's block. "Please," she pleaded. "I'll never ask you again." I was used to writing academic papers, she argued. I'd been able to complete a dissertation. It would be easy for me, she was sure.

For the rest of that day, I looked over her notes, through her highlighted and annotated books, and pondered. I was a professor. I was about to write someone else's paper. I tried to jot down some ideas. It was as though her writer's block had transferred to me.

The next day I told her I'd changed my mind.

"I'm sorry," I said. "It's impossible for me to do this."

She wrote the paper at the eleventh hour and got a B. After that, though, she seemed broken. Spent.

"Would you hate me if I dropped out of the program?" she asked.

"Of course not! All I want is for you to be happy." I meant it.

She took a leave from the program for a semester. She considered applying for a different MFA program, one in painting or sculpture. Then she decided to return to the creative writing program. She bought all the books and enrolled in choice classes with excitement— and then, partway through the semester, she dropped out.

"Are you mad?" she asked. "Do you hate me?"

"No, I'm not mad and I don't hate you. I swear."

I felt if she could immerse herself in what she loved—whatever it was—she'd be happy.

In the program, I developed a crush. On a man. He was both

a runner and a writer, a double whammy. He became my muse. I thought of him as I wrote my stories and poems, imagining his response. In one of the most obvious externalizations of my lust, I wrote a story about a lesbian who cheats on her partner with a man.

After ten years of a nearly sexless relationship, after feeling urgently hungry for Cole and then allowing that desire to chastely run its course, I thought I'd come to terms with an essentially celibate life.

But now I fanatically thought about sex. I imagined it in my waking and sleeping dreams. In my mind's eye, I saw my crush leaning over to kiss me then and forcing himself on me. I longed for, ached for, a body on mine, kissing me, penetrating me. That was something I missed about heterosexual sex: gazing into your lover's eyes during penetration. Years ago, Emily had put the kibosh on sex toys. If we were willing to try new things, would our sex life come alive? There had been a time when Emily and I had passionate, satisfying sex. It seemed so long ago.

I fantasized about hiring a male prostitute. There were those, weren't there? If I fucked a man as a business transaction, that wouldn't be cheating, would it? I imagined going to a bar and picking up on a stranger, just once, to get it out of my system. Then, satiated, perhaps I could retire into domestic, faithful, sexless bliss.

One afternoon, after obsessing over thoughts of sex, I became so agitated, so crazed, I thought I was losing my mind. I grabbed my cell phone, put our new dog on a leash, and rushed out the door. Walking through a grove of eucalyptus trees where monarch butterflies gathered during migration, I knew this was it. I needed help. I decided to call a therapist. I'd tried calling her once before but had hung up after one ring. Her number was still in my phone. All I had to do was hit redial.

She answered. The therapist, not a receptionist.

"How can I help you?" she asked.

"Can I see you today? Like now?"

"I'm sorry," she said. "I don't have an opening until tomorrow."

"What about in an hour or two?" I begged.

"I'm sorry. But I have a few minutes right now. Can you tell me what's going on?"

My heart went ballistic in my chest. I thought it might explode or come to a dead stop. I had never told anyone these feelings. Not my closest friends. Not a stranger on the Internet. I hadn't even written about them in my journal. I'd merely shot my desire all over my stories and poems in a sublimated spray.

"I'm in a long-term relationship," I said, "with a woman. We haven't had sex in a long time. I feel like if I don't have sex soon I'm going to die." I didn't apologize or backtrack. I didn't add the phrase, *This might sound silly.* I didn't say *I'm usually not this histrionic.* I poured it all out, right there under the trees, into the phone, the dog sniffing weeds at the end of the leash. A fat monarch drifted by, orange and black vivid against the blue sky. I knew it was time to admit out loud something I'd barely admitted in the darkest corners of the haunted house of my mind.

"I'm obsessing over having sex with a man. A specific man, one I have a big crush on. But I also feel like, right now, any man would do. I feel like I'll implode or explode without sex. But I know that if I do have sex, if I cheat, that will ruin my life. I mean, my relationship will die, and I don't want it to end. I can't image who we'd be without each other. She said if I ever left her, it would kill her. I could never forgive myself for betraying her. I love her. I love our life together except for this one thing. This one big thing."

I gasped, unable to catch my breath. Tears slicked my face. My skin tightened. I felt like I was on the brink of annihilation. A surreally orange monarch dipped and swirled. Where was I? Who was I? What was happening? Had I actually said all of this out loud?

"Oh my God," I wailed. "I can't believe this is my life."

Briefly, the therapist fell silent on the other end. Then she said, "Are you at risk of hurting yourself?"

"No," I said in a voice not quite mine. No, I wouldn't run my car off the road. I wouldn't slit my wrists. I wouldn't down a fistful of pills. I wasn't capable of hurting myself.

"Are you certain?" she said.

"Yes," I said.

"Can you come see me tomorrow at two p.m.?"

"Yes."

"In the meantime, if you feel desperate, call me back. If my machine picks up, I'll get back to you no longer than an hour later. Or call a suicide hotline. They are listed in the front of the phone book."

When we hung up, I stood in shadows beneath the bright open sky. Rozzie, the border collie mix who came into our lives after Mazie died, sat and looked at me with her pale blue eyes, waiting for me to make a move onward through the field. I dropped the phone in my pocket and wiped my tears with my fingertips.

There. I had said it out loud. I had stated my greatest fear—and it hadn't killed me. The words formed like bubbles, bursting and dissipating. I took a step forward, then another. Rozzie trotted next to me. I knew I would break the therapy appointment. I tightly folded my desire like an elaborate, tiny origami. And I tucked it into the hem of my life.

17

Thrill Seeker

If I took fear out of the equation, what would I change about
how I spend my days?
—Lissa Rankin

On the thirty-minute drive to Cape Cod Hospital, my memory returns in one fell swoop. I am now smack-dab back on Earth, fully inhabiting my body and mind. Kate the writer, Kate the wife of Dave (it's our first-year anniversary), houseless Kate on an odyssey, Kate who apparently just had a seizure.

I recall the state of not knowing, of free-floating—and before that, the dream of Gabriele. I recall surrendering to the force that took over my body. And then waking to a void.

As Robin pulls in front of the emergency room, she informs me I'll be well tended to. "This is the place, after all, that has taken care of Kennedys."

Several people sit in the ER waiting for treatment. I am rushed to the head of the line and taken by wheelchair into an exam room. I describe to the doctor what happened, that I awoke from sleep into some kind of fit or seizure or stroke. That I lost my memory but it returned. I tell him my name, my age, the name of my husband, the name of the president. I feel oddly calm, untroubled. This moment is what it is.

I feel such appreciation. For this doctor standing before me. For the kind intake nurse, and the even kinder one who took my vitals. For the fact of our medical insurance. For Dave, standing next to me, holding my hand.

An MRI establishes what's going on in my brain: a 2.6-centimeter tumor, the size of a walnut, is wedged beneath my skull.

"This tumor has all the characteristics of a meningioma," says the doctor. "That means that it's adhered to the meninges, the tissue that covers the brain. Yours is located on the front-left part of the brain, in the pre-motor region. The good news is, these tumors are usually benign and slow growing. But you will need further testing to determine your status."

I take in the news gently, objectively. I recall the time, years ago, when I sat in an ascending airplane and liquid started pouring from ceiling. Who knew if the plane was going down? But I had relaxed into calm acceptance.

The MRI shows you have a brain tumor.

I think if I can relax into the situation, rather than pushing against it; if I can be filled with love, not fear; if I can listen to my body; if can see myself as healed; if I can trust my intuition—then all will be well. No matter what.

Besides, Gabriele's words still echo in my mind. *There's no reason, ever, to fear death.*

A few days later, I write to Quentin in Australia, telling him about the tumor. He writes back: "You are surfing on the leading edge of human experience. Wow, darling, you really are a thrill-seeker!"

*

I decided to quit my tenure-track job in education and devote myself to writing. I wanted to plunge into my passion. I would teach writing, not education courses. The English Department chair offered me creative and academic writing classes.

When I gave my notice to the College of Education dean, I floated out of her office. The dean had tried to talk me out of my decision. I thanked her and declined.

A few friends and colleagues thought I was crazy (albeit brave) for relinquishing my secure job, one in which I was certain to be granted tenure. No one quits a tenure-track job! No one, I discovered, except Margaret Atwood and Wayne Dyer—and plenty others not so well known. Some people were happy for me. Some envious. Some puzzled.

By demoting myself from tenured education professor to English lecturer, I was following a pull toward freedom over stability. I felt like I was doing what Theodore Roethke, in his poem "The Waking," says: "Learn by going where you have to go."

I designed my English classes around themes drawn from

the works of visiting writers. When the humorist travel writer Tim Cahill came to campus, my courses incorporated a theme of literal and symbolic journeys. One semester, while the U.S. was embroiled in the Gulf War, I developed a course around the Middle East. We read work by two visiting writers that semester: Azar Nafisi (*Reading Lolita in Tehran*) and Salam Pax (*The Clandestine Diary of an Ordinary Iraqi*). Students were thrilled to be able to meet the authors. We read *My War* by Colby Buzzell, a book by a young American Iraq War veteran who'd grown up in the Bay Area. I contacted Buzzell, who happened to be in the area at the time. He said his publisher had wanted him to go on a book tour, but he didn't like the idea. However, coming to talk to college students was valuable, he thought. So he came.

He stepped out of his car, a tattooed guy in cargo shorts and a T-shirt. He gently shook my hand but avoided eye contact. I knew the students would relate to him, a guy from their generation who'd entered the Army because it promised structure and purpose in his life. Little had he known what he was really signing up for. Shy yet direct in his answering of student questions, he talked about many topics, including his PTSD. When a student asked him how the vestiges of trauma felt, he said at that very moment he was aware of all the escape routes in the room: the door, the windows. He also said he was focused on the cabinet in the back of the room. In his traumatized mind, he worried someone might be hiding in there, waiting to jump out.

I had the opportunity to develop a class from my own personal interests, Queer Film. We watched *Ma Vie en Rose*, the movie I loved so much about the boy who wants to be a girl. I introduced Harvey Milk to the students through the powerful film *Milk*. We watched *Fire*, an Indian movie about two sisters-in-law who fall in love. The class was alive with young people exploring constructs of gender and sexual identity. Two transgender students came in from the LGBTQ center to talk about their lives. They shared the amazing statistic that five percent of SJSU students identified as trans.

I had come a long way. Rarely did I feel tensions about being a lesbian and a teacher. The campus paper included my story and picture in an article about queer faculty. The fact that queer issues were more openly discussed paralleled my personal journey.

Yet, as in the College of Education, grievance was endemic among my colleagues in the English Department. I found myself lapsing into this culture of complaint: too many papers to grade, too many students in each class, low pay, low status of lecturers. Yes, these were real problems. Yes, there was an inherent unfairness in the system with tenured professors receiving better pay than their equally talented and qualified lecturer colleagues. But even the tenured professors carped. They, too, had valid reasons: a heavier teaching load at this university than many others, a top-heavy administrative hierarchy that made twice the salaries of most faculty, a tangle of bureaucracy.

Complaint felt like the water we were swimming in. Where was the joy? Wasn't becoming a lecturer in the English Department my *choice*? If so, why did I choose it? Oh yes, for the freedom. For the love of literature and writing.

I recommitted myself to all of these things. Instead of teaching summer school, I would reserve summer break to write and travel on a budget. Instead of going to meetings, which lecturers were not required to do for the most part but many did anyway, I declined—unless I really wanted to be there for some reason. As a lecturer, I didn't have to become involved in committee meetings and departmental politics. So I focused on my teaching. Gabriele's words echoed in my mind: *I stay out of departmental politics.*

I put into action all I knew about saving time on paper grading. When I did have papers to grade, I tried to recall I was lucky that I could grade them at home in my pajamas, or in a cafe. When I didn't need to be on campus, I appreciated those days, enjoying a long walk with the dog, cooking, writing. On my campus days, I took advantage of literary events and access to the library. I even began to appreciate the school grounds. Instead of blindly walking to class, I'd sit on a bench in the sun, watching students play Frisbee on the lawn and squirrels sprint in the trees. I thought about some of my students who'd come to the U.S. under dire circumstances, political oppression, poverty. They were grateful to be here. Why couldn't I be, too?

As I focused less on what was wrong with my job and more on what was right, my yearly departmental evaluations soared. I was offered better and better teaching schedules. I was offered more creative writing classes, a literature and film class, and the visiting authors seminar—a course for studying the works of writers coming to campus. A few years before, as an MFA student, I'd taken that course and loved every minute of it. Now I had the privilege to teach it.

I continued to write. Toni Morrison once said, "If there's a book that you want to read, but it hasn't been written yet, then you must write it." I'd always loved novels that read like memoirs, especially ones with a coming-of-age component: *Harriet the Spy, Catcher in the Rye, Go Ask Alice, Oranges are Not the Only Fruit, Bastard Out of Carolina, White Oleander.* Each one of these featured a young person who was faced with obstacles that challenged her (or in the case of *Catcher,* him) to find her way in the world. I decided to write *For the May Queen* based on my life in the dorms, which was the best of times, the worst of times. I wanted to write about what happens when a sheltered young woman is dropped into a hedonistic jungle.

In *For the May Queen,* the protagonist, Norma, is that young woman. By the end of the book, she is a writer who travels the world. When I wrote that last chapter, I stepped into the life of a traveling writer as though it were happening to me. Perhaps it was, in a parallel universe. Perhaps one day my vision would come true.

After Emily's mother died, Emily wanted us to buy her San Jose house. Because it would be a family transaction, we could finally own a house in the outrageously expensive Bay Area. Being a homeowner was a fetish in California, especially in those boom times when, it seemed, even felons were granted home loans. Discussions of real estate monopolized conversations wherever you were: at a party, on the bus, at a cafe. Wasn't owning a home the American dream? Wasn't it a great investment, not to mention an assurance of security? Most people never questioned the notion that home owning was a good investment, in spite of drastic fluctuations in the market that turned some people's finances and lives upside down. Owning a house represented a pinnacle of achievement and refuge.

I didn't completely reject those ideas. Yet there was something that irked me about the dream dictum of home ownership. It was a lot of responsibility. We'd have to spend time and money fixing things that, as renters, landlords dealt with. Most of all, I wasn't thrilled about trading Santa Cruz's small-town beach life for San Jose's land-bound urban world.

Yet eventually, I agreed. I liked the house, a 1930s Spanish bungalow in one of the more appealing San Jose neighborhoods. The streets were lined with old leafy trees, and there were a few restaurants within walking distance. Unofficially, the area was called the Gay Zip Code. The Lesbian, Gay, Bisexual, Transgender Center was housed down the street near a "men's water garden" (gay baths).

Two doors down from us lived a single gay guy, and next to him a gay male couple. A few blocks over lived another gay couple who threw New Year's Eve parties that involved mimosas and Giant Jenga. Toward the end of our block lived a lesbian couple with a baby. And around the corner lived a single lesbian, Liz, who became our friend.

Liz invited us to a party she threw in her back yard. The next day we were miserable with hangovers. We drank a lot, usually every day. I liked beer and wine. Emily was into single malt scotches and Grand Marnier. Life took on a hazy glow as we sipped our drinks. Hangovers became *de rigueur*. We downed aspirin like candy. We kept meaning to quit. Sometimes we went so far as to dump out our half-bottles of wine and distribute unopened bottles to friends. Our house would remain free of booze for days, but it always found its way back in, like a child sneaking into her parents' bed in the middle of the night.

When she finally quit the MFA program once and for all, Emily became more and more withdrawn. In the evenings, she donned earbuds and watched episode after episode of *Xena: Warrior Princess* while nursing a glass of Grand Marnier, poured from a crystal decanter. Behind her, on the bookshelves, were stacked dozens of her mother's unread books: gorgeous editions of the classics printed on Bible-thin, gold-edged paper. While Louise was alive, those books arrived monthly in the mail. Most of them were never cracked open. They were parked on the bookshelves, volumes of unrealized ideals. Of all Louise's possessions, these books remained in the house after we made it our own. One day, I pulled *Crime and Punishment* from the shelf, one of those classics I'd always meant to get to. I was as entranced by Raskolnikov's creepy musings as I was by the ethereal feel of the moth-wing pages. The books haunted me.

I didn't like collecting things we didn't use. I wanted to let things go. That's how I felt about all of Emily's art materials rotting away in her studio. I thought if she'd toss them she'd clear space for something new.

She thought I didn't value the energy of objects. Each one had a history, had a story to tell. Being an artist, she said, wasn't about buying the materials you immediately needed. Artists were inspired by objects, just as poets were by words. To be surrounded with stuff could stir an artist to make something in an unexpected, unplanned way. I respected that notion, but all I needed was a pen, paper, and my running shoes. I was the person who flung away everything I owned upon divorce and upon leaving for Japan. Maybe I didn't have proper respect for meaningful objects.

She did concede that a big portion of the U-Haul going to, and returning from, Seattle was filled with stuff she thought she'd use but hadn't. What had been meant to inspire seemed instead to weigh her down. Emily seemed burdened, struggling to move forward. She was scared about turning fifty. She was haunted by the loss of her mother. She was sad that her creative life—her writing, her art—fizzled. She didn't want to teach high school for the rest of her life. I hoped once her grief ran its course, she'd revive her sense of purpose. Perhaps she'd have an epiphany that would allow her to take a leap, as I had from education professor to writer.

Needless to say, our sex life was not renewed in her mother's former house. Our first year in San Jose, I poured my libido into writing, teaching, and running. I trained for a marathon. My goal was to run it in under five hours. I came in at four hours, fifty-nine minutes. After that, I stopped running. The guy I'd had a crush on moved away. Emily and I fell into recreating our Seattle habits of eating and drinking a lot and hardly moving our bodies. Corporeal amnesia.

We did what people do when their relationship is withering:

We went on a trip. Then we got married.

We had a friend who offered us a great deal on a Hawaii condo. I did the research and roused Emily about the opportunities to experience nature: whales and dolphins, volcanoes, and rain forests. She loved those things in the abstract. She read a lot of nature books and watched nature TV programs. The only drawback was the water.

She was afraid of swimming in the ocean, and she didn't like bathing suits. I told her we'd find calm, beautiful beaches where she could wade. She fashioned a swimming outfit she could handle: black, mid-thigh Lycra shorts and a black tank top. I bought a new one-piece turquoise bathing suit that made me feel something I hadn't in a while: pretty.

The Hawaii trip was a revelation of light. The sweet air smelled of flowers. Whales spouted with abandon. We hiked across a steaming crater, marveling that we stood in a spot where Earth was created. Spontaneously, we rented kayaks from a local and paddled the sapphire waters. One day, in her black swim outfit, she shouted to me. I looked up from the shore where I sat in the shadow of my straw hat, reading a book. There she was, floating on her back in the glittering Pacific, waving and smiling. I grabbed my camera and took shots of her floating on her back, floating in what she once feared.

One balmy, rainy afternoon, she sat on the shore while I went out to snorkel. Almost no one was around. I floated over coral, marveling at the colorful fish. I hovered over the word *Aloha* that someone had created on the ocean floor with rocks and shells. Underwater, I heard a funny noise, a clicking and beeping. Gliding up to my left, a dolphin appeared like a slab of soft gray stone. My heart knocked wildly. Another one appeared on my right. Then another and another. Before I fully understood what was happening, I was surrounded by a pod of spinner dolphins, including a baby at its mother's side.

As swiftly as they appeared, the dolphins swooped away, synchronized, like individual articulations of one large organism. My skin tingled, my hair spread out like a jellyfish on the water's surface.

Did that really happen?

I floated in awe in the abyss. Minutes later, they returned. Again they swooped up and surrounded me, so close my skin came alive in their vibrational embrace. After a few minutes, they again lunged away, leaving me afloat, alone.

At home we fantasized about moving to Hawaii. But soon we slipped back into our stale routines. And then another chance to reignite our love followed: the California Supreme Court overturned the ban on same-sex marriage.

Over the years, we'd registered as domestic partners in both California and Washington. Later, we were among the four thousand couples who married at San Francisco City Hall in 2004 when Gavin Newsom, the mayor of San Francisco, decided to break the law and let same-sex couples marry. When we heard the news on the radio, we raced up to the city with friends and participated in this act of civil disobedience—only to have the marriage licenses revoked by the state. Four years later, California legalized same-sex marriage.

We married on a boat in the Santa Cruz harbor in July 2008. Forty of our family and friends joined us, including my mom, my sisters and their families, and Emily's brothers and their families. As everyone arrived, Emily and I placed a purple orchid lei—our nod to Hawaii magic—around each person's neck. A good friend of ours, who was deputized for the ceremony, spoke of the power of love. Seagulls circled. Emily's brother and his teenaged son played their guitars and sang a song about having the "time of your life."

We kissed and the captain blew the horn. My mom, who had

Alzheimer's but was still aware enough to know what was happening, hugged us and cried. A reception dinner took place at an open-air restaurant. Afterward, a few of us met at our hotel suite overlooking the ocean, the same hotel where we'd first made love fourteen years earlier. In the distance, the lights of the Boardwalk sparkled in the night. Four of our women friends stripped and jumped in the hot tub. The only man there, our friend Wayne, laughed with delight. "No one will ever believe this!" he said.

It all sounds perfect. In many ways it was. Yet there were some alarming things happening to us physically, as though the wisdom of the body could not help but speak. Two days before the ceremony, Emily awoke with pain permeating the left side of her body. Weird red welts covered her skin. She was paralyzed in pain. The doctor diagnosed shingles. The next day, the day before the wedding, I contracted a horrible cold. I was engulfed in coughing.

Fortified with drugs from the doctor for her, and over-the-counter cold medicine for me (gulped down in non-recommended doses), we hid our misery.

I knew things were really bad when we didn't have sex on our wedding night. With her shingles and my cold—and sickened by eating and drinking too much—we fell into the California King bed of our perfect honeymoon spot where earlier we'd begged off from stripping and jumping into the hot tub with our friends. My body, my sexual libido, had become foreign, nearly to the point of being an alien enemy. I'd almost forgotten how to have fun.

The next morning we woke to a vista of sea. Barking sea lions echoed in the distance, as they had fourteen years before when we'd stood on that very beach, exchanging rings and promises to never squelch each other. Now we were legally married. We never thought we'd see the day this would be possible. I reached over the bed. Emily moved to me and nestled into my arms. A pelican hovered in the sky.

18

The Nest

Nothing belongs to me. Everything comes and goes.
Serenity is an open door.
—Byron Katie

Dr. Whittaker is marathon sinewy and I've-seen-it-all pragmatic. Wearing lime-green pants and a matching necklace, she seems like someone who, under different circumstances, would have been my friend.

I am in awe of the vast world inside me when Dr. Whittaker shows me images of my brain, the walnut-sized meningioma nestled in the left hemisphere. She says these types of tumors usually scoop right out but that some adhere to the tissues. Depending on the tumor's stickiness, surgery could take three to six hours. She mentions, but does not linger upon, possible complications. Yet her overall message is optimistic that things will go well. She tells me that ninety-five percent of meningiomas are benign. The only way to be certain mine is not malignant, though, is to remove the tumor and send it to a lab.

"When can you do the surgery?" I ask.

She calls in her assistant who, peering at a calendar says, "She has an opening a month from now. Oh, and one next week."

Dave and I look at each other, incredulous. We have been back in Santa Cruz from Boston only a few days, and things are moving fast. I quickly received a referral to this esteemed surgeon, who had an opening to see me the very next day. And now she can perform my surgery next week?

"Next week, please," I say, and I am penciled in.

Dr. Whittaker talks about the healing process, about how it will probably take me a while to feel normal again.

"We have plans to go to Hong Kong, India, and Sri Lanka in three months," I say. "Do you think that's possible?"

"I don't see why not," she says.

Dave drives us to the beach. We sit in the car, overlooking the ocean, a few blocks from the Love Nest. Who knew we'd be back here so soon after driving away in Chitty Chitty Bang Bang, heart-shaped sunglasses perched on my face?

Watching the waves, we talk about where we will roost after my surgery. I need to be in a quiet, comfortable place to heal, and it has to be in Santa Cruz for medical access and ease of transport. Should we find a place to rent for a while? Should we stay in a hotel? We have friends we can ask, but that feels like too much of an imposition.

We decide to drop it for now and take a stroll on the beach.

Before we get out of the car, though, I want to call my friend Roxy. We've been playing phone tag all week. When Roxy answers the phone, I update her on the doctor visit, including the date of my surgery.

She says, "You guys should come stay here."

They have a beautiful home in the redwoods of the Santa Cruz mountains. I tell her I appreciate her offer but I know that her house, with her twin boys, is vibrant with activity. She already has a lot on her plate, and I need a quiet place to heal.

"It's perfect!" she says. "We are going on vacation the day of your surgery. We'll be gone nine days. You guys should stay here."

As Dave and I walk the beach holding hands, we marvel at how things are working out. We decide the tumor is old news. It's time to get rid of it. It probably started in response to something that happened long ago. Who knows what?

Then it strikes me. We've been spending the past few months getting rid of stuff. Furniture, books, clothes—even our house. The tumor is just one more extraneous thing. For some reason, we are shedding, casting off, molting. We are transitioning into a new season of our lives.

We go to Gabriele's home to attend a gathering: a memorial and the scattering of her ashes. We are only able to be there because of my medical situation. Otherwise, we would have been on the road.

Dave and I stand in the living room, plates of food in our hands. Suzanne, Gabriele's oldest daughter, read about my brain tumor on my blog. She comes to me, concerned, and asks me about my condition. A woman standing next to me says, "Did you say you have a meningioma? I had one of those."

Her name is Mia. She is also a writer, a teacher, and a longtime friend of Gabriele. She was diagnosed with the tumor when she was fifty, same age as me. She had hers removed five years ago and, she tells me, was quickly able to resume her normal life. She looks vibrant, healthy. We lock hands and eyes, feeling Gabriele's presence.

"You'll be fine," she says.

Two days before the surgery, I wake up weepy. The sadness is soft and tangled and bittersweet. Why is this happening now, when finally, at age fifty, I've found my stride? Why now, after so many years of extreme highs and lows? Why now, when I've learned how to focus in the direction of my heart?

I go for a walk. It's another azure-sky California day. The neighborhood shimmers. Tall sycamores with leaves as big as hands cast cool shadows. Sorrow courses through my blood. My skull is about to be cracked open, my brain rooted around in. Am I going to be okay?

A man walking a dog approaches me. As he gets closer I see the emblem on his T-shirt: "B Strong."

B Strong. I think about two marathoners I read about who lost limbs in the Boston marathon bombing. They are happy to be alive and are already learning to use those incredible high-tech athletic prostheses. They both plan to run again.

B Strong. I smile, sniffing back tears.

*

Four months after Emily and I married, California voters passed Proposition 8, which banned same-sex marriage. Our marriage, along with several thousand others, was in limbo.

In San Francisco, we joined a march for Marriage Equality with eighteen thousand others. The next day we drove to Sacramento for a rally attended by fifty thousand. Christine Chavez, granddaughter of Cesar Chavez, spoke eloquently. We carried Emily's handmade "Love not Ha8e" poster.

It was powerful to be at Ground Zero of this movement that, fundamentally, was about civil rights. The queer community was my community, my tribe. And finally I felt like I'd hit my stride. Years out of my doctoral program and focusing on the literary life, I could talk about queer issues without so much anger. I felt less argumentative and serious, more apt toward humor and hope.

I went alone to Atlanta to participate in the Atlanta Queer Literary Festival. I stayed with my friend and literary compatriot, Martin. He picked me up at the airport and promptly took me to a diner for delectable greasy food. The next day when he went to work, I walked around midtown Atlanta. In the Carter Center and Presidential Library, I was overwhelmed to be in the midst of the life work of a president whose main interest was promoting peace and human rights. I prayed that if Barack Obama were to win the upcoming election, peace and human rights would be his focus, too.

I strolled around Little Five Point, a funky neighborhood

bulging with tie-dye, art, and health food. I loved wandering around new places. The world opened up. I kept thinking, *If only Emily were here to experience this.*

With poets Mark Doty and Franklin Abbott, I went to Emory University, where Mark led a workshop with graduate students. That evening Martin and I attended a reading at a queer bookstore. The evening's headliner was Sister So Am I, a founding member of the Sisters of Perpetual Indulgence, men who perform as flamboyant nuns to satirize issues of sexuality, gender, and morality. Paul Lisicky read a piece about his mother's dementia that moved me deeply in the face of my mother's condition.

One night of the literary festival, Kate Bornstein spoke. A writer and performance artist, Bornstein was born a man, underwent gender reassignment surgery, and now didn't identify as either a man or a woman—although linguistically she chose the female pronoun because, well, the English language offers two choices. Kate's message was one of radical acceptance, love, and freedom. I bought her book *Hello Cruel World* and read it on the plane home. Her book was written to encourage "teens, freaks, and other outlaws" to live their authentic lives without fear. "Do whatever it takes to make your life more worth living," she writes, "just don't be mean." It would have been hard to find a message that resonated with me more. I aspired to be as fearless and kind as she was.

That spring, Emily and I spent a lot of time outdoors. We were at our best in nature. Things seemed exactly as they should be when we hiked through the redwoods, the forgiving duff beneath our feet, or rode our bikes under blue skies. When we kayaked in Elkhorn Slough, the wildlife we saw was astonishing: harbor seals popping their heads out next to the boat; hundreds of pelicans swooping low, their massive outstretched wings skimming the water's surface; colossal translucent jellyfish ballooning past; and a party of sea otters rolling around, playing and breaking open shellfish. There was nothing like time on the water to be okay with life as it was, whatever shape it was taking.

One Saturday morning I sat up in bed with my coffee reading *Refuge* by Terry Tempest Williams. Williams, a Utah naturalist, writes about losing her mother and grandmother to cancer, which she attributes to the military toxic waste in the desert. In conjunction she writes about the ways of nature: the Great Salt Lake, the bird refuge, the marshes, and the human impact on the natural world.

That afternoon, Emily and I decided to take a bike ride. She'd heard about a route we'd never tried, so we hopped on our bikes and headed out toward the San Jose Municipal Airport, following a gravel trail north. Soon we came across a bird refuge, a marshland with salt ponds. Miraculously, the same flora and fauna that I'd read about in Williams' book that very morning surrounded us. Avocets glided around with beaks long and skinny as knitting needles. We spied two great blue herons, several white egrets with spectacular wingspans, and a huge falcon that landed right next to us on the bike trail. We rode around the marsh and salt pond, which was a bright mineral orange. Three mountain ranges hovered in the distance.

We rode twenty-six miles, a good training ride since we were doing a community thirty-six mile ride, the Tierra Bella, in two weeks. Having ventured out together to explore a sublime setting made me feel like we were pioneers, in awe of what we saw and reliant on one another.

Liz, our neighbor, also planned to ride the Tierra Bella. Liz was a petite, sinewy woman. Her most recent relationship had ended when her girlfriend began pulling *Fatal Attraction* antics. Liz was ready to put that drama behind her and start enjoying life again.

She hung out with us, helping us with gardening tasks since she had a green thumb. Emily and Liz both liked *The L Word*, a lesbian soap opera. We'd go to Liz's house to drink beer and watch. Often, though, I'd slip off into Liz's office and use her computer since I wasn't a fan of the show. I was doing a lot of online work to promote my new novel *Complementary Colors*. The book was a fictionalized version of how Emily and I had met and fell in love.

I thought of the novel as an homage to Emily and me. Her one complaint about it was that I made her character, Jamie, too good. I added a past drug problem to the character to make her more edgy. Still, Emily said the character was too benevolent.

"But that's how I see you," I said.

Emily and Liz started making beer, recalling the Seattle days when Emily hung out with our neighbor, Jim. Although I was Liz's friend, too, she and Emily spent more time together. For years Emily had talked about her desire to make new women friends. She wanted to befriend women who weren't her ex-lovers or weren't integral to that circle, which could feel like an exclusive club. She wanted to open up and meet women with whom she'd had no sexual bond. Liz seemed to fit the bill because, eerily, she resembled Emily's ex, the minister. That resemblance, said Emily, kind of creeped her out, so there was no possibility of attraction. I was happy that Emily had made a new friend. How cool that she lived right around the corner.

Emily was coming out of her dark mortality-focused slump. She seemed more joyful, more playful. She complained less about her job. She spearheaded our participation in the Tierra Bella.

The morning of the ride, bikes mounted on the back of our car, we followed Liz down the freeway. Suddenly Liz accelerated. Emily followed suit, stepping on the gas. Liz kept picking up speed. Emily tailed her. Soon we were speeding recklessly at eighty miles an hour.

"What are you doing?" I asked. I was scared. Emily never drove this fast.

"Relax," she said, "it's fun!"

I could see in Liz's rearview mirror that she was laughing. Emily was, too. My heart raced. Eventually when Liz eased up on the gas, Emily did, too.

"Jeez, you scared the shit out of me," I said. Emily didn't seem to care.

Liz was a powerful, fast bicyclist. Emily raced to keep up with her, and eventually I lost them both, riding the second half of the event alone. Not alone, really—there were hundreds of other riders. But I felt alone. Anxious. My skin crawled, like bugs squirmed in me. I tried to focus on my legs pushing around and around. I looked at the sky. It was a beautiful day. As I rode around Uvas Reservoir, the water was still, reflecting the trees like a mirror. Spring flowers were out in abundance, and the sky was Technicolor blue. I wanted to share this with Emily. My feelings were hurt that the two of them had left me in the dust.

Emily and Liz had nicknames for each other. They giggled together and drank together. It began to dawn on me that there was something going on between them, some kind of flirtation. I felt a stab of jealousy. But I recalled Emily's dictum to me early on in our relationship: *if you feel an attraction to someone else, just make it go away.* I figured she would do that. Perhaps, like I had with Cole, she needed to indulge the heightened feeling of a crush. And then it would dissipate. Nothing would happen. After all, we got married only eight months ago. We'd been together fifteen years.

One night Emily and Liz went to the wine bar around the corner with two friends. When the hour got late and Emily still wasn't home, I walked to the wine bar and peered through the glass. They weren't there. Along the shadowy sidewalks lit by dim streetlights, I walked around the corner to Liz's house. The house was dark. I banged on the door. I banged on the door some more. Like a wild animal sensing danger, I was shot through with electricity.

Finally Emily opened the door. Her face looked off kilter. She was drunk. But there was something else. I felt like I was falling down an elevator shaft. Behind her, in the dim room, a shadow of Liz said, "Good night."

My only protection was my anger. In a fury I asked her what the hell she was doing.

Nothing, she insisted, nothing, a sideways grin on her face.

On that short walk around the corner to our house, then in

our house, then in our bed, she maintained adamantly that nothing, absolutely nothing, nothing at all was going on. Yet she seemed secretly happy, like a child who sneaks into her parents' closet and discovers all she's getting for Christmas.

The bugs-beneath-my-skin sensation heightened. At my gynecology checkup, my doctor told me it was probably a version of a hot flash. I was, after all, forty-five years old.

Emily was spending a lot of time with Liz, and when they weren't together they were texting all the time. I finally asked Emily if she had a crush on Liz. No, she said, no.

Then I asked, "Would I be comfortable if I read the texts you and Liz send back and forth?"

She looked at me and said, quietly, "Probably not." Then someone—she or I or both of us—twisted that admission into nothing. The "probably not" was nothing. Nothing was going on.

We started talking in fits and starts, admitting little things to each other. I told her that yes, I'd had an attraction to Cole. She said she knew that. She wanted to know if I'd ever kissed him.

"No," I said. "Never."

"Really?" she said.

"Really," I said. I could tell she didn't believe me. I wondered if that was because she'd kissed Liz, but it was too scary to ask.

We talked about her hiking partner in Seattle, and she admitted there'd been some flirtation.

She aired grievances she had with me: I'd ruined her experience of her mother's dying because I'd put pressure on her to spend more time with me. Emily felt like she had to take care of both me and her mother. It was too much. I was shocked that she'd stored such resentment. Maybe now that she'd released it, there'd be some relief.

I admitted I'd been frustrated with her seesawing on the MFA and making art. She seemed offended. Had I pretended to be supportive? No, I insisted, I was supportive. That's why I hid my irritation. I truly just wanted her to be happy.

We talked about how we'd had a tendency to sweep things under the rug—that we should open up more, should make an effort to do more fun things together. We agreed these conversations might be helping us.

I asked her to go to marriage counseling. She said no. But still, the fact that we were shining light on dusty corners that had been neglected for years injected me with hope—which took the shape of an eerie mania. I could hardly sleep. I drank a lot of wine, which never knocked me out, only amped me up. One evening, I tried to seduce her into having sex. She refused.

As we lay in bed one night, Emily froze, morphing her into a stranger wearing an Emily mask, and she said, "I think I want to be single."

"You mean you want to be with someone else," I said, crying.

"No, I don't. I want to be single. I've never been single my whole adult life."

I cried like a wild animal had pinned me down and was tearing me open. I cried and cried and cried all night long, and she held me.

That became our way, night after night for a week: my unending crying, her unending holding. I'd drift off to sleep, but the minute I woke I'd break into sobs.

I could barely hold it together to teach. One afternoon, as I was walking the dogs in the neighborhood, I saw Liz. She crossed the street and bee-lined to me. With tears in her eyes, she wrapped her arms taut with ropy muscles around me and said, "I heard you and Emily have been having problems. I'm so sorry to hear that. I thought you were the perfect couple."

I allowed myself to believe her. If she could hug me and say that to me, perhaps she and Emily were only friends. Perhaps all of Emily's denials were truth. Was I crazy? Was my jealousy another of my character faults that Emily could add to the list she was building? Every day, it seemed, she drummed up a new grudge about our relationship. I was a horrible spouse. I was controlling. She couldn't believe it when I said yes to buying her mother's house; it was the only time in fifteen years she got her way. She said that because she was the only woman I'd been with that I'd hinged all my lesbian identity on her. It became too much for her to bear. She didn't want iconic status. She didn't want a relationship based on politics or popularity. She just wanted happiness.

I thought we could work through some of these things. I implored her to go to marriage counseling with me. Again she said no.

Then she told me that the next day she would be going away for the weekend with friends. She wouldn't tell me where or with whom. I thought I was losing my mind as I begged and begged and begged her to tell the truth. She remained steadfastly, powerfully mute.

The next morning I awoke not crying for the first time in a week. I felt anesthetized. My tear ducts were dead. My body was stiff. As Emily lay sleeping, I got out of bed and sat in the dark living room on the Colonial style rocking chair that my parents had bought in 1963. I sat there like a ghost of a ghost. The room lightened as the sun rose. This was the room where Emily's mother had died. Right there, near the sofa, next to the window, gripping the bars of a hospital bed.

My parents bought the rocking chair because President Kennedy had one. It had been reupholstered, and Kennedy had been gunned down, and my father was dead, and my mother was withering from Alzheimer's in a nursing home.

I heard Emily utter "Leen?" My nickname, the one she'd called me for years, the second syllable of my childhood name, Kathleen. She said it again, a tinge of panic in her voice. I didn't answer. I didn't rock in the chair. I sat pale as the sky, as nothing as a wisp of a cloud.

"Leen?"

Emily appeared in the threshold between the dining room and living room, her face sleep-creased in anguish. She looked thin, drawn. I looked at her, saying nothing.

"I thought you were gone," she said.

I wondered why she cared. She, herself, was leaving in a few hours, to an undisclosed place with undisclosed people.

"I can't be here anymore," I said. "I need to go somewhere today. Anywhere but here."

"I understand," she said softly.

I called Fran. She said I could come spend the day at her house. Fran and her partner had to go out for the day. But it was quiet there, and there was a comfortable couch and snacks and a big-screen TV. I was welcome to hang out.

Fran was the woman Emily had discovered in her and TJ's bed, the woman who'd been TJ's partner for many years, the woman whose heart was later broken by TJ, the woman who now was central to the circle of lesbian friends. Fran was a powerhouse personality. Among the friends, she was the most financially successful, having diligently worked her way up the corporate ladder. She learned to play golf so she could fully participate in the male-dominated business world. On her fiftieth birthday she climbed to the bottom of the Grand Canyon and back up. In this time when I felt so vulnerable, like my skin was being stripped off, Fran felt like the one to turn to. I hoped to soak in ripples of her strength.

A week before, I had called Fran from my cell phone as I walked the neighborhood. I told her what was going on, that Emily said she wanted to be single.

"That's such crap," Fran said. "Someone doesn't decide out of the blue they want to be single. Something has sparked this. She's having an affair, right?"

"I don't know. I think, maybe," I said, trembling. I told her about the way Emily and Liz hung out, about the pet names and texting, about the wine bar night.

"Have you checked her phone, her email, read her messages?"

"No," I said.

"Why not? You should. Clearly she's messing around on you. You need to confront her with solid proof."

I didn't believe in snooping around in my partner's computer or phone. I believed in trust.

"Don't be a fool," Fran said. "You know this is Emily's pattern."

"But we've been together for fifteen years!"

"So? Listen, I'm going to call her. She's clearly messed up. I will find out what's going on and talk some sense into that woman."

Fran had tried multiple times to call Emily, leaving her messages, but Emily didn't return her calls. Emily was doing the same thing to TJ. Over the years, in spite of our conflicts, TJ and I had developed a kind of truce, a tentative fondness for each other. TJ was livid that Emily was treating me like our long-term relationship was expendable. Besides, TJ didn't like Liz, and I sensed that was mutual. Liz was a stranger. At least I was a known entity.

Fran came to the door and gave me a hug. I melted into her, sobbing. I lay on the couch. She covered me with a blanket and handed me the TV remote.

When she and her partner left I felt more alone than I ever had in my life. Like I lay in a grave, half-alive. It wasn't cold, but I shivered beneath the blanket. How was it possible everything had come to this? I glanced at my phone on the coffee table. Emily might call or text, to see how I was. But no, she wouldn't. She was off with her new lover. She wasn't thinking about me at all.

I flicked on the TV. Erratic images and sound assaulted me. I turned it off. I watched the second hand of the clock on the wall. Each moment lasted an excruciating year, decade, eon.

I remembered the despair I'd felt after my divorce from Ray, after Harry had told me he didn't want me anymore, when I'd frozen in a crosswalk as I walked across the street. That was a pinprick compared to this. A piece of me was shocked this was hitting me so hard. Hadn't I fantasized, sometimes, about our breaking up? Once or twice, I'd even indulged, to my horror, in a daydream that Emily died, leaving me free.

How could it be that after all we'd been through, Emily wasn't willing to try marriage counseling? Hopelessness punctured my heart. She no longer loved me.

I must have drifted off because when I opened my eyes, a thought suffused my brain like the remnants of a dream. A robotic calm engulfed me.

I wonder where Fran keeps her knives? I wonder what kinds of pills are in her bathroom cabinet?

Killing myself made perfect sense. It was the next logical step.

Then suddenly, as though an intruder barged through the door, terror swarmed me.

Oh my God, I could really do it. I could really end my life.

I reached for my phone and dialed the operator, asking for the Suicide Hotline.

A woman's deep, calm voice answered.

After I breathlessly spilled out the story, she said: "Of course you thought about killing yourself. You wanted relief. And it makes sense that such a thought would reach the surface of your consciousness as you were waking. That's the time our subconscious is most accessible."

It made perfect sense? I wasn't crazy? I was merely in need of relief from excruciating pain?

We talked a while longer. Once we were both sure I wouldn't be offing myself, I asked her if she counseled private clients. She said sometimes, and gave me her number.

When I got home, there was a letter on the table, a full page written in Emily's handwriting. She told me she wasn't coming home. She was going to stay, temporarily, in the guesthouse of our friends in Santa Cruz, Kiki and Elizabeth. Elizabeth had officiated at our wedding.

It was May. I zombied my way through the trailings of the semester. I couldn't eat, couldn't sleep. Friends came by, commiserating. They couldn't believe this was happening. What had come over kind, sweet, loving Emily? Emily wouldn't answer my calls. I called Kiki and Elizabeth. They said ostensibly Emily was staying in their guesthouse in their back yard, but they'd seen her only once. They didn't know where she was spending the night.

Anger and despair rolled through me like monster waves. I fantasized about breaking out the windows in Liz's house, about crushing holes in the kayaks that sat in her driveway.

A friend gave me Pema Chodron's *When Things Fall Apart*. Chodron's wisdom brought blessed relief, even if for a moment or two. She wrote that "to live fully is…to be willing to die over and over again."

My suffering was integral to the human experience. No one escapes. And there is wisdom in no escape. Pema promised that suffering leads to growth. I clung to her words like a life raft.

Finally Emily called me and came by, agreeing to talk. Bolstered by Chodron, I was able, for once, to remain calm around Emily, to not attack her, to not beg. We sat on the couch. Calmly, I asked her a straightforward question:

"Are you in love with someone else?"

She looked down. "Yes," she said.

I took a breath, thought of Pema, who said to not fear or avoid the pain, but lean into it as into the tip of a sword.

"Okay, then," I said. "What are we going to do about this?"

Emily looked stunned.

"Wow," she said, "Something has happened to you. You seem, I don't know, enlightened." Funny she used that Buddhist term. At that moment I was breaking a pattern of avoidance or attack that had shaped our dynamic for so many years.

"Emily," I said, "you can't keep doing this to people." I didn't specifically say it but we both knew I was referring to those left in the wake of her serial-monogamy-with-overlap.

"I know," she said.

"Of course, I don't give a shit if you do it to Liz," I added.

She half-smiled. Then she agreed to go with me to a marriage counselor.

By the time we got to the counselor, though, it was clear my "enlightenment" wasn't enduring. Emily still had not told me the truth about Liz. She'd didn't, wouldn't, even in therapy. Deeply perturbed by her unwillingness to talk things through, I lost it. I yelled and begged and cajoled. She said another person had nothing to do with what was going on between us.

The counselor said, "It's clear your marriage is over, the one that you've been in for fifteen years. Now you two have to decide if you want to start again, if you want to enter into a new marriage." After all we'd invested, I thought we should try. Even if we didn't end up together, at least we'd learn a lot. At the second counseling session, though, Emily told me she was done.

Yet she wanted to remain friends. At one point—I'm not sure when—I recall we met for a hike in the redwoods. She held my hand. I remembered thinking that if we were friends, she'd rediscover all the good in us and change her mind. A sliver of me had brainwashed myself into believing that she wasn't with Liz, that she was truly doing what she'd said she wanted to do: being single.

I knew I was fooling myself. I felt like I would explode with insanity. Why wouldn't she tell me the truth? Was she really going to end our marriage without even trying? The betrayal was colossal. Could I be friends with someone who treated me this way? I knew befriending exes was the way of the lesbian tribe. I wasn't sure I had it in me. I tried to stay calm, to breathe. Holding hands, we walked down the mountain, through the shadows of towering redwoods, Emily's favorite kind of tree.

Soon it became clear that Emily was living around the corner at Liz's house. She never directly told me. Her car appeared in Liz's driveway. She did convey to me, though, via emails, that we should start on the legal process of divorce. We'd fought so hard for marriage equality. We now had divorce equality.

I said I'd agree to go to mediation. She gave me the name of a lawyer, Tara Helmer. Wait a minute, why did I know that name? And then I realized, Tara Helmer was Liz's friend, a lesbian who lived across the street from Liz. No, I said, we should choose a neutral mediator. Emily refused. Her stonewalling was ruthless. She told me I had no rights to the house because she'd used her inheritance for it. She said my contributions were akin to a roommate's rent, language I was sure she'd been fed from Tara Helmer. When I asked her if her brothers knew what was happening to us, she insisted I not contact them. They and their wives and kids had been my family for fifteen years, yet I followed her wishes. Whenever I spoke to our common friends or sent out an email revealing what was going on, she slammed me with anger, telling me I should keep our private life private. I lashed back, accusing her of lying to and bullying me. The brief notion that we might remain friends disintegrated into a stereotypically ugly divorce.

My sister Sheila flew up from San Diego. She was worried about me. Both of my sisters were nearly as upset as I was. Emily had become the fourth sister in a family of three daughters. Now she was washing her hands of us all.

One morning Sheila said to me, "I can't take it anymore. We need to get the hell out of this house." She scoured the newspaper and discovered that down the street was a Greek Festival.

"We're going," she said.

I couldn't imagine attending a celebration, but I agreed. The place was alive with people and music. A group of dancers snaked around a stage. People poured ouzo into each other's mouths. Sheila bought us each a glass of red wine then pulled me into the food line. For weeks my stomach had been clenched. Eating offered no pleasure.

As we waited in line, smiling people passed by, carrying plates heavy with Greek salad loaded with cheese and olives, thick chunks of spanakopita, hunks of baklava shiny with honey, grape leaves stuffed to bursting. A guy in front of me ordered a mammoth, aromatic sausage. I said, "I'll have one of those."

I'd been a vegetarian for twenty years. I had no idea why I was suddenly ordering a sausage, other than that it looked good. It had been a while since anything edible was appealing.

My sister and I sat on folding chairs near the dancers. She held up her plastic cup and bumped it against mine. I sipped my wine then bit into the sausage covered in chopped tomato and herbs. My teeth broke through the savory skin and into its spicy center. It was delicious.

The dancers smiled and swayed and jumped to the exotic music. I wondered how many of them had experienced anguish.

The answer came to me: all of them.

Certainly, each one had had their heart broken—or would. Everyone suffered. Yet here we were, gathered together, celebrating life with music and dancing and food. As though pain was nothing. As though anguish could not win. As though we had the power to live though anything.

The group of dancers held hands, forming a circle. Other people jumped up to join. Each time the circle broke open then restored, absorbing the newcomer. It had been years since I'd danced. I used to love moving my body to music. When had that fallen away?

As though my body had a will of its own, I walked to the stage. On one side a young man with dark eyes gripped my hand. His fingers were warm and coarse. On the other side, a beautiful, ageless woman—was she thirty? fifty?—slid her damp palm over mine. People's bodies twisted one way, then the other. I wasn't sure how to follow suit.

"What am I supposed to do?" I asked the guy.

"Don't worry about it!" he shouted over the music. "Just have fun!"

19

Alchemy

I sing the body electric...
You are the gates of the body, and you are the gates of the soul.
—Walt Whitman

Being wheeled down the bright hospital hall, I see looming over me Dave's face, a medical guy in scrubs, and the white institutional ceiling—like one of those point-of-view shots often used in soap operas, designed so you sympathize with a doomed character. I smile, remembering my friend Hank's droll words: "Sweetie, your life is like *Knots Landing* these days."

In the pre-op room, the anesthesiologist, who looks like a surfer with a hangover, asks me a few questions. I answer them, calmly, having given myself over to this thing that is bigger than me.

"I'm going to inject your IV now with something to get us started," he says.

I watch him do so, then close my eyes. I open them. Dr.

Whittaker stands over me in scrubs.

"Hi," I say. "When are we starting the surgery?"

"It's over," she says.

That afternoon in the ICU, a memory comes to me, a memory of something that happened during surgery. My body was stoically enduring the breaking open of my head, and my spirit decided it was going to take off. *I'm outta here. I could be anywhere right now. I want to be free.*

And my body, like a dog trainer, commanded my spirit: *stay!* Then, more calmly, *Hang around. You just might learn something.*

A few hours out of brain surgery, covered in bandages and tubes, and I'm astonished at the image of my body ordering my spirit around. It seems ludicrous. It seems comical. Yet it feels true.

I realize I always thought of my spirit as being higher-ranking than my body. I now see their relationship is symbiotic. The spirit needs the body to experience this sensory plane, this here and now. Perhaps the spirit can learn from the body—not just the other way around.

Released from the hospital after one night, I lie on Roxy and Tim's sofa, redwood trees towering out the windows. The surgery is like an exclamation point on a sentence I've been composing since we left the Love Nest. As a wanderer, I am becoming more and more aware of how my body is my true home. If that is so, then I've spent a lot of my life feeling not at home.

I wonder why I haven't been nicer to this miraculous spacesuit that propels me through the world. I've judged my body harshly, berating it for being too much *this* or not enough *that*. Judging my body creates agitation, ongoing dissatisfaction, an inability to be fully at peace. Any time I judge my body, it's as though I am trying to jail break. My discontent has led me to abuse my body through extreme exercise, numb it through too much booze or food, and ignore it by spending all my time in my head.

Now, as I focus on healing, I want to comfortably inhabit my home. To create a gentler, more peaceful relationship with my body. As the bumper sticker says (according to Tosha Silver), "If you were in your body, you'd be home by now."

I focus on feeling myself from the inside out. I meditate on my organs, thanking them for doing their work. I begin to understand more deeply how my heart doesn't need me to beat it, how my digestion happens without my conscious effort, how my lungs will continue to breathe even if I'm unconscious.

Due to the nature of brain surgery, I can't use avoid-my-body strategies. I've had to give up alcohol and caffeine. I can't focus on screens: no TV, no computer, no tablet. Talking on the phone makes me dizzy. I can't read a book. Music hurts my head. Dr. Whittaker went so far as to say, "Don't think too much. Let your mind rest."

I can't take a walk or do yoga. I can't even escape into sleep because sleep is elusive. I nod off for an hour or two then jolt awake.

The challenge: *just be.*

But be here? In a body that had been sliced open at the top? The one where the scalp was peeled back and the skull drilled through? The one with a gap in the brain slowly, and noisily, filling with spinal fluid?

For days after the surgery, I hear creaks and groans and pops in my head. Only they aren't solely "in my head." Dave can hear them, too.

All that surgical poking around in the pre-motor region of my left brain has affected my right hand. I can't hold a coffee cup or remove the toothpaste lid.

I have to decide: is inhabiting this body going to give me the heebie-jeebies? Am I going to feel like a haunted house? Am I going to think dreadful thoughts that might hinder my healing? Am I going to freak out each time I experience a weird noise or sensation? Am I going to go to the dark place and imagine there are so many things *wrong*?

I consciously cultivate the notion that nothing has gone wrong. That all is well. That something good is coming from this. Even in the dark of night, waiting for dawn to light up the room, I gently dwell inside my body. I think of the knocks and pings in my head as a symphony of healing. What a miracle that my head is being held together with medical versions of glue and staples. My body is a healing machine.

I thank my right hand for all it has done for me over the years. Lovingly, slowly, I touch each finger to my thumb, back and forth like practicing scales on the piano. Like a child, I press Silly Putty into my fist. I think about the miracle of my shaved hair beginning to sprout forth like little leaves of grass.

My biggest challenge to loving my body comes in the form of

shit. Because of the painkillers and lack of physical movement, I am constipated. Dave brings me laxatives. I drink a ton of water. Dizzy, I pace the floor. Nothing works. One night, I lie awake on the couch in the living room while Dave sleeps in the bedroom. I can't catch even a minute of sleep because of the pain in my gut. I worry that if I can't go to the bathroom, I'll have to go to the ER. I've heard of fecal impactions but I never comprehended their excruciating extent. It's three in the morning. I drink hot water. I take another laxative. I eat a prune, then another, then another. I drink three tall glasses of room-temperature water. My stomach bulges. Pain skyrockets through me.

My mother was constipated her whole life. It was a constant battle for her, mornings drinking tall glasses of water with stool softeners mixed in, constantly eating fruit. A few months after my father died, she contracted a bacterial infection in the hospital and suffered the opposite: months of uncontrollable diarrhea. I saw her screaming in pain on a gurney, her arm broken after a fall. It was as though, during all her years of working as a school nurse, caretaking for my father, mothering us, and caring for her dying parents (even her father, who had sexually abused her as a girl), she'd clamped down to hold it together—and as soon as my father died, she unclenched her fingers from the cliff and fell into a chasm of grief.

I try to divert my thoughts, but as my gut pain increases, my mind is a tornado, sucking up every image of anguish it can attract to its funnel. I am engulfed in memories of my mother's decline and death. Then images come to me of my father—of his yelling out when his heart stopped, of his lungs pumping out their last air.

I imagine that the pressure of pushing my bowels will split open my head wound, which has been seeping blood all day. I beg the clock to pick up its pace so I can wake Dave and implore him to run to the store to buy me an enema. Either that, or take me to the ER.

At the first peek of light, I rouse Dave. Sleepy-eyed, he grabs his keys and takes off. Every second he is gone, I tell myself, anguished, to hang on. Just hang on.

When he returns, I administer the suppository then rail at the directions that say results will take up to thirty minutes. Crazed, I tell Dave about the sinister machinations of my mind. Why is this happening?

He says, "I don't know. But whatever it is, you need to let it go."

Oh, my God. He's right. The physical gripping of my body mirrors an emotional clenching in my mind, my heart. Instead of watching my fear float by like bad weather, I've been standing amidst its fierce winds, buffeted by terror.

Thirty minutes pass but I am still backed up, still in racked pain. Over and over I say softly to myself, *Let it go, let it go.* I lie on the bed in the dark, earbuds in my ears, listening to a guided healing meditation.

Let it go, let it go.

I send love to my parents, to my body, to my mind.

Let it go.

Still in pain but in a calmer state, it comes to me that when women give birth they take in deep breaths, inhaling and exhaling with the waves of contractions. In the bathroom, I do that very thing. After three breaths, everything releases. I release. I let it go.

For more than a week, I rarely sleep. Night goes on and on and on. I lie on the couch, my head and back propped up by a half-dozen pillows, and imagine a bright egg breaking over my head, golden light oozing down my scalp, face, body—all the way to my toes. I watch my breath do its thing, softly, gently. I invite space into my body and heart. I invite the face of every person I love to flash before my closed eyes.

Suddenly, Oscar—my college friend who died of AIDS twenty years ago—is there, chatting me up. He says he has a song to play for me. Whitney Houston's soaring voice sings "The Greatest Love of All." I suddenly understand that song to be about something other than romantic love. It's about what Whitney would have called God; it's about what I call the eternal love of the mysterious universe. I begin to laugh and cry simultaneously. It's just like Oscar to play for me something so theatrically corny and perfect for the moment, especially Whitney Houston, since he introduced her to me.

Are Oscar and Whitney together in the firmament? Has he requested a special concert for his friend?

The next morning, Dave lowers me into the bathtub. He gently rubs shampoo into my hair, avoiding the gash on the top of my scalp. He pours warm cups of water over my body, rinsing away the suds. When I rise, wobbly, he dries me off, helps me knead lotion into my skin, pulls my nightgown down my body. He guides me to the deck, where I sit on a chair, the sun drying my hair. The yard is alive with birds and wood and sun. This simple beauty is all I need. I can't ever imagine wanting more.

When I am ready to come inside, he sits with me on the couch, holds my face in his hands, and kisses each cheek and each eyebrow, then my lips. He wipes away my tears with his fingertips.

*

When I left Emily's and my house, I did two things. First, I tore up a copy of *Like All We Love*, my poetry collection dedicated to Emily and filled with pieces about our love. The two women's faces on the cover disintegrated as my hands, with superhuman strength, shredded the paperback book. I threw the shards beneath our bed. The next thing I did was haul our photo albums to Emily's backyard art studio.

For years I'd meticulously assembled pictures of us, our animals, our friends and families, our travels, our holidays. I smashed these chronicles of our shared existence, one after the other, against the walls of her studio. The fat albums exploded. Pictures rained down over unfinished paintings, demolished knickknacks, and collapsed a mountain of art supplies. I threw against the wall, screaming at the top of my lungs, our wedding portrait taken by Rich, Gabriele's husband—a black-and-white of our womanly faces touching. Its glass frame burst, splintering like a supernova.

I held in my hand a ceramic box Emily had made for me for my fortieth birthday. On the outside were engraved words from a poem I'd written about us: *stars plant themselves in our yard*. On the lid, Emily had fashioned brightly painted stars nestled in dark grass. When you opened the box, dozens of those little stars jostled inside like tiny, pointed dice.

I heaved the box against the wall. It shattered. Stars dropped like stones.

My sister Brooke invited me to live with her for a while in the East Bay. But I wanted to be in Santa Cruz. Kiki and Elizabeth invited me—as they had Emily—to stay in their guesthouse in Santa Cruz. They were distressed over what was happening between Emily and me. Elizabeth, especially, felt invested in Emily's and my love because she'd officiated at our wedding.

They'd had a wedding, too—actually a commitment ceremony, since same-sex marriage was not legal at the time. They asked all the guests to wear white so *all* one hundred of us would be united as the wedding party. They were very creative. They never just threw a party; they created fun and meaningful communal gatherings that engaged guests in wearing costumes, building Christmas baskets, or stuffing envelopes for one purpose or another. When Emily and I returned to Santa Cruz from Seattle, we lived with them for a few months. They were instrumental in helping us find the yellow Victorian to rent. We'd been kayaking together. We watched *American Idol* together, voting on the contestants. They were great cooks and wine lovers. They'd done a major remodel on their house virtually by themselves, and they were powerful businesswomen who ran a successful company. I knew they'd had times when they'd struggled in their relationship. Who didn't? But I also knew they always found ways to make it work.

It was surreal being in their guesthouse, especially since Emily had recently stayed there. One night they asked me to come to the main house for dinner. As always, they made a fabulous meal and opened a bottle of wine. Candles and music lit up the room. I did my best to eat even though my stomach was clamped down.

I remembered when Kiki and Elizabeth were first together, they came to visit Emily and me in Seattle. They'd been so in love. One morning they walked out of the bedroom, rumpled and flush from intimacy. I'd wondered if Emily and I would ever regain sexual affection.

Now they'd been together ten years. I sensed they deeply respected each other. They were bewildered about Emily's treatment of me. They concurred that she'd suddenly turned into a stranger. Was this a classic midlife crisis, we wondered? I didn't know. I couldn't figure it out. I was struggling to understand how to move forward. They held up their wineglasses and toasted me, telling me they loved me and knew I would be okay. At that moment, the disco classic "I Will Survive" poured out of the stereo.

"This is your song!" pronounced Kiki.

She jumped from the table and pulled me up after her. In their living room, we danced. Years ago, before Kiki met Elizabeth, Kiki had gone through a difficult breakup. Her heart had been broken, but look at her now: she'd built a beautiful life with a woman who seemed like her soul mate. Was that possible for me?

Laughing, we jumped and sang. Kiki and Elizabeth changed every "I" to "you." *You will survive! You will survive!*

I stayed in Santa Cruz for a few weeks, searching for a place of my own. The places I could afford were abysmal: dank, dark, invaded by loud traffic noise and inhabited by shaggy, stoned roommates. I was not quite two months out of a fifteen-year relationship that had ended brutally, one that was locked in a drawn-out, agonizing divorce. I was exhausted. I awoke one morning remembering my sister had been kind enough to offer me a refuge. Why not take her up on it? It was summer. I wouldn't have to worry about commuting to campus. By the end of vacation, I'd figure out my next step. I intuited that being around my nieces and nephew could do me some good. I would be too concerned about their wellbeing to mope around fingering a knife or a noose. Perhaps living with my sister would be comforting. She'd known me all but the first six years of my life. Besides, I was sure the advantages could be mutual. Another adult around can offer a buffer in the chaos that is child rearing.

I had held deep in my being for years a resistance to my sister's lifestyle. They lived in a four thousand square foot mini-mansion on a cul-de-sac in a community rife with country clubs, California Distinguished Schools, plastic surgery, and swimming pools. Like most of her friends, she was a housewife and a mom to her three children while her husband worked at a technology-related job, raking in bucks big enough to support their lifestyle. That was not how I lived. I was a writer, an artist, an academic, a lesbian, an iconoclast. My low-level buzz of judgment about my sister's world had probably permeated our relationship for a long time.

But now that I'd been mown to the ground, I didn't have the vigor it takes to perpetually judge. I was softer. I took in her life without comment. It struck me that the way she chose to live was none of my damn business. Besides, she was so generous to invite me to stay in her guest room for as long as I wanted.

I began to reap pleasures from her world that reached into my injured life and soothed me. It was pleasurable to sprawl on the soft wall-to-wall carpeting in the living room, wrestling with my nieces. It was comforting to open the refrigerator and stare at the abundance, even if I was still unable to eat much. I loved watching my nieces in a gymnastics meet, their strong bodies flinging around fearlessly. I loved kissing my nephew goodnight as he sat up, reading. (I loved that he said, "You know what I love? Big fat books.") There was something appealing about the nonchalantly masculine air of my brother-in-law in his white shirt and tie, fresh-faced from a shower, reading the paper distractedly before work.

Brooke encouraged me to enjoy looking good again. She had a lot of great clothes. My judgments about her vast walk-in closet evaporated, along with my general disregard for my appearance.

For years I'd been wearing mostly black, no makeup, and very little jewelry. It had been years since I'd worn a dress or a skirt, and years since I'd shaved my legs and armpits or plucked my eyebrows. Ever since I had come out as a lesbian, wearing a dress made me feel like a drag queen. That feeling disappeared. I shaved and lotioned my body, reveling in the smoothness of my skin. I bought skirts and sundresses. I bought shorts and flowery blouses in soft fabrics. I bought earrings that bounced against my neck. I bought lavender and green and blue eye shadow, brown mascara, peachy lip gloss. Memories of clothes shopping as a teenager seeped in, a visceral pentimento of high school: the smell of a leather purse embossed with flowers, the feel of high-waisted jeans, my favorite lavender blouse that I wore to cafeteria dances.

I bought a bikini. I hadn't worn a two-piece bathing suit in almost thirty years. It was a green-and-blue beauty with a bandeau top. The first time I wore it I sat on a lounge chair next to my sister at the country club, watching the kids scream with joy as they plunged into the turquoise pool.

I swung from euphoria about being free to despair about having been so cruelly betrayed. The way Emily and Liz were treating me was beyond the pale: Emily changed the locks on the house. I couldn't retrieve the rest of my things. Her attorney was after me, wanting to gut me. Emily wouldn't give an inch. There would be no mediator that wasn't Liz's buddy.

Anguished, I cried on my therapist's couch. How could she do this to me? I obsessively thought about Emily and Liz having sex. After all those years of denying me (or was it the other way around? I wasn't sure), how could she fall into the arms of another woman?

My therapist said, "When you think of the two of them having sex, you are telling stories. You have no idea what's really going on. How about picturing them having awkward sex, where one of them has an upset stomach and the other one turns away? Maybe all this stress of your breakup is affecting them, too? Why do you torture yourself with imagining they are blissful? How do you know?"

I dabbed my eyes with a tissue. The minute I imagined Emily and Liz struggling with their sex life, I laughed.

Wow, I could make myself feel better merely by telling the story in a new way.

I sat in a bar next to a jockey. He had the face of a young Robert DeNiro and the manic, witty energy of Robin Williams. He was jockey short because, well, he was a jockey. He was in his early thirties and had already been married four times. He'd been in trouble with the law on several occasions. Now he was working to reclaim his decade-old former glory of a top-winning jockey.

And me? I told him I was a lesbian. Or maybe bisexual. I wasn't sure there was a label for me anymore. It had been a long time since I'd had the opportunity to face my desires head on. After so many years of ignoring them or subverting them, I was in a bar with a man I found attractive. It had been two months since Emily left me.

I accepted another screwdriver from the bartender and reveled in the morphine quality of booze. I felt less pain than I had in a long time. The jockey was a great distraction. But I couldn't quite imagine anything happening between us. It had been fifteen years since I'd had sex with a man. Fifteen years since I'd kissed anyone other than Emily. Fifteen years since anyone other than my wife had touched my face or held my hand.

As a jockey, he loved winning. He burned bright. I'd been in the dark for so long that I basked in his blaze. He made me laugh. In this small-town bar that allowed smoking through some loophole, I was smoking one of his cigarettes. I wasn't a smoker, but he made it look sensual, so I joined in.

We were a study in contrasts. I was a non-smoker, and he smoked like lung cancer was a rumor. I had three graduate degrees.

He had dropped out of high school. He rode a motorcycle. Not any motorcycle, but a crotch rocket, shooting it down the freeway at 150 miles per hour. I drove a silver four-door Avalon that used to belong to my parents.

I was five-eight, 150 pounds. He was five-two, 105 pounds—110 pounds when he gave into the temptation to eat a sandwich or two. I learned from him that most jockeys have eating disorders. He regaled me with stories of bulimia, of riding a stationary bike for hours in a hot room, of eating nothing for as many days as he could stand it. I was familiar with those tactics but only as performed by women.

His life kind of creeped me out and kind of fascinated me. Sipping beer, he told me his last wife was blond and five-ten.

"Wow," I said. "How did you two fit together?"

Over the lip of his beer bottle he fixed a grin at me. "I'm strong," he said. "I can climb anything."

What a rush to be flirting with a man, and to have him flirt back. Guilt free, without feeling like I was betraying my wife or my identity. I wondered if he thought I was hot. It had been years since I cared about whether or not a man looked at me with desire. If a man expressed interest in me, I was sometimes flattered, but I felt protected by my lesbianism. As a lesbian, I didn't have to care about the approval of men. I didn't have to dress for them, discipline my body to their tastes, or worry that they didn't want me anymore when they looked at another woman on the street or at a Victoria's Secret TV commercial. Was I backsliding? If I started up with men again, would I be at square one, an angry heterosexual feminist who's not happy with men and not happy without them?

But this moment with the jockey felt like a relatively safe foray back into the heterosexual dance. If he didn't want me, who cared? He may have been handsome, but he was also crazy and very short.

When I finally got off the barstool, it wasn't easy to walk. That he was several heads shorter than I was undeniable now that we were standing. Very soon we were sitting again, in my car. He in the driver's seat, me in the shotgun, sunroof open. It was a cool, ocean-air night with pinpricks of stars. He said we should go watch the waves. He drove us through the dark night to the other side of town and parked at an overlook I knew well, a place my wife and I used to walk with our dogs.

He was swiftly on top of me, kissing me. I was kissing someone who was not my lesbian lover of fifteen years. I was kissing someone who had a prickly face, not the creamy face of a woman. I loved the harshness of his skin, his tongue in my mouth, his hands on my body. I loved that we were like teenagers, drunk and frantically making out in a car.

It was surreal. But I was so drunk it was like being in an altered state within an altered state. Time collapsed. I was sixteen, making out with an eager boy. I was a girl who loved the foreign scents and mysterious behaviors of boys, an adolescent whose adulthood had not yet congealed.

I was so ready for him to do what he did so deftly. Somehow most of his clothes were off, then mine, too. The next thing I knew, I was absolved of all lesbianism and engulfed in the dreamy, drunken wonders of sexual intercourse with a man. It was all so wonderfully strange yet familiar. He rode me like he was aiming to win the Triple

Crown. Bruises bloomed on my arms. Stigmata of my ecstasy.

The jockey and I spent the night at his place. He had to get out of bed early to make it to the track for training exercises. That morning, handsomely decked out in Wrangler jeans, black chaps, motorcycle jacket, and boots suitable for a moonwalk, he quickly kissed me good-bye as I lay in bed, half asleep. Then he pushed onto his head a motorcycle helmet, concealing his face in fiberglass. He exited my life like a tiny astronaut.

It was hard to see the clock. My eyes were gluey from makeup I'd neglected to wash off the night before, and the contacts I'd not removed. It was dark and cold. I was suddenly wide awake, and stunningly not hungover. It had been a long time since I'd slept so soundly. Static shocks of energy coursed through my body. All I wanted was to get in my car and drive.

It was dawn as I drove north on the freeway. In this early Sunday morning, only a car or two accompanied me on the stretch of interstate usually packed with traffic. The Bay Area was smeared with a wash of gray and white. I was driving home. Well, not quite home. I didn't have one of those anymore. I was driving to my sister's house. A sensation of new understanding crept up with the rising sun. After two months of barely being able to breathe through the pain of loss... after two months of torturing myself with the fantasy that my wife would beg my forgiveness...after two months of twisting around in a tornado of grief...after fifteen years that ended in *this*...I'd had sex with someone else. A man.

My marriage was over.

Emily left our marriage months ago. And now, finally, I left it too. Fidelity had been the last uncut string. I didn't have to feel shame or guilt. My body was mine. My mind was mine. My sexual fantasies were mine.

It was six a.m. on a Sunday, and no one knew where I was. I wasn't the focus of anyone. I didn't belong to anyone. I had spent a night doing whatever I wanted to do, feeling whatever I wanted to feel. I didn't have to call anyone. I didn't have to explain anything. Not even to myself.

Gripping the steering wheel, I sped by California emerald hills that in a week or two would turn gold overnight. Nature's alchemy.

20

New Life

Illness sets the stage for the opening of our hearts.
—Judith Orloff

Dr. Whittaker's assistant yanks all ten staples from my scalp with no anesthesia. I feel the tug and pull but no pain. Dr. Whittaker walks in and says, "Good news! The lab results show your tumor was benign, grade one. The best possible result."

I'm taken aback. I've been so focused on seeing myself as healthy, I'd forgotten there was a remote possibility that the tumor could be malignant. I have to have another MRI in a few months. And I can't submerge my head underwater for a while. But I'm healing well.

After almost two weeks in Roxy's house in the Santa Cruz mountains, we are headed to the home of other friends for a few weeks. Being in the car has a spaceship quality. I'm a little dizzy but happy to be in regular clothes on a regular day doing a regular thing like taking a ride.

Dave stops off for lunch. Here we are, sitting in a restaurant. It's the most astounding thing.

Two weeks later, we drive south to L.A. When Natasha, my oldest friend, opens the door to my knock, she envelopes me in a hug and whispers, "Thank you for not dying."

"You're welcome," I whisper back.

A few days later, we land in Leucadia, a beach town north of San Diego where my sister, Sheila, lives. Dave and I stay next door at the home of her neighbor who's away.

Sheila and I shared a bedroom as kids. Back then ours was a kingdom of stuffed animals and Barbies. We read Nancy Drew and the Happy Hollisters into the night, summer air drifting through the screens. We listened to Dr. Demento on flat speakers under our pillows. We wrote stories about girls solving mysteries and traveling the world. We captured polliwogs and watched them sprout legs in jars on our windowsills.

Now we are sharing her neighborhood friends and beaches. Being in Leucadia means living an indoor/outdoor life. I like hearing my sister on the phone through the window, or my brother-in-law Jack calling the dog. I see my nephew walking up the hill, surfboard under his arm. People leave their doors and windows open. They gather at dusk for wine in each other's back yards. They spontaneously share dinners, each person bearing food that multiplies like loaves and fishes.

Sheila and Jack's house sits in what is fondly known as the "surf slum," a couple of blocks from the beach amidst other small houses. There are no towering condo complexes shadowing the sunny yards. You can regularly hear neighbors' conversations and music.

When I'm in my sister's living room, I think about how by most American standards, their eight hundred square foot house is tiny. But it has everything one would need: furniture to relax and read on, a kitchen table to eat and play games on, a bed to rejuvenate in, a stove and fridge to feed everyone, a computer desk to email on, a backyard to barbecue with neighbors, and a vegetable garden to nourish family and friends.

The more I focus on the bounty of their house, the bigger it appears. It literally grows before my eyes, as though I am Alice who ate the cake. The rich patterns in the rug emerge. The painting of an American Indian in a canoe at sunset vibrates. Thick with impasto, that painting used to hang on the wall of the house where we grew up. It throbs with history.

At age nineteen, I lived in one of my favorite spaces ever. A bedroom in a tract house shared with other college students. I loved being in that room, its white walls adorned with posters of my favorite bands, its bookshelves filled with lives I intimately experienced. In that space, I had a rich sense of being on my own, of inhabiting a private, uninterruptable world. I also loved my apartment in Japan, even though my knees hit the wall when I sat on the toilet.

I grew up in a big house. Split level, five bedrooms, redwood decks, swimming pool. Mostly, I loved that, too. But at an emotional level, it wasn't any better than the one bedroom in the tract house.

I wonder what kind of house will be Dave's and mine some

day: large with wood and glass like the ones we grew up in? Small like my sister's with easy access to the beach? Medium sized in the mountains?

For now, every house we stay in is our home.

Holly and Dan, neighbors up the street, throw a party in their yard, a field filled with fragrant lavender and fringed with grapevines. Dogs run between our legs. We clench our wineglasses. As the sky darkens, Holly lights candles. Dan sets up a large screen to show slides from their recent trip to Australia. I marvel at the fact that on the screen they stand in the same places we recently visited—and now we stand here together on the other side of the world, under the stars. Somewhere in between, I had brain surgery. The stars are coming out. I hear my sister's laugh. A dog yips. Dave's hand touches mine.

*

At age forty-six, I was a single woman living alone in an urban apartment, worlds away from my previous incarnation as committed partner in a fifteen-year relationship with a home in suburbia. My mom's piano sat in the small apartment living room. In the dining alcove I'd placed the dining room table I grew up with, the one where we ate family meals for decades.

I was beginning to appreciate my autonomy and solitude. My time was my own. I could grade papers at two a.m. I could spend all day in bed, writing on my laptop. I swung from feeling nervous, empty, sad, and abandoned to free and happy. I was still seeing a therapist and reading a lot of self-help books. Weekly, my friend Hank and I went to "Buddha and Beer." First we'd attend a meditation class, then we'd go drink. Life felt like a blank slate, exciting and unnerving.

With a sycamore reaching its branches up to the sixth floor, my apartment had the ambiance of a treehouse. Every weekend at two a.m., I was awakened by laughing and yelling bar patrons leaving the clubs on the streets below. Trucks rumbled by and airplanes drew white lines in the sky. Crows congregated in the tree, startling the leaves. My two little dogs, Max and Spokey, curled on the futon.

One afternoon, I rooted through a box and pulled out a photo of me wearing my graduation regalia. And another of my friend Oscar and me from 1983 at a college Christmas dance, him dipping me back in my purple dress. Here was one of my parents, sisters, and me in 1969, the Grand Canyon multihued behind us. And me at a writing conference, standing next to two of my literary heroes. I rooted out an acceptance letter from a magazine for a story I published, and two synchronized swimming first-place ribbons. My accomplishments, my passions, my life having nothing to do with Emily. I pasted them carefully on butcher paper, and hung the collage on my refrigerator. A visual representation of my self-worth.

I recalled how, at the mediation class, the teacher talked about the ending of long-term relationships. Eyes closed, we were to envision a time before we knew that person existed on the planet. What if Emily and I had never met? And it came to me, washing over me like a warm wave: I'd still have journeyed the past fifteen years living a meaningful life. I'd still be me.

All my life, I could now see, I'd sought a relationship to complete me. I'd idealized love. I'd believed someone else could make me whole. And when that failed, it was as agonizing as having a limb hacked off.

When I was a girl, I listened over and over to a romantic album by Bread, fantasizing that the boy of the week was singing to me, mooning over me. *Baby I'm a-want you.* The belief that I was valued because someone longed for me had been planted deep in my young psyche. It was time to root it out.

Now, when love songs came on the radio, instead of turning them off in disgust (which I had for months), I started singing them to myself. Lyrically I promised myself I wouldn't go breaking my heart. That I would love myself to the end of time. That in my eyes, I was complete.

I sang how wonderful life was because I was in the world.

I vowed no matter what, even if I fell in love again, I would always sing love songs to myself. I vowed that no one's love for me would ever usurp my love for myself. I promised I would never again consider taking a knife to my beautiful wrist.

I threw a housewarming party, which doubled as a new-academic-year party. Gabriele and Rich came, as did Mary and Wayne, Carrie, Cathy and Hank. TJ—who was more upset about Emily's and my breakup than most of our lesbian friends—showed up with her girlfriend. And Jen, a former student of mine, came. We danced for hours in the living room. My energy was high, bordering on manic. I drank glass of wine after glass of wine. At the end of the evening, Jen and I agreed to go dancing at a club sometime.

Jen had taken my freshman composition class and several of my creative writing courses. She was now a twenty-two-year-old graduate student with a full-time teaching job. The week after my party, we met up at a flashing-lights-thumping-music queer club. When Jen and I began dancing and laughing, others responded to our energy. Soon we were jumping to the beat with groups of people, exchanging partners, dancing with men and women, then reuniting every few songs, singing every lyric we knew.

The lights went up in the bar. Could it be closing time already? Two guys we'd been dancing with—William and Brett—and Elaine, their self-proclaimed fag hag friend, asked us if we wanted to keep the party going.

We followed them out into the cool night and onto the city sidewalk. All the bars were closing down, so people walked around in their party clothes, drunkenly laughing and talking—the sounds I usually heard from my apartment in bed.

Elaine was probably in her fifties and looked great in her short black skirt. William and Brett were in their late twenties. William was tall and catalogue gorgeous, with blond hair and dark eyes. Brett was short and cute, a little pudgy. He talked in a train-speed, flamboyant chatter about how San Jose was a boring town, how Brittney Spears was white trash, how he wanted a joint and probably had one in his car. Jen and I giggled like teenagers. She looked cute in jeans and boots, boyish with short red hair and bangs brushing her eyes. I wore jeans, too—with rhinestones on the pockets—and a slinky black blouse and heels. Clothes of the new me.

We stopped at a high rise. Elaine passed a card through a

scanner. The door slid open. When we entered, she said hi to the security guard behind the desk. We followed her, taking an elevator up to the eighth floor, and went into a boardroom that was almost entirely filled up by a big table surrounded by padded chairs on wheels. The plate glass windows looked out over the dark city bejeweled with lights.

A boom box and wine appeared. Before I knew it, Brett and I were dancing on the table to the Commodores' "Brick House." I moved my body, reveling in the feeling that I could dance forever. Elaine and William were talking by the windows, their backs to us. Jen sat in one of the chairs pulled away from the table. I looked down at her, caught her eye. I could see in her look all of this: there I was, her teacher, her professor. The first out lesbian she'd ever met. When she'd come to college, she was escaping strict, religious parents who thought homosexuality was an abomination. She had matured into a beautiful, confident young lesbian who was staring at her former professor with adoration. A nudge of desire crept into my booze-soaked body. She was so young. Did that matter? I wouldn't exactly be pulling a Mary Kay Latourno, would I? I was no longer her teacher. She was an adult. I'd been with one woman my whole life. Jen, on the other hand, had had a number of girlfriends. I was the more virginal one.

We left the boardroom and were in a car, passing around a joint. Elaine drove with William in the shotgun. I was crammed in the back between Brett and Jen, their thighs pressed against mine. Soon we were leaving the car and walking into a McMansion somewhere outside city center. When we entered the house, we were led into a dark bedroom. As my eyes adjusted, I saw a single bed against one wall and a large futon against the other. On the back wall was a large desk with a computer, where Elaine sat and started up music. Beer and snacks appeared. Jen and I leaned back on the large futon, the guys next to us. That's when I saw a lump under the bed across from us shift. A guy with bed head sat up.

"Hey," he said.

"Hey," Elaine said. "Want a beer?"

He leaned against his headboard and accepted the beer. In the dark, I couldn't see his features. The guys next to me talked in low whispers. Jen leaned into me, and the next thing I knew we were kissing. Soft face. Soft lips. I touched her hair. Soft. Ran my hand up and down her arm. Soft.

I pulled back and whispered, "Do you know you're only the second woman I've ever kissed?"

"You're shitting me!" she whispered back.

I smiled. "Nope."

She came at me with a vengeance. Like she wanted to consume me. I reciprocated, somewhere in the haze of my mind realizing we had an audience, although I wasn't sure they could see us in the shadows. We made love, navigating around our half-dressed bodies.

I floated off into a kind of sleep when I felt something next to me, on the side other than Jen, who was fast asleep. Something was touching me, touching my hand. I realized it was Brett, trying to place my hand on his penis. I pulled my hand back.

"What are you doing?" I said.

"William passed out on me," he whined. "Help me out here,

girl."

"Aren't you gay?" I said.

"A hand is a hand," he said.

"No, thanks," I whispered fiercely and turned my back to him, curling up next to Jen. Again I drifted off, only to be awakened by Jen's whisperings.

"Come on Kate, let's get out of here."

She handed me my shoes and purse. I grabbed them, not bothering to slip on my heels. The guys were asleep. Elaine was nowhere to be seen. We quietly snuck out of the room and out the front door, Jen leading. The sky was dark gray, lighter at the edges. Dawn. I had no idea where we were, but Jen said she knew. It would be a trek, but we could walk back to my apartment.

The cold sidewalk felt good under my feet. At first we were silent, walking beneath streetlights that began winking off. It was Sunday morning. The residential neighborhoods gave way to streets with silent stores. Soon, we began to talk in a whisper. What was that boardroom about? Remember the disco music on the boom box? Who the heck is Elaine? Whose house was that? Who was that guy in the bed, drinking a beer while we made out?

That one sent us into spasms of laughter. A car drove slowly by. I told her about Brett waking me up, wanting a hand job.

"No way!" she shrieked.

After more than an hour, we reached my apartment building. I realized she had been the mature one, the one who had taken care of me, of us, by paying attention to where we'd been going then navigating us back home. I was the one who'd behaved like a wild youth, going wherever with abandon.

I was looking forward to diving into my bed to get some real sleep. But I felt Jen was waiting for me to ask her up. All I really wanted was to be alone, to sleep and then meditate on all that had happened. I'd had sex with a woman who wasn't my wife. I'd had sex with a woman even though I'd already been with a few men. What meaning might that hold for me? Who was I?

I invited her up. We crawled into my bed, her in a T-shirt and underwear, me in a nightie. She curled next to me. I felt such affection for her, but my desire had waned. I suddenly knew very, very clearly that I wanted to be alone.

We slept a little. I woke and saw her sleeping there sweetly like a pretty child. I couldn't stay in the bed anymore. I got up, made coffee and scrambled eggs. She must have smelled the food because she rose and smiled a sleepy smile. We ate breakfast. Sitting across from her at the table, I had a feeling I was in the wrong place, in the wrong skin. She was a wonderful woman. And smart. And pretty. And a writer. But this wasn't me. I didn't know what was me. But this wasn't it.

After we finished eating, I told her I had things to do, that I'd walk her to her car. We hugged good-bye.

On my forty-seventh birthday, I woke alone in my apartment. It was also Thanksgiving Day. In sunlight that poured in from my bedroom window, I pulled on my jogging bra, tank top, running shorts, and new running shoes. It was still early when I stepped into the morning air.

As I walked several blocks toward Discovery Park, more and more people gathered on the streets, dressed in running gear. A banner strung across the park entrance reading "Silicon Valley Turkey Trot." Hundreds of people sprawled across the lawn, stretching, warming up, chatting. I got in line to pick up my bib when I heard someone call my name. Standing there were Fran and her partner. The last time I'd seen them I'd nearly offed myself in their condo.

We exchanged light hugs that resonated with uncertainty. It had gotten around that I was dating men, and I knew they knew. Both of them had unfriended me on Facebook. Fran had been married to a man years ago but had been a lesbian for more than twenty years. Like me, her partner had been with only one woman, Fran. I wondered if they now thought of me as a different species. I wondered if they thought I was a traitor.

They told me they were running the race with another couple. They had to go meet up with them.

"Good to see you," Fran said. "And happy birthday."

They disappeared into the crowd like ghosts.

The streets were packed. I was alone. But not. Thousands of other runners were my companions. For the first time in years, no one was going to make me a cake, or give me a present wrapped in decorative foil. My sisters were out of town, and a bunch of my friends had celebrated with me the previous week at a party. Just like my thirtieth birthday in Japan, I was flying solo. Later I planned to pick up my mom from the care facility to take her to my cousin's house for Thanksgiving dinner.

I followed the pack of runners through the downtown streets, thrilling to the clapping and shouting from spectators. My legs and lungs were my friends, launching my body forward. We ran down a major street when I noticed we were bee-lining toward my old neighborhood, the one where Emily now lived with Liz. My pulse already cranked up from exertion, my heart began to beat even faster. At the cafe where Emily and I used to drink coffee and write in our journals, the pack turned left and I followed.

For the second time that morning, I heard my name shouted out. My former neighbors, the gay couple who threw New Year's Eve parties, waved me over. I ran to them, my body wet with sweat. They both hugged me, smiling, and said I looked great. I gazed at them through a scrim. They stood on one side of my life, and I on the other. I gave their golden retriever a pat on the head and waved good-bye, rejoining the stream of runners.

And there I was, running through my old neighborhood, the Gay Zip Code, past Craftsman houses and Spanish bungalows, beneath soaring trees with leaves like a grandmother's hands. I felt a little dizzy as I passed Liz's house, where Emily lived now. The house was dark.

Past it all, past it all, my muscles pushing me through the old life and beyond. With the strength of thousands buoying me, I looped around the high school field where Emily and I used to run our dogs. I turned away from all that history and with every step headed toward downtown. Toward my new life.

21

The Story

There are advantages in having access to multiple
versions of your life story.
—*Gabriele Rico*

"My advice to you is to forget this ever happened and move forward with your life," says Dr. Whittaker. It's my three-month post-surgery appointment. My MRI looks great. She wants another MRI in six months, but she doesn't expect any problems.

Later, Dave and I laugh about Dr. Whittaker's injunction to forget the tumor and surgery, and to move forward with life. Could a message be more fitting? We believe in the power of letting go of the past, of not allowing yesterday to determine now. Each moment we have the chance to start over.

At the same time, I know I will be writing about my experiences. I will not forget what happened. Instead, as a meaning-making being, I will examine my story, shape it, illuminate it. There is a difference, though, between suffering the past and accepting it, even thanking it. The past, after all, led me here.

Stunned, I come across this journal entry from September 27, 1992, written twenty-one years before my brain surgery: "Every time I think of a spiritual experience, I think of the time I felt a hand on my head when I was distraught and crying on my bed. At first it was pressure, then a kind and reassuring stroking that felt like a loving presence. If I were Kafka or Woody Allen, I'd write about it becoming a brain tumor. But that hasn't happened, as far as I know."

A year or two before my seizure, I saw a remarkable TED talk on YouTube by Dr. Jill Bolte Taylor, which led me to her book, *My Stroke of Insight*. A neuroscientist who had a stroke, Taylor was in a unique position to understand and later describe the event. Her stroke had incapacitated her left brain, the same side of the brain affected by my tumor. Without a functioning linear left hemisphere, Taylor could actually *see* that she was "made up of energy particles that are woven together into a universal tapestry."

Was that why, during my seizure and the disruption of my left brain, the veil dropped? Was that why I could so easily connect to Gabriele? And what about in Australia, a month or two before my seizure, when I had my first dream of Gabriele? She hadn't spoken but happily waved to me from behind a huge glass window, and the most incredible shot of energy blasted through my body. It remained coursing through me after I woke up. It strikes me that the intense, electric sensation was similar to the bodily sensation of the seizure. Had I been having a preview of the seizure? Had I been able to experience that first Gabriele dream/visitation because my linear, logical left hemisphere was compromised, overridden by my holistic right brain? Had the dominance of my right hemisphere opened the door to a spiritual encounter?

I'd felt connected to something greater, an electrical outlet linked to its source. We are vibrational beings. Walt Whitman sang of the body electric. Emily Dickinson wrote, "The brain is just the weight of God."

A biological explanation for the dream would be this: during the trauma of the body, my mind created a soothing scenario intended to help me deal with the physical and psychological pain. Is consciousness a bridge between science and spirit? I don't pretend to have an answer. But I do know that I trust in the nonphysical, just as I trust my nose to smell and my eyes to see. If my mind was helping me to deal with the seizure and the possibility of dying, I like knowing that something nonphysical was invested in soothing me.

I wonder about the time my father, three months after his death, visited me. At that moment, I'd been lost in the flow of writing. When Dad "appeared," my skin tingled, alight with static electricity. When writers are lost in the flow, the holistic right brain dominates. Time no longer matters because the linear left brain is not ticking out the moments. That experience is what Mihaly Csikszentmihalyi calls "flow," when "the ego falls away. Time flies. Every action, movement, and thought follows inevitably from the previous one, like playing jazz."

So perhaps when I was in the flow of writing, with my right hemisphere reigning, I was unguarded. The door swung open, and my father walked in.

*

Now that I was interested in meeting men, my sister Brooke encouraged me to try online dating. At first I resisted. It was too soon. It was embarrassing. It might be weird or unsafe. After a few sister pep talks, I lightened up and thought it might be fun.

But how would I position myself on dating websites? Would I mention I'd been with a woman? If not, how would I break the news? Most people I talked to said guys wouldn't care. In fact, they'd be intrigued. I didn't mind intrigue, but at the same time I didn't want men to think I was the automatic door to their *ménage a trois* fantasies.

Then again, would I reject a group sex situation if the opportunity presented itself? I didn't think it was my bag, but I couldn't be completely sure. After living so long with rigid sexual rules, I had to relearn how to listen to my inner voice. I was free to create the tenets I wanted to live by. I could consider what appealed to me and what didn't. I could pick my preferences without angrily rejecting others. I didn't have to judge. I could organically, naturally lean toward what felt right for me.

I did know I wanted to date men—to play, to flirt, to have hot sex. Once I found someone I wanted to be in a more meaningful relationship with, and who wanted to be with me, who knew what that might look like? I was a work in progress.

I found myself savoring the ways men were different from me.

The fleshiness of a flaccid penis and the electrifying phenomenon of its rising. The depth of voice, the tendency toward monosyllables, the force of an unmediated opinion. The proliferation of hair on the body, the muscles, a rounded belly. The scraping graze of a five o'clock shadow. The loveable vulnerability of the back of an exposed neck (which I also found appealing in butch women). The male rituals of the handshake, the face pulled taut, the sports and job talk.

Many of these things had bothered me years before. Now they compelled me, excited me, softened me. Perhaps I was romanticizing straight men—just as I had lesbian women years earlier—but it felt good. These days, I veered more or less without judgment toward what delighted me.

As I connected with men online, we'd usually email for a while then eventually talk on the phone before meeting in person. We'd write or talk about our passions, our jobs, the configurations of our families. There were so many men in the world with such an array of different lives.

I had yet to talk to anyone about my lesbian past. But then there was a guy named Greg. He emailed me regularly. He was intrigued that I was a writer and professor, and that I loved to travel. I was intrigued that he owned a restaurant, and that his dream was to sail around the world as Cole's had been. Eventually, he called me. We talked about places we'd travelled and books we liked. He told me about his two teenaged daughters, one a ballet dancer, the other a blossoming writer. I began to feel a building pressure that I needed to tell him that the person I was getting a divorce from was a woman. I hadn't lied, but I'd avoided gendered pronoun references.

What was I worried about? If he didn't like it, he wasn't someone I'd want to see anyway. I didn't know why it was hard to spit out. After all those years of coming out as a lesbian to family, friends, students, and strangers, you'd think I'd be used to it. For the most part, I'd liked how coming out as a lesbian wasn't only personal but served a larger social purpose. Coming out as a woman with fluid sexuality might do the same thing. Then again, I was exhausted after all the upheaval in my life. My heart had been so broken I felt black-and-blue inside. I wanted to live without justification, explanation, or drama.

Once, talking to Greg, I let slip the name of the university where I taught. Generally I avoided specifics so I didn't reveal my identity until I was ready. Sure enough, the next day, I received an email from Greg: "Kate, I played fast and loose with Google, and I found out some very interesting information about you. You are much more complex than I'd imagined."

As I read, my heart picked up its pace.

"I hope you don't mind. I didn't mean to invade your privacy. It's just that I am so curious about you. I like you; I wanted to find out more. And now I can see why I felt you were holding back a bit. I can understand why it might be hard to tell people. But I would be the perfect person to tell. Here's why: we have much more in common than you could even have imagined. My mother was a lesbian."

My assumptions boomeranged right back at me. Of course there were men out there—men everywhere—who knew and loved lesbians. These women were their mothers, their aunts, their sisters, their friends, their colleagues. I could no longer assume anything about the men I met. What I would now assume was this: they would have no problem with me unless proven otherwise.

Greg and I dated awhile. Our first meeting was explosive. We kissed for an hour, and I experienced something I never had before: an orgasm without genital stimulation, with my clothes on! But eventually it became clear we didn't jive in other ways, and after a few months we stopped seeing each other. I altered my online profile to include the fact that I'd been married twice: once to a man, once to a woman.

I never received hostile or sexually forward communication on the dating sites. I enjoyed assuming that most people are generally good, that most people will creak open a new space in their minds when faced with novel information. I liked expecting the best of people.

I decided I wanted to say yes to life. I'd spent a lot of years saying no to so many things. On impulse I'd started eating meat again—at the Greek festival where I ate a sausage—and my body responded well. Maybe my body knew what it wanted. My heart, too. It was as though the trauma of losing Emily, of being so deeply rejected, opened up new space in me. I was ready to try things the old me would have rejected.

A guy asked me to go to a boxing match. Instead of balking I thought, *Well, that could be a new experience.* He and another couple picked me up in a four-door one-ton truck. Everyone but me wore jeans and cowboy hats. A jockey, now this? I laughed to myself at how my determination to be open was mirroring my growing-up years in a small town when I dated cowboys. I wondered what my lesbian friends would think if they saw me now.

Because of the jockey, I attended horse races for the first time. With another date, I rode my bike seventy-two miles around Lake Tahoe. I saw movies and TV shows, and read books and magazines, and tried food and drink I would have rejected in the past.

The phoenix was rising from the ashes. Living the life I wanted was up to me. Even though it was late fall and the divorce was still dragging on, I made plans to travel. On winter break, I'd go to Southern California to hang out with my friends and my sister. I bought a ticket to Hawaii for spring break, and a ticket to Europe for summer. I was determined to live the life I wanted to live.

Eventually, I tired of the online dating scene. I wanted to spend less time on the phone and computer and more out in the world. I deactivated my accounts and joined a hiking club. I figured I'd go out and do what I loved. Maybe I'd meet guys to date. If not, at least I was enjoying life.

One day I received a message from a guy on Yahoo Personals, a free site I'd not deactivated because I'd forgotten I was on it. The message was simple. He lived in Sausalito and worked in San Jose. He asked if I'd like to meet for dinner. Well, that was different. No long email describing himself and asking about me? No back and forth for weeks before meeting?

His picture looked cute. There were a few details on his profile: that he liked to travel and scuba dive, that he liked music and kayaking, and that he worked as a business developer (whatever that was). His name was Dave.

We met at a Japanese restaurant. I walked the two miles from my apartment. I loved walking, and the city made it welcoming. He was there when I arrived. He had a warm smile and striking green eyes, one of which was a little sleepy in an endearing way.

He told me this was his favorite Japanese restaurant. We discovered we had Japan in common. He'd worked for the Japanese phone company for ten years and had traveled there many times. He now worked for a startup.

He ordered tea, not beer or *sake*, with dinner. That was surprising. I'd yet to go out to dinner with a guy who didn't order booze. He earnestly talked about his spiritual beliefs—not religion, but his belief that a broader intelligence infused us all. He liked to meditate and do yoga. I liked those things, too, but I wondered if he was too woo-woo for me.

He told me he'd been married once before and had been divorced for ten years. Surprisingly, he didn't have kids. All the men I'd dated had children, some young, some teens, some adults.

I told him about Emily. He didn't bat an eye. He told me he'd dated a woman who'd at one time been a lesbian. We shared our travel stories. He'd been all over the world to scuba dive and, intriguingly, to see music. He told me about his favorite band from New Orleans. He'd seen them live more than a hundred times. This was all fascinating, but I wondered if it was true. So many guys had regaled me with stories of their exciting lives, only to find out they'd done all their traveling in their twenties with a backpack slung over their shoulder.

He was wearing business attire, a button-down shirt and slacks.

He was sincere but a little too serious and square. When he found out I'd walked to the restaurant, he seemed surprised. I wondered why a guy who purported to love hiking would be shocked that I walked two miles. He offered to drive me home. I declined. He offered again. It was getting dark, and the neighborhood could be a little sketchy. I finally agreed.

He had a BMW and a new iPhone. Definitely square. Did he even drink? He dropped me off in front of my apartment. I thanked him and went in, thinking I'd probably never see him again. The evening had been pleasant but not remarkable.

A couple of days later, he called and asked me if I wanted to go to a blues club in San Francisco. I thanked him but told him I already had plans.

A few days after that, when I was walking across campus, my phone vibrated. A text from him read: *I'm off to kayak in the bay on this gorgeous day. Wish you could join me.* The air was crisp and the sky pure blue. I yearned to be paddling across the bay rather than sitting in my office. I guess he hadn't been bullshitting me. He really did like to do things, not merely sit in front of his computer.

The second time we met was at brunch. Again, the conservative clothes and no booze. I tested him, asking if he drank. He said he didn't drink much but that he liked dark beer. He also enjoyed wine tasting. As he talked, it was clear he knew a lot more than I did about the subject of wine.

When we talked about our past relationships, instead of wallowing in their problems, he said something interesting: "Well, it's good to know what you don't want, so you can learn what you do want." I liked that. It focused on the past not as a problem but as a path for growing.

While we drank post-lunch tea, he reached out across the table and held my hand. My skin buzzed. When we walked to his car, he leaned into me, kissing me softly, almost imperceptibly, on the lips. Then he drove away. I wasn't sure how I felt about that kiss. I wanted a man who wasn't too passive. I'd spent too many years in a relationship where I felt I had to steer the boat. I wanted a co-captain, not a passenger. The kiss, while sweet, didn't seem like the forceful kiss of a man who'd take charge, much less be powerful in bed. Never again would I be in a sexless relationship. He obviously was interested in me, but he hadn't been pushy. I wondered if that meant he was respectful, or docile.

At that time, I was also dating another guy who had drifted in and out of my life for a couple of months. He wanted me to go away with him for a few days. I thought it would be a good opportunity to see if something more might grow between us. When Dave called again to ask me out, I decided to be honest. I told him I liked him but that I was also dating someone else. I was going away for a few days with him to see if there was anything worthwhile between us.

"Well, that's not what I'd hoped to hear," he said. "But let me know how it goes."

That was the most honest, mature response I could have imagined. Dave had a calmness about him that appealed to me. The three days I was with the other guy were unremarkable; Dave often drifted through my mind. When I got home, I called him. We made a date to meet the next night at a restaurant down the street from my place.

I got there early to sit at the bar with a glass of wine and struck up a conversation with the woman sitting next to me. Dave walked up behind me. I could sense his closeness, felt a sweet vibe. I leaned into him as he gave me a hug and a soft kiss on the neck. After the woman left, he teased me, asking if I was "into her." I laughed. It was the first time he'd joked with me, said something edgy and funny. I was happy.

At the end of the evening, I invited him up to my place. He pinned me against the kitchen wall and kissed me voraciously. That was more like it.

The next week, Dave took me for a hike along a path with a magnificent overlook of the Golden Gate Bridge. We sat on a large, flat rock, which he said was his favorite spot for meditation. I asked him what he did when he meditated. He said he thought about everything and everyone he appreciated.

"You *think* when you meditate?" I said. "I thought you weren't supposed to think."

"I like focusing on appreciation. It's really great. Want to try?"

I did. He held my hand lightly, and we took a few deep breaths. The tiny red bridge in the distance spanned the blue and white water. I closed my eyes and gave thanks for the air, the ocean, the birds. Dave had suggested I allow faces of people I love to flash through my mind. They did, one after the other. A deep peace laced with joy filled me up. I squeezed his hand and whispered, "I think you're going to be good for me."

That night we danced and danced in his living room, pulling off pieces of clothes until we were in our underwear, dancing and laughing and kissing. Then we fell into bed in each other's arms.

In the middle of the night I awoke, panic shooting through my body. I slipped out of bed and wrapped a blanket around me. I felt my way into the dark living room and pulled open the sliding glass door. Dave's place was perched on the top of a hill, overlooking the bay. The water and sky were dark, a few boats and stars twinkling. I reclined on a lounge chair, gulping air.

Oh my God, I was falling in love with this guy. I was terrified. If we ended up together, would he one day have sex with someone else behind my back? Would he spend years with me and then be unwilling to work on our relationship if the shit hit the fan? Would he break my heart?

I looked up to the stars and started talking to my dad, a telepathic phone call. *Please, Dad, help me. What should I do?*

I'd never initiated a conversation with my father. I'd had only that one experience of his visiting me unbidden. As clearly as if he were sitting right next to me, I heard his voice say:

Don't worry. Dave's a good guy.

Then I felt, running through my bones, this reminder: *I'm a whole person, with or without a lover in my life.*

The next morning, I told Dave that I was falling in love with him and that it was freaking me out. He said, "Well, you have a choice. You can fight it or go with it; it's up to you."

The message that I was whole, that I was in charge of my own feelings, that I was the creator of my life, was coming at me from all sides. Perhaps it was time I believed it. Perhaps it was time I fully embraced my one true love. Me.

Later, I asked Dave if he thought it was strange that I talked to my dead father. Not at all, he said. He told me that when he was twenty-three, his father fell ill and was put on life support. Dave and his stepmom stood vigil in the ICU. It was quiet except for the churning machines. Suddenly, Dave sensed his father up in the corner of the room, conveying that everything was okay and that he was moving on. Even though he'd never experienced anything like it, Dave had no doubt that the presence was his father, and that everything was, indeed, okay. At that moment, a nurse who'd been monitoring Dave's dad walked in and said, "I'm sorry, he passed." Dave remembered thinking, *No kidding. I already know that.*

I was stunned. The corner of the room? That was exactly where I'd detected Wes at his funeral. Dave and I talked about how these experiences felt so real at the time. There was nothing strange or surreal about them. To us, they were calming. And they were proof that we were more than our bodies, that our spirits somehow live on.

I soon learned that Dave was no square. He was an intriguing mix of businessman and bohemian. Like me, he married young and launched into the life of a professional right out of college. He worked in the corporate world for years. In his late-thirties—after a turbulent marriage and a sticky divorce—he began to look closely at his life. How, and why, was he repeating patterns that led to unhappiness? How could he stop blaming others and become the conscious creator of his life? That quest led him on a personal and spiritual transformation. He quit his job and began to travel. He spent a lot of time in nature and with family and friends. And he discovered the jam band music scene.

Most of the live music I'd seen took place in huge venues where people sat and listened, hoping the band would play each song exactly as it sounded on the album. I'd loved those concerts as a teenager, but now I found them lackluster. The music Dave loved, and introduced me to, was more improvisational. Jam bands fit under a wide array of genres and were usually some mix of rock, blues, pop, jazz, bluegrass, gospel, reggae. Bands might play a tune from a CD but then break out into an ad-lib riff that could go on for ten or fifteen minutes. Such grooves were entrancing, meditative, elating. Many jam shows took place in small-to-medium clubs where people danced and danced and danced. I immediately loved the scene. Finally I understood the hoopla about the Grateful Dead. The Dead songs I'd heard on the radio were okay, but I didn't get why some people went crazy over the band. I hadn't understood that it was all about the concert experience, about the audience and band morphing into one big organism.

After years of mostly not working—except for embarking on a few entrepreneurial endeavors—Dave was back in an office, working long days at a technology startup. Yet he was the man who loved nature and animal encounters, who loved to hike and swim and scuba dive, who enjoyed cooking, who enjoyed being Uncle Dave to his friends' children, who loved to laugh and was the master of wackiness and puns. At a music event, he could party like a hippie with his friends, while the next night might find him playing board games or kicking back on the couch with a book. Dave soaked up my book recommendations, reading contemporary novels and memoirs for the first time in his life, and enjoying them.

For years I'd swung wildly from a life of married domesticity to a freeform life dominated by edgy merrymaking. I saw that no such binary governed Dave's life. He did both, and it was all one life.

We fell into a rhythm of seeing each other mostly on the weekdays. He'd spend nights at my place since it took only ten minutes for him to get to his office, whereas it took over an hour from Sausalito. But he still had a home to tend to, so on the weekends he'd go there. Sometimes I'd join him, but I too had weekend things to take care of at home. One day I told him I wished we could spend more time together on the weekends.

"Well, you know how that could happen," he said in his signature understated way. "I could move in with you."

I looked at him. Really? He wanted to live together after only three months of dating? And even though I wasn't yet legally divorced? He'd lived in that awesome house in Sausalito for eight years. He was willing to give that up? We were in love, no question about that. But wasn't it too soon?

Dave didn't believe in arbitrary timelines. What might be too soon for one person, might be just right for another. He was all about trusting his feelings. He sat there calmly while I talked about my thoughts. I told him I wasn't sure.

"That's okay," he said. "Give yourself some time to think about it."

I awoke the next morning with a fresh breeze flowing through an open window in my heart. It was crystal clear what I wanted. As we sat at the kitchen counter for breakfast I said, "Okay, I thought about it. I want you to move in."

"Kate, are you sure you don't want to give yourself more time to think about it?"

"No," I said. "I know it's the right thing."

In one month he dismantled eight years of Sausalito life and moved into my apartment—our apartment. We jettisoned my hodgepodge furniture to make room for his antiques. Still, he had to downsize from a three-bedroom house to a one-bedroom apartment. But he didn't bat an eye. Change had been building for a while. He knew it was time. We were going on pure instinct.

I was sitting in the living room, surrounded by piles of legal documents, my head in my hands. The whole thing was horribly overwhelming. Emily's and my divorce was dragging out. I was stuck in a mire. I had fired my costly attorney and was representing myself. I was no lawyer. I hated all the legal mumbo-jumbo. Fine print was my nightmare.

Emily was still represented by Liz's attorney pal, Tara Helmer. If we had mutually agreed on a mediator, the divorce would have been final months before. I couldn't see beyond the legal morass, with its emotional underpinnings. Tara Helmer was a strange woman. Even the judge had been impatient with her ramblings.

I'd had one triumph through self-representation. The judge ordered Emily to pay me spousal support. The thrill of that success was short lived. I wanted the whole thing to be over. I could tell as long as we were involved in a divorce battle, the past would never be history. Emily's biggest concern was that I would be given a stake in the house. Stupidly, I had agreed for only her name to be put on the title when we bought the house. I didn't recall the reasoning, but now my trust in our relationship had blown up in my face, in more ways than one.

At the same time, the house felt like a dark relic of sorrow and demise. Even after we'd remodeled, I could smell the past in the floorboards. That was the house where her mother had died, and where our relationship had died. Perhaps money from that house would be infested somehow. I ran the gamut between gripping to what I thought was fair, and wanting to let it all go.

Sitting there on the couch surrounded by a mound of paperwork, I told Dave it felt like I was losing my mind.

"Kate," he said, "there will come a time when this is all over. How will you feel then?"

"I'll feel great. Free. Hugely relieved."

"Okay then," he said, "imagine that it's over. Picture it. Feel the feeling of it being over. The only reason you want it to be over is so you can feel better. Feel better anyway."

There it was again, the reminder that I could create my own reality. I closed my eyes. I saw the papers signed. I saw myself walking free. I felt liberated. I knew it was up to me to convert this whole mess from a horrible experience into a transformative one. The power was mine.

When I opened my eyes, my hand reached into the pile of papers for the exact one I needed for an upcoming meeting. Over the next week or two, the pieces fell together much more easily, like a wheel had been greased.

In a conference room, I met with Emily, her attorney, and a supposedly neutral judge. I say *supposedly*, because when Tara Helmer and the woman judge talked, they joshed with each other. It was clear they were friends. Whatever. I didn't care. I had tasted the freedom of the divorce being final, and I knew it would be soon. Tara Helmer tried to coerce me into signing papers to end the battle right then and there, with no more money coming to me and no stake in the house. I said no. Emily asked if she could talk to me alone. Reluctantly, the judge and attorney left the room.

The minute I was alone with Emily, I felt overtaken by grief that I hadn't known still lived in my body.

"You ripped apart my life," I said.

"I know," she said. "And I'm sick about it."

"Then why did you do it?"

"I don't know."

"Are you happy?" I asked. "Is Liz your soul mate?" Maybe I asked the question because I wanted her to admit her misery to me. I knew they weren't happy. At least that's what a few friends had told me.

She looked down, then back up, her lips in a tight half-frown, her eyes red. She moved her head side to side, saying nothing, but the message was clear: she didn't love Liz. Or at least, that's what she wanted me to think. I had no way to know what truths, and what lies, she'd ever told me.

"Tara's going to kill me," she said, "but I want to make an offer to you. She thinks I shouldn't pay you a dime." Emily stated a number.

She would write me a check, and it would all be over.

Her offer is paltry, said my left brain. *Abundance and freedom are yours*, said my right brain.

I went with freedom.

I walked the mile back to the apartment. It was spring, the season Emily left. Now it was a new spring, a Technicolor spring, the spring of the final cut. A riot of birdsong lifted from the city trees. A car blasted a few bars of a rap song as it whizzed by. The past ghosted up through the present like pentimento, as though *now* was painted over an old canvas of *then*. I walked past the restaurant where Emily, TJ, and I had first sat over beer to talk after Georgia's poetry class. Then I swung open the door into the apartment building where I now lived, walking up six flights of stairs and into my new life.

After the divorce was final, and Dave and I were moving to Santa Cruz, I dumped two fat boxes of legal files into the apartment complex's garbage bin. I also deleted an email file where I'd kept correspondence from Emily for many years. I let it all go. The past was over.

Then one day, months later, I received an email from Emily. I opened it up and read the opening: "Really, Kathleen?" I scanned it and realized it was an incensed letter, a page or more long. She was outraged about something I'd written on my blog. For the first time, I'd told my truth, publically. The piece focused on telling a new story: what I'd thought was the worst thing that ever happened to me was actually the best. The betrayal had opened my cage.

With the anger in Emily's email staring me down, I knew I had a choice. Engage or disengage. Part of me was curious about what she had to say. But another part of me knew that curiosity killed the cat. Why infuse her fury into my heart? I had my reasons for writing my story. If she didn't like it, she could tell her own version. I wasn't out to deliberately hurt anyone. No longer did I have dreams of revenge. I was a writer. I was the creator of my life, my life story.

Without reading beyond the first line or two, I hit delete. Then I blocked Emily's email address. A machine would now delegate the past to the past. Over the next year, I went a step further. Whenever Emily came into my mind, which was rarer and rarer, I wished her well. Whenever I did that, the impulse to grasp or defend or explain dissipated.

For a long time this was my line: "Emily and I needed to split up. I just wish it hadn't happened the way it did. I wish she had been truthful with me."

Then I began to realize even wishing it had been different was a kind of clinging. Our split couldn't have happened any other way. Its brutality stripped away my ego so violently that I was gifted the chance to be reborn. Emily and Liz had done me a favor. They were angels in disguise.

It took some of my friends longer than it took me to accept what had happened. As I got happier and happier, as I dated and then fell in love with Dave, several of my friends—reeling at the change—asked me, "Don't you miss her?" I knew it was they who missed her, missed us. I understood. But I no longer needed to tell the story of betrayal. I now told the story of renaissance, of transformation.

Years later, two weeks before Dave and I were about to embark on our odyssey, I received a text from Emily. I'd long ago deleted her from my phone, so no name appeared, only a number. The text began "Leen," so I knew right away it was her. She asked if I would please meet with her. She knew I was leaving California to live as a nomad. She didn't know if or when she'd ever see me again.

I mulled it over then let the text sit unanswered for a while. When I was ready, I wrote back: "Why do you want to meet?"

She texted back that she had so much she wanted to tell me, so much to say. She said if I wouldn't meet with her, would I at least read an email if she sent it? I didn't want to read a one-sided missive from her. A monologue.

I asked Dave what he thought.

"Do whatever is best for you," he said.

When Emily saw me walking toward her on the downtown Santa Cruz sidewalk, she cried. When I got close enough, we hugged. While she waited at a sidewalk table, I went inside the cafe to order a tea—the cafe where, years ago, Emily and I sat for hours, writing and sketching in our journals. The memory was like a movie I'd seen.

When I got back to the table, she wiped away tears.

"Thank you for meeting me," she said.

"You're welcome." My chest felt tight. I breathed in, focused on opening it up. On being in that very moment.

She cried a bit more.

"It's hard to see you," she said.

I nodded, took a sip of my tea. There she sat, the woman I'd once thought completed me. Now I knew that was impossible. No other person belonged to me. She had been free to go. If I'd known to let things end, I would have suffered less. Yet the suffering had been my greatest teacher.

"I wanted to say to you that I'm so sorry," she said. "All those things I said when we were breaking up—that you were a horrible partner—they weren't true. You were a wonderful partner, loving and supportive."

My eyes misted. In spite of it all, it felt good to hear that.

"I don't know what came over me," she said. "I feel like I was crazy in those days, like the death of my mother and turning fifty and everything else made me, I don't know, just crazy. I hope you can see that the Emily who did all those mean things—well, that's not me. I hope you know the real me is the kind, gentle Emily you thought you always knew. That's who I really am."

I believed she was both. We all are. We all have the capacity to be kind and cruel. I thought about her pattern of leaping from one relationship to the next. That was part of who she was. It had been part of me, too. She was the woman who locked me out of the house, who had an affair and lied to me. And she was the woman who bought food for a hungry homeless man, the woman who was deeply perceptive about the way light changed in the sky, the woman who was afraid of swimming in the ocean but, then, one day swam in Hawaii, waving from the shore. She was the woman who'd loved me. She was all of that.

She wiped away more tears. "And what we—what I—did to you…Leen, it was horrible. Just horrible."

A spectral memory of betrayal, of devastation, seeped through me then disappeared like a vapor. I thought of how happy I was, how I loved Santa Cruz, how joyful I was about Dave's and my decision to live as nomads, how nothing could hold me back unless I let it.

"Yes," I said, listening closely to my heart. "Yes, it was horrible. But it's not anymore."

We were silent for a few minutes.

"I also wanted to say, I'm so sorry about your mom." Her tears came again. She had left our relationship while my mom was disintegrating from dementia. She'd not been there for my mom's death, for the release of her ashes into the sea.

"Thank you."

She told me about the deaths of our dog and cat, the ones she'd taken with her. She said she'd heard Max had died, the sweet Pomeranian I'd taken with me.

"I read your blog," she said, half smiling, her eyes glinting. She didn't mention the angry email I'd never responded to. I wondered if she'd changed her mind about what I'd written.

Her phone buzzed. She looked at it and quickly responded with a text. I was sure it was Liz. I was also sure Liz had no idea Emily was meeting with me. I thought about all those texts they'd exchanged years ago, behind my back, when they were falling in love. I thought about when Emily used to call me surreptitiously from a pay phone when she lived with the minister. I thought about my slipping out of Michael's life and into Emily's arms. And I thought of Dave: he knew I was here with Emily. He had left my decisions up to me, and I had no desire to lie to him, or to tell him a half-truth, or evade anything. Thank God, I thought, thank God I was learning how to live in a brand new way. The past was all necessary, every single bit of it. As John Tarrant said, "Every step in the dark turns out, in the end, to have been on course after all."

When she tucked her phone away, she looked at me. She knew that I knew. The irony was poignant, if irony can be.

As though to counteract the intensity of it all, we chatted about a few inconsequential things like neighbors who unexpectedly bumped into each other downtown.

"Can I ask you something?" she said.

"What?"

"Please don't write about this on your blog."

I paused. I guessed that meant Liz also read my blog.

"Okay," I said. "Not on my blog. But I can't promise I won't ever write about it."

"I understand," she said.

I took the final sip of my tea.

"What are you thinking?" she said.

"I feel like I want to give you some advice."

"What?"

"Well, I feel like I want to tell you that it's possible to be happy."

She leaned back in her chair and ran her hand through her hair. "I know it is," she said. "I know."

We stood for a good-bye hug.

"Have a great adventure," she said.

"Thank you," I answered. "You, too."

As I walked away down the sidewalk, I heard her call my name.

I turned.

"Maybe I'll see you in Paris," she called out.

I waved at her and turned toward home.

22

Water

Do you have the patience to wait until your mud settles
and the water is clear?
– Byron Katie

I want to live within walking distance of swimmable water.

This thought comes to me not as a conscious creation of my construction but as a gift, a fully formed object—like a stone, a heartbeat, a breath.

When Dave and I headed out on our odyssey, I had consciously allowed myself to inhabit the fertile void. I trusted that the footholds would appear. While I was healing from my surgery, I swam a lot—head up—in our friends' pool. Then we spent weeks by the ocean in southern California. Our times in and near the ocean in Australia and Cape Cod had been magical. Before all of that, of course, we'd loved beachy Santa Cruz—and the sweetest part of our downtown San Jose apartment life had been the swimming pool and Jacuzzi.

Then there were our times in Hawaii snorkeling and swimming, and my years as a synchronized swimmer. It's as though my psyche gathered up all my watery love like pieces of thread and wove them together into a tapestry of revelation:

I want to live within walking distance of swimmable water.

Yet when I ponder the message, I wrangle with it. Does this mean when we decide to settle down again that I'll want a swimming pool? Or that I'll need to join a gym that has a pool? Would a pool be enough? Is it a call to buy a place in Hawaii? But we'd have to win the lottery to afford a Hawaii pad within walking distance of the beach. Does it mean living on a lake in a more affordable place? Where might that be?

The more I wrangle with the details, the more uncomfortable I feel. I decide to let it go. To trust. To allow the answer to appear as easily as the desire did.

Soon, the perfect opportunity arises to buy a ridiculously affordable casita in a small town in Baja California Sur, Mexico. For years, my sister Sheila and brother-in-law Jack have been going down there, a two-day drive, where they own a small surf shack with no electricity. Sheila calls it "camping with walls." For many years, Sheila has enjoyed it, but lately she has become less patient with the lack of basic comforts. Several straws broke the camel's back: a swarm of attacking wasps, a scorpion in the bedroom, and—the biggest straw of all—a rattlesnake in the living room.

Like the bedbug infestation that led us to the Love Nest, this plague led Sheila and Jack to buy a casita in a small, new resort. It's their kind of place, not big and flashy but with a three-story condo tower and surrounded by other individual casitas. Some people live there full time, others use their places as vacation rentals. The resort has a pool, a Jacuzzi, and an open-air restaurant. And it's a five-minute walk to the best swimming beach in the area.

When Sheila tells me about it, she mentions that another one-bedroom casita under construction is for sale right next door to theirs. The cost is a fraction of the price for the Love Nest.

I know immediately this is the answer to the question raised by my revelation. It isn't only a knowing but a profound recognition. Dave agrees. More and more, we are apt to trust in the genius of our intuition. And that assurance is affirmed as we look into the details. With a pool, Jacuzzi, and swimmable beach, there is water, water everywhere! There is also an abundance of sea life, some of our favorite creatures: dolphins, whale sharks, sea turtles, and at least five species of whales.

While we've both spent time in Mexico, neither of us has been to the exact spot of the small resort. Given that we are scheduled to leave for Asia soon, immediately going to Baja isn't feasible. We are making our decision completely on faith, bolstered by the validation of my sister and her husband. Besides, the casita is number eleven. That is our special number. A number of alignment.

Sight unseen we buy the place, wiring the first payment days before we leave for Hong Kong. The vision is clear in our hearts. My medical and spiritual adventures have sharpened my instincts. I trust my intuition like never before, and I know more deeply than ever that living life now—flowing with waves of faith—is the way to go.

The W Hotel in Kowloon has the highest pool in all of Hong Kong. Spread out over the seventy-sixth floor rooftop, the infinity pool and Jacuzzi seem to spill into the spectacular skyline.

The sky is purple. Typhoon Haiyan's tail whips up a hot wind. Dave and I are the only ones crazy enough to be up here. We are here for a baptism. For the first time since the surgery, I submerge my head. Rain pelts us at a slant, and the pool water rises and falls in waves. The wind is so strong it almost topples us over as we move from pool to warm Jacuzzi.

Dave shouts, "We'll be okay as long as the building stands!"

I think about the surgeon busting open my skull. I think about all those elevators and jets and boats and taxis and subways that, over the past months, have hoisted our bodies up and down, whizzing us through space and time. I think about the faith it takes to live life in the face of complete and total impermanence. I think about Gabriele and my father, and how we all survive, in some mysterious way, the final fall.

I say, "Even if the building falls, we'll be okay."

We hold out our arms like wings and yell into the howling winds: "To infinity and beyond!"

*

Before I met Dave, I had bought tickets to travel to Hawaii for spring break and Europe for the first month of summer. I asked him if he wanted to come with me, but he was entrenched in working long days at the startup. He knew the job would come to a natural end at some point—perhaps within the year—but it was impossible to know exactly when. While we were sad we'd be apart for a while, he knew I needed to travel for myself. He urged me to have a grand adventure.

The trip to Hawaii felt like an important step, like coming full circle, closing a gap. It was my first solo flight since my divorce from Emily. I'd tried to go to Hawaii after my first divorce, but that trip had been aborted by the airplane's broken water line. Then I'd gone with Emily; the trip had been a revelation of light and dolphin love. This time was about me, my decision to go to the islands, alone.

When the airplane doors closed, to my pleasant surprise, I didn't feel an inkling of claustrophobia. I sat, looking out the window, same as I would in my apartment. I ordered a small bottle of champagne and toasted myself, a honeymoon with me.

My most remarkable adventure on the trip was this: I decided to take a long hike by myself across a volcano, a more arduous trek than I'd ever attempted. I met with a ranger at the Hawaii Volcanoes National Park Visitors Center. She issued me a back-country permit and marked on a map the hike, which would take about five hours.

I made a conscious decision. I was going to release all fear. As much as I'd pointed at Emily's fears and claimed I didn't want to live in dread, fear had been my companion for a long time: fear of my parents' illnesses and deaths, fear of flying, fear of being suffocated in my relationship, fear of being deceived, fear of being alone. My whole life I'd regulated many of my actions because of the messages I'd absorbed: women are vulnerable, women get attacked and raped, women shouldn't go places alone. I had done enough in my life, like living in Japan, to counter those fears. But I'd "felt the fear and did it anyway." On that aborted flight to Hawaii twenty years before, I'd embraced my mortality. Accepting the ephemeral nature of life alleviated fear. I decided for this hike I was going to cultivate that feeling. I wasn't going to fight fear. I was going to release resistance to death so that I could fully live.

That morning there was a light rain. I pulled a rain poncho from my backpack and slid it over my hiking clothes. I knew that this hike would involve the disorienting feeling that a volcano can engender because of its monochromatic landscape. I'd have to keep an eye out for the small cairns placed to mark the path. Sometimes their verticality tricked the eye, collapsing to horizontal like an Escher drawing.

Soon I stood alone on a massive rock, like a woman on the moon. Vast craters rose from nowhere; the tips of my boots hovered over an abyss. Sulphur steam misted from the ground, and rain tapped at my plastic covering. For an hour, then two, I walked across the ethereal landscape.

Pausing to look at the map, I descended into a rainforest on a narrow trail, branches tugging at my poncho. Then I saw a man walking toward me. A hat shielding his eyes, he ducked beneath the low limbs. Out here in pure isolation, one of us would have to turn sideways to let the other pass. Fear welled up. I let it go, like one might release a helium balloon.

As he approached, he tilted back his hat and caught my eye. He moved to the side of the narrow trail and signaled for me to pass.

"Hi," he said. He looked to be in his twenties.

"Hi," I said.

Then I saw there was another person, a woman turning the corner toward me. I stood aside. She smiled as she squeezed past, joining her man on the trail. They disappeared. I was alone again in the canopy of trees. The rain dwindled to a mist. Streaks of sun pushed through the overhead green, illuminating my way.

That summer, it was hard to say good-bye to Dave. I would be gone a whole month. We'd been together six months. I was going alone to Italy and Spain, two countries I'd never been to before.

In Rome, the beggars were biblical. They had deformities only Jesus could cure. They knelt in the streets not flinching when I dropped a coin in their cup. I saw a guy on a skateboard with shriveled legs and a shoe on one hand that propelled him across the cobblestone. He said *thank you* instead of *grazie*. Was it that obvious I was an American?

At a sidewalk cafe, an old man who spoke little English began to chat me up in a mix of languages. Smoking a hand-rolled cigarette, he called Obama a capitalist. I understood him to say he lived in Russia for a while but left because it was so cold. He had nieces and nephews who lived in California. He asked me to guess his age. I thought he might be eighty, so I said seventy-five.

"Ninety-one!" he exclaimed, pulling out his passport to prove it to me. An old black-and-white photo of a young, dark-haired woman drifted onto the table. "My mama," he said.

I stayed in a pension. The small but comfortable bed was shoved in a corner. I lay there, feeling waves of joy and loneliness sweep through me as a couple down the hall made riotous love.

After a week in Rome, wandering the streets and ruins and museums, I took a train to San Sepolcro, Tuscany, where my friend Jill lived. We hadn't seen each other in thirty years but had reconnected through Facebook. My greatest memory of her was that as a freshman, she had won the lead in the spring musical, *Babes in Arms*. Usually upperclassmen were given such roles. But her singing voice, acting ability, charm, and beauty surpassed her age. Best of all, the role required she kiss a foxy senior. I'd been in awe of her.

When I stepped off the train, there she stood, a blond teenager embedded in an elegant woman with a dazzling smile. She embraced me then ushered me into her car. We talked as she navigated us through a maze of roads and, then, through acres and acres of farmland. We talked as she parked in front of her big stone house, Santa Croce, an eight-hundred-year-old former monastery. We talked in the kitchen as the room darkened and she lit candles and poured wine. We talked as she prepared homemade Tuscan linguini with a spicy picante and a mouthwatering Chianti. We talked as we ate, and then afterward for hours, over more wine. We'd talked for seven or eight hours, straight through, and we had more to say—when Jill held up her hand and said, "Shhh. Wait a minute. There's something I want you to see."

In silence, she led me to her front door. She swung it open to the night. Her vast, dark yard was lit up with thousands of fireflies, like dancing stars fallen from the sky.

An artist, Jill had an eye for accentuating the beauty of her ancient home. Every corner looked like a still-life painting, with aesthetic arrangements of furniture, flowers, candles, and curios. A former monastery, Santa Croce had originated as a medieval watchtower given its proximity to the Tiber River, an essential trade route flowing all the way to Rome. She lived in a valley, surrounded by mountains, one of which was embedded with a medieval village called Anghiari. We walked along Anghiari's archaic, winding streets, fingering objects for sale spread across long tables in the square.

Jill took me to Umbria, to the home of her former art professors who, upon retirement, had moved from California to Italy. Their house—San Zeno—was a huge, ancient, restored convent. We toured the castle-like abode, walking down long hallways past heavy furniture and copious books and works of art. We explored their jam-packed art studio. Paintings filled the easels and wall space. A few of their friends dropped by, and we gathered on the back deck, wineglasses in hand, overlooking a vast valley filled with buttery light. I wondered about the nuns who'd lived here hundreds of years ago. Could they even have conceived of a life like ours?

One afternoon, Jill and I trekked to the river Afra, named for the goddess Aphrodite. To get down to the water, we scaled a small cliff, clinging to a rope set there for that purpose. We reclined on a rock in the sun like mermaids, the water rippling past our feet.

Alone in Florence, I escaped the heat and sat in a cool dark church, the stained glass shedding shards of color on my lap. I decided to try praying, a vestige of my Catholic childhood.

I wanted wisdom, guidance. Silently I asked, *What is the most important thing for me to know right now?*

An inner voice responded, a voice that sounded like an elderly, wise woman. She told me not to look outward so much, to not impetuously follow my impulses. Her advice reminded me of what my therapist had said to me: if I slowed down and got quiet, I could better hear my intuition.

What about writing? I asked. *What place does that have in my life?*

Writing, she said, *is your spiritual practice.*

I took an overnight ferry to Spain, disembarking in Barcelona. I checked out Gaudi's creepy, astonishing, unfinished church, *Temple Expiatori de la Sagrada Família.* I walked the streets, passing vendors, listening to musicians, watching boisterous, drinking crowds gathered around televisions as Italy played Spain in the World Cup finals. At the beach, I followed the native tradition and removed my bikini top.

In Madrid, I stayed with my friends Nicole and Lucía. Like me, Nicole had been a student at San Jose State and worked with Georgia Constantino. We knew a lot of people in common yet hadn't known each other well. But via the magic of Facebook, we'd followed each other's lives. She had been living for years in Spain, teaching English, where she met and fell in love with Lucía, a native of Madrid. Same-sex marriage was legal in Spain. They planned to marry soon. They took me all over for great food and sightseeing. My favorite place was Retiro Park, a massive public park at the edge of the city center, not far from the Prado. I wandered for hours among the sculptures and monuments, past the lake and the magnificent Palacio de Cristal, a glass-and-metal structure built in 1887 to exhibit flora and fauna from the Philippines.

In Madrid I met up with my sister Sheila and her friend Lori, who were in Europe to celebrate Sheila's fiftieth birthday. My friend Gabe joined us, too. By chance, he happened to be coming through Madrid at the same time. It was astounding to be in a place so far from California with people I knew well. The world was big and small.

Later, Sheila and I took a train to the south of Spain, to Costa del Sol. After a few days of beach time, we took a ferry to Tangier, Morocco. On a group tour we wandered the narrow ancient streets past colorful buildings, glimpsed men in long robes watching us, touched beautiful rugs, ate rice and lamb, and rode a camel. Two Dutch women, Margreet and Lia, were also on the tour. On the returning ferry, we sat with them. They were both married with children, and every year their husbands watched the kids while they went away for a girls' week. As can happen in exotic locales far from home, we all bonded immediately, sharing our life stories. When I mentioned I'd been married to a woman, our new Dutch friends were fascinated and plied me with questions. We were still talking when the ferry docked and agreed to meet the next night for dinner, Sheila's fiftieth birthday.

After an outdoor paella-and-wine dinner, the four of us walked the cobblestone streets, randomly entering stores to try on coats and hats. We linked arms, laughed and sang, landing in an intimate bar where we sat on thick couches and ordered a bottle of sparkling Cava, then another, to toast Sheila's birthday.

While Sheila and Lia were engrossed in conversation, Margreet—a gorgeous blond who reminded me of the young Olivia

Newton-John—leaned into me on the couch. In her lilting accent, she confided that she'd always wanted to make love to a woman. She said her husband knew. He was open to it if he could be involved. But she didn't want him to be. It wasn't something to be taken lightly. She thought that maybe she was a lesbian.

"How long have you felt this way?" I asked, my head spinning from the bubbly booze.

"I think my whole life," she said. "I probably never should have gotten married." She talked about how her husband was insensitive and never really understood her. She said her once-a-year trip was a gift, but that the rest of the year he expected her to have no life other than wife and mother.

"I think if I made love to a woman, it would help me to know for sure who I am and what I really want. Kate, would you make love to me?"

I almost laughed because the way she put it was so charming, like Ingrid Bergman speaking to Humphrey Bogart.

"Oh, Margreet," I said. "You are beautiful and sweet. But I'm in a different place in my life right now. I love my boyfriend, and the idea of making love to someone else right now doesn't seem appealing—no matter who that person is."

"Really, Kate? Are you sure you can't do it, just this once? I don't think your boyfriend would care."

Was this really happening—an insanely sexy woman begging me to sleep with her?

"No, Margreet, I'm sorry."

She set her glass on the low table in front of us.

"Well would you at least, then, kiss me? I've never kissed a woman. You wouldn't have a problem kissing me, would you?"

I glanced over at my sister, who was drinking and laughing with Lia. If she saw me kissing a woman, I wondered what she'd think.

"Please?"

"Okay," I said, smiling. "A kiss."

I was sure Margreet had no idea she'd be only the third woman I'd ever kissed. I wondered if I'd feel a spark.

Margreet wrapped her arms around me. I draped my arms over her shoulders. Our lips met. She ran her fingers through my hair, pulling me closer, kissing me deeply. It was lovely, sweet, almost innocent, like two girls practicing to kiss. No desire shot through me, just a tender affection for a woman I hoped would find her happiness.

The day after I flew back from Europe, Dave took me to the High Sierra Music Festival. I'd been to music festivals before—where multiple bands play over a long, full day—but never anything like this. Four days of jam band music that ran from morning into late night set amidst tall trees and broad skies, incorporating workshops, food booths, glittery costumes, hula hoops, fire play, themed camps, and storytelling. Children's events were set up for families who attended. Love was the vibe. I felt like I'd been transported into another world, amplified by the fact that a few days before I'd been wandering the ancient streets of Italy and Spain. Best of all, I was experiencing this event with Dave, who was happy to be sharing this part of his life that meant so much to him.

The playful nature of the festival mirrored the experiential nature of jam band music. Every set of songs took the audience on a journey. I had never been so blissed out dancing to music for hours and hours. It wasn't the kind of manic dancing I'd done in the past in clubs. This was about moving our bodies to music that carried us along, about being surrounded by friends and friendly strangers, about the intoxicating fresh air and towering trees. It was about feeling the love.

I tried ecstasy for the first time. Dave told me to enjoy it because if I ever took it again, it would never be as good. As the Black Crowes played, Dave stood behind me, wrapping his arms around me. I was already high from the music, from love, from life—and the drug built in me a gorgeous pleasure, then elation, that built and built until I had an orgasm. Just standing there, fully clothed, in Dave's embrace, enfolded in music.

On our way back home, we stopped at Rock Creek, a hidden gem of a spring with crystal clear waters, deep in a rocky canyon. In our swimsuits, we dropped our bodies into water so cold it took my breath away. Then we lay out in the sun on hot slabs of flat rocks.

This time, I wasn't on a drug, but a sensory ecstasy built in me, an accumulation of the incredible festival and now the embrace of nature. Glimmering beads of water trickled down our skin. A feeling rose in me, shocking and amazing, as though once again an orgasm were building. Lying there next to Dave, our arms touching, that's what happened: without sexual stimulation, I came and came while Dave held me.

Later I read about sexual climax as a spiritual experience. The libido is life energy. Perhaps so many years of denying my sexual nature had hindered my spiritual growth. Or perhaps another way to think about it was this: so much sublimation had held my sexual/spiritual self in escrow where it grew and grew in the dark. Those years were not wasted. I may have felt stuck, but I had been expanding in the dim recesses of my psyche. Now I was a butterfly bursting from my chrysalis.

As Greg Levoy writes, "With the whole world as the apple of your eye, all of life becomes an aphrodisiac."

23

Where We Are

Let's pay attention only to where we are.
There's enough beauty in being here and not somewhere else.
—Fernando Pessoa

When Dave and I walk into the yoga center with our friends Bella and Vasdev, a little white cat sneaks in from the street. The windows are open to the sounds of thunder, crows, and a barking dog. The room smells of lemongrass.

The teacher begins the class with an evocative chant. We are in India. We are doing yoga in India.

My body leans into the positions, surrendering. My monkey mind makes lists, wonders if I brought the right clothes, rehashes a morning conversation, considers whether or not I should try a headstand on my scalp scarred from brain surgery four months ago. I allow the chatter to float by.

During final relaxation, my body starts to buzz. Suddenly I am observing myself from above. There I am, lying on the mat. There I am, hovering near the ceiling. I'm not separated into two parts but expanded into a vast version of me. This has never happened before, but there's nothing odd or scary about it. It's as though I'm loosened, as though I'm multiplied like a blown dandelion.

After class, we are given a snack: half a banana, a ball of sweet sticky rice, and tea, because it is a special day, Kartik Poornima, a Hindu festival coinciding with the full moon. "Kartik" means "star." Today is the festival of lights of the gods. We dip our forefinger into pastes of three colors—yellow, red, and black—and dot our foreheads. The black is ashes from burnt offerings.

On our walk home, we weave along crumbling sidewalks through throngs of people, dogs and cows, and the occasional water buffalo. Cars and auto-rickshaws zigzag, horns beeping. Motorcycles dodge children and goats. In an empty lot, a group of guys plays cricket.

We stop at a cart where a vendor sells pekoras. For fifty rupees, we get a handful. He wraps the deep-fried potato, onion, and herb balls in newspaper. We eat them on the warm and drizzly walk along the beach.

Kids run up to us shouting, "Photo! Photo!" After we take their picture they say, "Zoom! Zoom!" They want to see their faces in our camera. On the sand, kids kick around a ball. Three boys play with pieces of a Styrofoam cooler.

That night, from Bella and Vasdev's rooftop, we watch the golden full moon rise. Fireworks light up the sky in celebration of Kartik Poornima. Off in the distance, the haunting Islamic call to prayer echoes. That morning I'd been awakened by the bells of a nearby Christian church. Hindu, Christian, and Muslim braid together, here in this spot of the world.

On November twenty-sixth, I celebrate my fifty-first birthday in India by teaching poetry to Bella's third-grade students. We read Shel Silverstein with words omitted and make guesses about which words fit in. Bella brings me an armful of flowers and, in the school tradition, I don a wacky birthday cake hat while the kids sing the birthday song.

For Thanksgiving weekend, we go with Bella and Vasdev to Pondicherry, a couple of hours south, to a resort on the Bay of Bengal. We sleep in the rainforest beneath a palapa roof, in a bed draped by the otherworldly scrim of a mosquito net. In the open-air yoga center, we do an hour-long meditation and the next morning take a yoga class.

We meet Miles, his wife Opal, and their daughter Starla, who is almost two. Miles, too, had a brain tumor—but his was not benign. He has undergone two craniotomies, chemo, and radiation. He's doing well, but a recent scan was questionable. I try not to worry about him, just to see him whole and healed. I watch his daughter play with her fork, her water glass, so confident, so in her body in that way children can be. We eat our Thanksgiving meal together, giving thanks for this moment.

One hot, humid evening, we walk with our friends along the

beach, where people gather on the ledge of the promenade. Cows, down for the night, sleep in groups of three or four along the road near street dogs and goats.

Vasdev leads us on a detour down a dirt road through a fishing village filled with shacks. Most have their doors open to bare rooms and dirt floors. People nod as we pass.

A group of girls comes running up to me, squealing and laughing. They grab my hands and reach up to touch my hair.

"What's your name?" asks the tallest one.

"Kate," I say.

The girls chant, "Kate! Kate!"

I ask each of them their names. They stare into my eyes. I do my best to repeat each name. They laugh and caress my arms.

As we pull away, I wave and they chant, "Good-bye, good-bye, good-bye."

*

One fall evening after I finished grading papers, Dave and I—having lived together in the San Jose apartment for not quite a year—sat on the couch, eyes closed.

"I see us getting in our car, equipped for snow, all our gear piled inside. We drive into the Sierra, a fun and easy drive. We're in a warm house in the snow, fire going, food, friends."

I saw it all as Dave described it. I smelled the smoky fire and heard the flames click and pop.

"Now we're gliding down the mountain," he said. "It's a beautiful, bluebird day. Tons of snow, air pure and fresh. We are smiling, loving every moment."

I felt the movement in my body, wind against my face.

Our first year together, Dave had gone skiing on winter weekends with his friends. He always returned, glowing from the fresh air and buttressed by exercising for days in the thin atmosphere. I'd tried to ski a few times as a kid but I'd never liked it much. My Scotchgarded jeans would get soaked, hanging heavily from my hips, my fingers and toes growing numb. Just a few times skiing—or more like tumbling—down the slopes would end with my shivering in the lodge. But Dave's enthusiasm for skiing was infectious. Maybe I'd missed out on something essential about it as a kid. Dave learned to ski in his forties, why couldn't I?

Dave told me it was all about having the right equipment and learning how to square your shoulders while facing down the mountain. It was about following the lead of your parabolic skis, not spending all your energy resisting falling. He also said going skiing a few times wasn't enough. If I really wanted to learn, we'd need to go as much as possible during the ski season. I felt an urge to give it a try, even though I had no ski equipment or clothes. We didn't have a car that could withstand snow conditions, we had no place to stay, and we didn't even have ski passes. I had six weeks off during winter break, but Dave was working long days. If we did it, we'd need to drive up to Tahoe on the weekends.

Instead of making lists and worrying over the details, Dave suggested we visualize our desire. He wanted us to focus on the feeling of skiing, just as he'd once told me to focus on the feeling of my divorce being settled. I knew about the magic of lining up with positive emotion. As Abraham-Hicks says, "The reason you want every single thing that you want, is because you think you will feel really good when you get there. But if you don't feel really good on your way to there, you can't get there."

So instead of getting uptight about all we'd have to do to make skiing happen, we decided to visualize the experience and to luxuriate in good feeling. It's almost impossible now to remember how all the pieces fell together so easily, but they did. A ski swap popped up on our radar, and we went, buying me gear at a discount. With remarkable ease, we sold our cars and bought a brand-new blue, all-wheel drive Subaru outfitted with seat warmers, puddle lights, and snow tires. We named her Chitty Chitty Bang Bang. Then, seemingly out of nowhere, came the opportunity to rent a ski house for the season with another couple.

The *pièce de résistance*, though, came the day before Thanksgiving. I was cooking dinner, happy that Dave would soon be home from yet another long day in the office, happy that we had a holiday ahead of us.

The phone rang. "Hi, baby," Dave said, calling from his cell phone. "Do you want the good news or the bad news first?" I detected playfulness in his voice.

"How about the bad news?" I said.

"I got laid off." We knew this had been coming, that his job would be phased out. It was funny how the "bad" news thrilled me. Ever since I'd known Dave, he'd worked long hours. I intuited a whole new version of life opening up. While his severance pay would only go so far, and we didn't know financially what would happen next, we trusted it would all work out.

"Okay, I said. "What's the good news?"

"It's ski season!"

The big piece of our visualization was unfolding before our eyes. We'd be able to spend weeks up in Tahoe in the ski house. We'd be able to ski on weekdays, not only crowded weekends.

"Hurry home," I said, "so we can celebrate."

I enjoyed the contrasts of living in a snowy world: warm under my clothes with a bite of cold on my face; orange fire in the living room while white snow floated out the window; breathing hard while moving my body in the icy high altitude, followed by a warm indoor yoga session, wine and food and games of backgammon, our friends' dogs curled at our feet.

Everything was novel. Donning equipment that made me feel like an astronaut, riding the funitel that glided up the middle of the mountain, whizzing down slopes that would be a challenge to walk down, and experimenting with form.

Our friends, one of whom was an expert skier who'd been in a ski movie, were kind enough to slow their pace and offer me tips. My favorite was to move to the rhythm of a song in my head. My choice was "Peaceful Easy Feeling."

My biggest challenge in learning to ski mirrored what my life had been teaching me for years: don't resist, allow. Going with the flow while on skis wasn't easy because the fear was primal, visceral. Speeding down a steep mountain, the wind in your face, was not natural. I could easily do it on a bicycle, though, so I conceptualized skiing in that way, which helped. Something else that helped was Dave's advice to look around at the beauty. What a privilege to be able to stand at the top of a snowy mountain, surrounded by emerald trees, a cobalt lake spread below. Why were we out there, after all, if not to have fun, appreciate our bodies, and commune with nature?

I wanted to get better every minute, every day. Finally I was able to walk through the lodge without feeling like an alien. I found my excitement build about getting out on the slopes as I put on my gear. By day six, I skied down a slope I refused to try day one. Skiing was visceral, symbolic, empowering, expansive. I had to be fully in the moment to respond spontaneously, naturally, to every curve and lift of powder or ice or berm. The flutter of the wind matched the flutter of my heart. The adventure of living pulsed through me.

One time when I fell, my left knee snapped. Pain shot through my leg like hot lightening. I lay on the snow, screaming. Then a mantra came to me: *freak out or get curious*, closely followed by its twin, *I wonder what good will come from this?*

I stopped trying to get up. I relaxed into the snowy mountain like a feather bed. I thought, *This is a new experience, lying here on the snow, not able to move. I wonder what will happen next? I'm going to watch this unfold. Something good will come.*

The minute I relaxed, the pain alleviated. It didn't disappear; it softened. When the medics arrived and hoisted me onto a gurney, I was filled with appreciation for their skill and care, not to mention their hunky good looks. As I was pulled down the hill by a snowmobile,

357

I marveled at how I was able to watch the blue sky. Never before had I glided down snow on my back. What an interesting perspective. My ego tried to butt in: *you look like an idiot on this thing. You are a loser for falling while skiing.* It stung briefly until I swerved my mind back to appreciation.

In the warm medical hut, I took in everything the medic said as he examined me. I was grateful for his training and insight. I thought about how cool it was that his assistance was free.

I arrived to our hotel room hobbling on crutches. There, I gave thanks for everything Dave did, from helping me get comfortable on the bed to bringing me food. He placed his hand on my knee and, Reiki-style, channeled healing energy.

Something good is going to come from this. I wonder what it is? That wonder blossomed into the kind of excitement you feel on the brink of a voyage. A mere thought transformed a "bad" experience into an adventure.

The medic said I may have snapped the tendon in my knee. If so, it would get weaker and weaker, eventually requiring surgery. The other possibility, he said, was that I had hyper-extended the tendon. If this were the case, it would eventually heal on its own, perhaps taking months. Either version could be true. I also imagined a third option: the knee could heal within a week or two, on its own. I provided the knee with direct attention: Dave's Reiki, my kind and loving thoughts. And then I distracted myself by watching TV.

The next day, I still could not stand on my leg. When despair or fear came, I thanked them for their concern and watched them pass like clouds. Dave and I got in the car for the four-hour drive back to the Bay Area. We figured he would probably drive me right to the urgent care near our house.

In the car, I watched the sky, loving and appreciating California's beauty, and thinking of how our true natures are vast and clear as the sky. We listened to a favorite CD. Whenever my knee drew my attention, I sent it love. I was in pain, but I wasn't suffering.

About two hours into the drive, we passed through Auburn, my hometown. At that moment, I felt a shift in my knee. Unmistakably, something had changed.

"Dave," I said. "I feel like I could stand."

"Really?" he said.

"Pull over."

He did. I got out of the car and, tentatively, stood. Even though my knee felt tender, my leg held me up.

I got back in the car and said, "Let's go home."

Over the next few days, I was able to take short walks. I gently stretched my knee, listening carefully to my body. It told me what it wanted. A month later, I was back on the slopes.

24

The Path

The highest goal one can achieve is amazement.
—Goethe

Krish, our Sri Lankan guide, is driving Dave and me on a dirt road through Yala National Park. Yesterday in the park, on a group safari, we saw elephants, crocodiles, jackals, red-faced macaques, gray langurs, mongoose, prehistoric-looking monitor lizards, colossal peacocks, and elk-sized deer. Today we are headed to a Buddhist shrine.

Krish slows the car and yells out, "Oh my God, a leopard!" He creeps the car toward the beast, which is sitting in the middle of the road, grooming himself.

Under his breath, Krish says over and over, "Oh my God, oh my God!"

The leopard looks up, hunching his back, predatory eyes boring into us.

"Maybe we should roll up the windows?" I whisper.

"Don't worry," Krish whispers back. "I have my foot on the gas."

The leopard stands like he has all the time in the world and walks slowly off the road and into the jungle. My skin is buzzing.

Little by little, Krish moves the car forward.

"There he is!" Dave says.

The leopard is weaving through the trees, walking parallel to the road. Monkeys chatter wildly as the leopard passes. In a small clearing, as though to offer us a good view about fifteen yards from the car, the leopard sits. In feline style, he begins cleaning himself elegantly. When he lifts his hind leg to lick, his foot looks the size of a frying pan. His muscles ripple beneath his spotted pelt. As he had on the road, the leopard stops and looks directly at us, hunching his shoulders. He gives us his direct, full attention, a moment of undeniable presence and power. Eventually he stands, in a slow-motion, stealthy way, and disappears into the jungle.

"I can't believe it!" says Krish. "My father has been taking people into this park for more than twenty-five years, and he's never been that close, for that long, to a leopard."

At Kataragama—a pilgrimage town sacred to Buddhists, Hindus, Muslims, and the indigenous Vedda people of Sri Lanka—people draped in flowing clothes walk the paths, buying flowers and fruit as offerings. Monkeys scramble over the shrines.

A bald Buddhist nun sitting in the shade of a building overhang calls out "hello" to me. I go to her. Her orange robe is stained, her hands and face creased with age. With a smile of brown and crooked teeth, she asks me where I'm from. I tell her and ask her where she's from. She says she has no home. Some nuns belong to monasteries, she says, but she does not. Bulky bags surround her, slumped against the wall. I wonder if her American equivalent is the homeless woman, pushing a grocery cart swollen with garbage bags. She says she'd like to bless me. I call Dave over so he can be blessed, too.

She reaches into one of her bags and pulls out a roll of white yarn. She loops a piece around my wrist then ties it. She places her hand on my forehead and says, "You are already healed. You are well." I inhale her words; it has been four months since my surgery. She ties yarn around Dave's right wrist and blesses him with a long and happy life.

Given the beauty of Sri Lanka, and the ease of traveling around, it's hard to believe a recently ended civil war raged there for almost thirty years—and that the island was hit hard by a tsunami in 2004, just nine years ago. Krish grew up with the war. He has a cousin who lost a limb, and he knows a number of people who died. There were certain areas of his small, island nation that he'd never been to until a few years ago.

On our last night, Krish invites us to his home for dinner. He drives us beyond the urban whir of Colombo, down rutted dirt roads into his rain forest neighborhood. Krish pulls up into a driveway for two houses, where a motorcycle is parked. He leads us into the smaller house where his wife, Shali, shyly nods at us. His daughter Seneshma, a six-year-old with large dark eyes and wearing a yellow-and-white dress with ruffled sleeves, jumps into Krish's arms.

"Welcome to my castle!" says Krish, smiling. The house is about the size of an American garage. There are gaps between the walls and ceiling, and the walls are draped in colorful cloth. The tiny front room is dominated by a table with three chairs. The only other piece of furniture is a desk that holds a computer with a bulky monitor.

Krish shows us his yard and neighborhood. He points out the well and pump that provide the family with water. He points out the huge king coconut tree in their yard. "Nature provides," he says.

We walk down the dirt lane, Seneshma joining us on her bicycle. We nod at neighbors who stare at us from their yards. I have a feeling some of them have never before seen white people. A few homes display vegetables and fruits out front for sale or trade. In front of one house, an old woman leans on her fence.

"Hello!" she calls out.

I go to her. She is a dark-skinned version of my grandmother. She takes hold of my hands, and peers at me, her eyes shining. She says something I don't understand. I squeeze her hands, nod my head, feel a connection beyond words, beyond cultures.

Back at the house, Shali tells Dave and me to sit so she can serve us dinner. We insist they join us. Shali declines, but Krish sits in the third chair with Seneshma on his lap. As is the Sri Lankan way, he eats with his fingers and every so often pops morsels into his daughter's mouth. The food is a huge dish of rice, spicy chicken, and vegetables. I grow sweaty from spice and humidity. I wonder how much this meal cost them to prepare—and am glad we brought a bakery cake.

After dinner, Krish takes us into the front house to meet his parents, sister, brother-in-law, and their baby son. They speak Sinhala, and Krish translates for us. When the baby sees us, his eyes grow wide and he wails. Everyone laughs.

They bring us into the kitchen, where Shali had cooked our meal over an open flame. Roots, herbs, and vegetables with soil still clinging to them line the pantry shelves. Krish shows us how coconut milk is made by grating coconut and pouring water over it, mashing it around. Krish's mother excuses herself and lights incense and candles, reverentially moving around the house to pray at various shrines affixed to the walls.

"My father has something he wants to show you," says Krish.

By now night has fallen. We follow Krish and his father out the back and around to the side of the house. His father shines a flashlight up into a tree at a low-hanging limb, talking in Sinhala to Krish.

"Look," said Krish. "My father wants you to see the nest."

We peer up to see the bottom of a bird nest, made transparent by the flashlight beam. A small bird sits atop three shadowy eggs.

When it's time for Krish to take us to our hotel, Shali and Seneshma come along. At first it looks like Seneshma might get in the front seat with her parents, but I tell Krish she's welcome to join us in back. She was shy with us when we first arrived, but she has warmed up. She jumps into the back seat between us. I feel a little hand reach over. Seneshma stares straight ahead, but her hand touches my leg. I put my hand near hers and she wiggles her fingers into mine. We hold hands in the dark the rest of the drive.

*

On my forty-ninth birthday, Dave took me away for a few days for a trip up the coast. It was Thanksgiving break. I made sure I brought no student papers along so I could soak up being with him on the last days of my forties.

We walked along the beach in Half Moon Bay, Dave carrying a backpack filled with what I imagined to be lunch and a blanket. Sure enough, when we stopped he pulled out a blanket and spread it across the sand. Even though it was late November, it was a cool, sunny day. The waves were huge and the horizon hazy, making intangible where land ended and sky began.

As I lay there in his arms, Dave started talking about how great we were together, how much he loved me and enjoyed the life we created. Then he pulled a white gold ring with a deep blue stone from his pocket and asked me to marry him. The ring looked like the sky, the sea, the world from afar.

My friend Roxy said, "Aren't you glad you went through what you did a few years ago? Because you needed to in order to get where you are now. And you certainly wouldn't have wanted to miss out on *this*." She wrote me a poem:

Restoration
How reassuring to know
passionate love
still exists. Once blackened rubble
now sweet scented blooms
so vibrant, strong

alive
one can hardly remember
that rocky desolation
out of which they grew—
Old decay
now new food
for boundless
roots.

I thought of Camus' words: "In the depth of winter I finally learned that there was in me an invincible summer." I knew that marriage would not bring me happiness. I would bring my happiness to it.

That weekend Dave and I hiked in Butano State Park, a place of towering redwoods, filtered light, and banana slugs. For the first time ever, I was able to watch one of those bizarre, bright yellow creatures eating, slowly munching on slimy fungus.

We spent a night in a tent bungalow at an eco-resort. It was kind of like camping but instead of a tent and blow-up mattress, we had a wooden floor, canvas walls and windows, and a cozy nest of a heated bed.

One night we stayed at the home of a friend who was out of town. A five-star hotel couldn't have been better because the pad came with a sweet cat named Digit and a deck overlooking the town and sea. That night, at a sushi bar, we met a local couple who'd been married for almost forty years. I asked them their secret to a long marriage. They said, "Enjoying the same food."

On our way back the next day, we stopped for a hike in an open-space preserve. We took a ten-mile loop on a duff-soft, well-tended trail. The place was otherworldly, fragrant and damp, a cathedral of redwoods. A few miles in, we passed through areas of oak woodland and then ascended from the creek back up to the ridge. Tingling with the sweet sweat of exertion, we got back to Chitty Chitty Bang Bang and headed home.

In a few weeks we would be moving from downtown San Jose to Santa Cruz. Finally I would be back in the beach town of my heart. My birthday and our engagement felt like a preview of coming attractions: a life together amidst the ocean and forest. A life of walking the path together, sometimes downhill, sometimes up. And always among the trees, with their boundless roots.

25

My Forever

I'm ready to live my forever.
—*Anders Osborne*

A huge, age-old sea turtle lounging on the beach became our impromptu best man as we gathered with family and friends, fragrant leis encircling our necks. Four of our friends' children showered the sand with petals. The sun hung vibrant and low in the sky. A light breeze blew.

Our officiate, Cheryl, welcomed everyone. Pas, her husband, played the guitar and sang Iz's version of "Somewhere Over the Rainbow" blended with "What a Wonderful World."

Cheryl mentioned those who would be with us if they could: Dave's parents and mine, and Gabriele, who was undergoing cancer treatment. The sweet scent of plumeria filled the air, my mom's favorite flower.

Our friend Martin, who brought his guitar from Mexico, sang:

You must give yourself to love if love is what you're after
Open up your hearts to the tears and laughter
And give yourself to love, give yourself to love.

Garry, who brought his conch shell from Santa Cruz, stood out on the lava and blew the shell in all four directions. The sky opened up in purples and oranges as the sun flared, then dropped into the Pacific.

*

After leaving Sri Lanka, we fly to California and make our way to Sebastopol, north of San Francisco. There we house- and dog-sit for our friend Anders. His house—a glass-and-wood seventies custom home—is reminiscent of the one I grew up in. There are large living room windows and a deck overlooking the valley. Wild turkeys and deer meander through the yard. One day as I do yoga on the back deck, a fox walks by on the railing.

Christmas morning dawns bright and cold. We cook breakfast, filling the house with the aroma of coffee, bacon, and oatmeal with warm blueberries. In the quiet, I sit before the window with my laptop and look at friends' Christmas mornings on Facebook: the glittery trees, the kids, the dark and shiny churches.

Dave and I don't exchange presents. What is there to buy? And where would we put new stuff, anyway? These days we spend our money mostly on gas and food. There are a few exceptions. For my birthday, Dave bought me a ring in Sri Lanka—blue topaz, my birthstone. For his, I bought him books that he leaves wherever he finishes them.

Now we are in Tahoe, in a house in the snowy mountains. Most days I write. We ski, hike, read, do yoga, play Rummikub.

The vision of spending a winter in the mountains was part of our brainstorm last year when we'd gotten news that the Love Nest was up for sale. I feel like I'm living parallel lives: *We are in the car deciding to spend winter in the mountains, and we are spending winter in the mountains.* As though time isn't linear but is a folded-over piece of paper where events touch, where thought and outcome occur not in sequence but in a flash.

It's peaceful here. The gremlin voices occasionally burrow into my brain, telling me I need to do more, plan more, worry more—that it's not enough to trust in life's unfolding and to follow my passions.

The other day, a message popped into my email from a former student. She was raising money to, as she put it, follow her dream to teach in Kenya. I grabbed my credit card and donated.

Soon after, I received this message from her: "Thank you so much. Kate. This means a lot to me that you donated! Following you and your adventures on your blog is one of the many reasons I took the leap. I want to live the journey like you are."

This mountain house has three bedrooms. Our friends come in droves, bearing groceries and wine. Cathy and Carrie come by for a few days. One night, Cathy hands us copies of the play she's working on. We sit around in the living room near the fireplace and read it aloud, taking different parts. I watch my friends' faces bright with firelight. Years ago, Carrie helped me move out of Emily's and my house, loading her van with my things. Years before that, Cathy organized a standing-room-only campus reading and book-signing for me when my first novel came out. It was a highlight of my life. Gabriele was there that night. She had introduced me, invited me up to the podium, eyes shining, proud like a mother, like a dear friend.

Our friends Steve and Catherine come to Tahoe with their three kids. I volunteer to take the youngest—eight-year-old Allegra—skiing. The rest of the family tours the mountain with Dave.

Allegra follows me down the hill each time, just as I usually follow Dave. Being the coach, the guide, I feel myself relax more deeply into the mountain.

As Allegra and I sit on the chair dangling over the bright white, we talk about animals and art. We talk about pictures she can draw back at the cabin. We watch other skiers go by, commenting on their form and outfits. A guy skis while juggling three pins. Amazing! We've never seen anything like that before.

On one fairly steep run, she whispers to me that she's scared. "I understand," I say, "But you don't have to be. Follow me, and you'll be fine." I take wide, sweeping turns—and she stays with me the whole way down.

After living in this house for months, I forget it's not ours. Then in a flash, I grasp the limited time and I look more closely at the tree out the window, smell the dinner Dave is cooking, feel the computer keys beneath my fingers.

In less than two weeks we will leave. I'm excited, yet a little nostalgic. It's similar to how I felt before we left the Love Nest. I remind myself that I don't regret leaving Santa Cruz. I like the flowing motion of life. I think I was born to evolve. Transformation is who I am, who we all are. As Gabriel García Márquez said, "Life obliges us over and over to give birth to ourselves."

We will head to Mexico, to our casita, toward the end of the year. It remains to be seen how long we will stay there. Will we use Baja as a temporary perch while we continue our nomadic ways? Or will we fall so in love with the area that we want to make Mexico our permanent home? I've friended on Facebook our future Baja neighbors who write us little updates and entice us with pictures of the beach and marine animals. Every so often the builder sends us photos of the progress. In mañana style, they don't seem to be in a hurry. Neither are we.

Deeply, I feel the paradox, the temporary yet eternal nature of existence, bounded yet porous. The unknown as infinite possibility, the fertile void. I want to keep returning to this sacred moment, to this eternity that is always present. I want to love every day, no matter how exotic or mundane. As did Ralph Waldo Emerson: "I wish the days to be as centuries, loaded, fragrant."

Maybe this means being patient with life. Maybe, as Eric Weiner once said, happiness is "not feeling like you should be somewhere else, doing something else, being something else."

We sit in the hot tub that overlooks the forest. It's an ethereal afternoon. The sun lightens the sky and snow drifts down. How can it be sunny and snowing simultaneously? But it is.

I lean into Dave. Warm water surrounds us. He reaches his hands into my hair and massages the scar that runs the length of my scalp.

Ground squirrels scrabble over a fallen tree trunk that is decomposing into duff. Tiny snowflakes swirl. From a pine, birds lift like dark fragments, ascending into the muted sky.

Off in the trees, something moves. In a few seconds, we realize it's a coyote strolling by. We watch him until he disappears in the woods.

The Trip of a Lifetime

1)
My dad has become much more spiritual
since he's become a spirit. Maybe his blue eyes
and handlebar mustache signaled he always had angel
potential. He'd been gone only three months
when, as I sat at the computer, he—
I don't know how else to put this—
came over for a visit. My body filled with
a warmth I recognized as him. My fingertips
froze on the keyboard. I resisted saying,
"Hi Dad!" because I worried he'd
evaporate if I spoke or moved. A
softening cupped my heart. He spoke
without language, filling me with this message:
Everything's fine. Fine as in whole, as in
flawless. Fine as in don't worry—as in lovely
and pure. As fine as the sand on an endless beach
that spreads toward the eternal horizon.
A few days before he died, he said if the afterworld
was real, he'd find a way to pinch me.
This wasn't a pinch, though. Maybe spirits
don't have fingers. I remember Dad's fingers,
thick fingertip pads that fumbled as he

turned newspaper pages. Yet he grasped a hammer
so resolutely that he built redwood decks in record time,
laid down railroad ties and hauled thousands of
buckets of firewood. He'd always slide
his ring back on after his shower, before dinner.

2)

A week after the funeral, Mom and I found
Dad's wedding band in a drawer
next to the bed, gold and round as a tiny halo.
"Toss it," Mom said. All afternoon she'd been saying
"Toss this, toss that" about most of Dad's things.
The geriatric psychologist asked my mom:
"In what way are a rose and a tulip alike?"
Mom said: "They are not alike."
He said: "How are a watch and a ruler alike?"
She said: "They both measure time."
"A bike and a train?"
"They are both machinery."
"A corkscrew and a hammer?"
"I don't know."
He asked: "What would you do if there was a fire in your house?"
She answered: "I'd close and lock the doors."
Patient described as showing a change in cognitive status. Her husband
of forty-eight years passed away two months ago. She worked as a school
nurse for many years but doesn't recall when she retired. Patient is a poor
historian.

3)

The doctor wrote: "Patient is a poor historian."

Pablo Neruda wrote: "Love is so short, forgetting is so long."

4)

Hospice literature says:

"One week before death,

the average patient

still has

a 40% chance

of living."

It says:

"There is no medical definition

of terminal."

It says:

"There is no medical definition

of dying."

5)

The next time Dad popped in for a visit

I was jogging through my neighborhood.

"Wow," he said without words, "Look, look,

look, look, look!" As my feet metronomed

on the pavement, the colors brightened. And I saw

through new eyes the crystalline winter day,

the razor-sharp infinite blue of the sky, and the

preposterous fuchsia blossoms as unabashed as the sex of
the world. Mom gave me the same gift once:
a ViewMaster in my Christmas stocking.
I'd spent hours peering in,
atingle at the Wonders of the World in 3D—
azure seas and golden windows, lush veils and drapes
and rushing waterfalls—places my mother dreamed of.

6)
Mom began to leave long before she died.
Her language left word by word
as though she were packing a suitcase.
She hadn't spoken in almost a year.
But when I showed her my engagement ring—
sapphire blue like my father's eyes—
she reached out and touched my face.
She doesn't visit. I can still feel the release
of her last exhalation, like the lift of a plane.
She's off on the trip of a lifetime.

—*kme*

Appreciation

Thanks, mom, for bringing books and writing into my life. And thank you, dad, for helping me embrace a life of passion. Love to my sisters, who are always there.

Gabriele, thank you for taking my parents' gifts to the next level. Big hug to Suzanne, Stephanie, Simone, and Rich.

Huge thanks to friends for reading this manuscript and offering me feedback: Janelle, Dawn, Nancy, Julie, and Jennifer. And especially Ellen—who helped me relearn how less is more.

Thanks, Patricia, for sweeping up those last typos and for your support of me and my work. Thank you, Bill, for your blurb—and for all you do for writers. Karen, thanks for your keen eye. And Jan: You rock!

To all the students, colleagues, friends, family, and strangers who've crossed my path: Thank you for teaching me.

To all the friends who've generously welcomed Dave and me into their homes and lives on our journey: We love you.

"This very moment is the perfect teacher." Thank you, Pema Chodron, for that wisdom and all you've given to me through your work.

Dave, the ultimate co-creator, I love you. Thank you for listening to me read my pages aloud, for shopping and cooking while I was immersed in writing, and for being a loving and an adventurous soul.

Kate Evans lives half the year in Baja California Sur, Mexico, and travels half the year. She writes about her adventures on *Living the Journey* (beingandwriting.blogspot.com). She is the author of *For the May Queen* (Coyote Creek Books) and *Negotiating the Self* (Routledge). Her stories, poems, and essays have appeared in more than fifty publications including *ZZYZYVA*, *The Santa Monica Review*, and *North American Review*. A recipient of a PhD from the University of Washington and an MFA from San Jose State University, she taught at U.C. Santa Cruz and San Jose State. She leads writing workshops worldwide and serves as a private writing coach. Visit her website: www.kateevanswriter.com.

Made in the USA
San Bernardino, CA
14 July 2015